Interpersonal Group Psychotherapy for Borderline Personality Disorder

Interpersonal Group Psychotherapy for Borderline Personality Disorder

Elsa Marziali
and
Heather Munroe-Blum

BasicBooks
A Division of HarperCollins*Publishers*

Designed by John Chung

Library of Congress Cataloging-in-Publication Data

Marziali, Elsa.
  Interpersonal group psychotherapy for borderline personality
disorder / Elsa Marziali and Heather Munroe-Blum.
    p. cm.
  Includes bibliographical references and index.
  ISBN 0–465–08893–7
  1. Borderline personality disorder—Treatment. 2. Group
psychotherapy. I. Munroe-Blum, Heather, 1950–.   II. Title.
RC569.5.B67M36 1994   94–18148
616.85′8520651—dc20   CIP

94 95 96 97 ◆/HC 9 8 7 6 5 4 3 2 1

Contents

Preface

This book is the culmination of 10 years of clinical investigations of the diagnosis and treatment of borderline personality disorder. My motivation to pursue this work stemmed from my own therapeutic failures with patients so diagnosed. I also would hear repeatedly from other therapists about their anxieties and frustrations in their work with similarly diagnosed patients. I did not believe that the available theories for understanding borderline personality disorder, in terms of both etiology and diagnosis, were sufficient for working effectively with these patients. The study and analyses of clinical experiences with borderline personality disorder eventually resulted in the design and testing of several pilot approaches to treatment. Finally, with the collaboration of Heather Munroe-Blum we were funded to carry out a treatment comparison trial in which the experimental treatment, interpersonal group psychotherapy, was compared with psychodynamic individual psychotherapy. The study was funded by the Ontario Mental Health Foundation and by the National Health Research and Development Program. We thank Dr. David Dawson, who developed the original treatment approach for use in individual psychotherapy and who gave us considerable direction in adapting the model within a group context. He was available for consultation for the duration of the project. Dr. Munroe-Blum had been trained in the Dawson model and thus provided important direction for its implementation with the rigor needed for a treatment comparison trial. We thank the research staff who worked with us during various phases of the project. They were highly talented and shared our strong commitment to carry out the trial as effectively and efficiently as possible. We are grateful for the support of the McMaster University Medical Centre and its Department of Psychiatry for housing the study. The cooperation of all of the hospital and clinic staff within the network was essential, and we thank them for their support. The therapists who carried out the treatments gave generously of their time, experience, and good humor. We thank them for their loyalty, endurance, and hard work. Our greatest gratitude is extended to the patients who agreed to participate in the study. Although the patients provided informed signed consent prior to engaging in the project, their stories in this book have been thoroughly disguised so that there is no likelihood that they would recognize themselves. Their stories show that they kept us "on course"; they taught us to listen, observe, and withhold judgment. They were impressive in their intelligence, forthrightness, and high motivation to benefit from the therapeutic experience. They too worked hard, and we thank them.

ELSA MARZIALI
Toronto, Ontario, Canada
April 1994

1

Introduction

Although numerous books on the subject of borderline personality disorder (BPD) have recently appeared, the utility of the concept's diagnostic specificity, usefulness in guiding treatments, and contribution to etiologic formulations continues to be questioned. What is undisputed, however, is the high prevalence of people diagnosed with BPD in outpatient psychiatry caseloads (approximately 15%) and using inpatient services (approximately 20%) (Gunderson, 1984; Kass, Skodol, Charles, Spitzer, & Williams, 1985; Piersma, 1987). Borderline personality disorder is encountered in multidisciplinary mental health treatment contexts, and there is every indication that patients diagnosed with BPD are well represented on the case-rolls of community social service and welfare agencies. This disorder is thus the concern of a broad range of mental health and social service professionals, and the development of effective, broadly applicable intervention strategies to respond to the problems of BPD is a high priority.

Senior diagnosticians have been known to comment that the most direct way to arrive with some certainty at the diagnosis of BPD is to measure the size of the patient's clinical file. If it is over 3 inches thick, a diagnosis of BPD is likely to be warranted. Although such an approach might appear glib at the surface, what these experienced clinicians know is that the BPD diagnosis captures a meaningful cluster of features with a strong behavioral emphasis that, taken together, point to a person who experiences significant distress, is at high risk, and uses multiple services often unbeknownst to the range of service providers while typically benefiting little from what mental health practitioners have to offer.

Treatment difficulties have generally been associated with three major factors (Munroe-Blum & Marziali, 1988): problems in the classification of the disorder (Gunderson 1977; Perry & Klerman, 1978; Spitzer, Endicott, & Gibbon, 1979), the very nature of the disorder itself (Gunderson, 1984; Kernberg, 1975; Masterson, 1976), and the paucity of empirical data supporting particular treatment strategies for BPD. Several scholars have raised the important question of whether traditional approaches to the treatment of BPD may not, in fact, do more harm than good (Frances & Clarkin, 1981; Vaillant, 1992). A few efforts have been made systematically to assess the contributions of psychotherapy, and findings from these studies indicate substantial early treatment dropouts and limited gains for those who remain in treatment. Where improvements are demonstrated, these appear to be primarily in the realm of behavioral change, but changes in the structure of the personality are rare (Waldinger & Gunderson, 1987). With few exceptions (Linehan, Armstrong, Suarez, Allmon, & Heard, 1991; Munroe-Blum & Marziali, 1986–1992), studies of the treatment of BPD have focused on long-term individual psychotherapy (Clarkin et al., 1992; Kernberg, Burstein, & Coyne, 1972). Given the clinical prevalence and related high costs of the disorder, the associated burden of suffering for both patients and their significant others, and the only moderate beneficial contributions of traditional psychiatric treatment, the development and testing of new models of BPD treatment and other service responses are needed, including modalities other than long-term individual psychotherapy.

Challenges in the Development of Effective Treatment Models

The development of effective treatment models for any disorder, although of critical importance when none have been established, is a time-consuming and difficult task. A National Institute of Mental Health (NIMH) workshop on treatment development identified a rigorous program for such efforts. The stages of this program include:

1. The articulation of a treatment strategy with theoretical and clinical promise;
2. Treatment standardization (including the development of treatment manuals, therapist training procedures, therapist competency measures, and patient and therapist adherence measures);
3. Pilot studies with small sample sizes to demonstrate treatment feasibility and potential efficacy;
4. Comprehensive clinical trial research to demonstrate treatment effectiveness (see the 1993 Department of Health and Human Services Public Health Service National Institutes of Health NIMH Program Announcement PA-93-093).

Although such a comprehensive, scientific approach to treatment development is necessary to help clinicians to be confident that they are doing more good than harm in practice, it is no wonder that new treatment models for BPD treatment have been slow to emerge.

The introduction of new BPD treatment models corresponds to such a comprehensive treatment-development approach. This will entail some reconciliation and resolution regarding the lack of agreement on the definition, diagnosis, and etiology of the disorder; lack of continuity between diagnostic and etiologic approaches; problems in integrating therapy techniques with the relational and contextual features of psychotherapy; and problems with testing the reliability and validity of treatment models. Although we address these in detail in subsequent chapters of this book, we introduce each briefly here in the context of discussing the development of new treatment models.

Definitions and Diagnosis

With the introduction of DSM-III criteria for the diagnosis of BPD (Spitzer & Williams, 1980) and a range of semi-structured interview and self-report approaches to BPD assessment (Gunderson, Kolb, & Austin, 1981; Hyler et al., 1989; Loranger, Susman, Oldham, & Russakoff, 1985; Millon, 1987; Spitzer, Williams, & Gibbon, 1987; Zanarini, Gunderson, Frankenberg, & Chauncey, 1989), standardized approaches to ascertaining the disorder have been emerging. The pervasive overlap of this disorder with others and new information on subgroup and severity of the disorder underscore the fragile nature of current conceptualizations.

Considerable agreement exists about the external boundaries of the diagnostic entity; however, there is still intense debate regarding the meaning of variations within the disorder. In order to be effective, it follows that a treatment must remedy the problems inherent in the target condition (Munroe-Blum & Marziali, 1988). It is likely that effective BPD treatment models will emerge in the context of increased understanding of the prognostic implications of the various dimensions and subgroups of the disorder.

Etiologic Models and Implications
for Treatment Development

Historically, much emphasis has been placed on the links between knowledge of the etiology or cause of a condition and the development of effective treatments. This results from an assumption that the study of causes is the best way to determine how to intervene with a condition. This assumption is based on a linear, unidirectional model of disease promotion, initiation, and course, in which factors that are viewed to predispose to or initiate a disorder also sustain (or, in their absence, reverse) the condition.

In fact, most disorders from across the spectrum of medical specialties, including psychiatry, have a complex, multifactorial pathophysiology. Often, a range of factors will contribute to the predisposition and onset of a disorder, causal factors will lack disease specificity, and different factors will play a prominent role in the various stages of disease predisposition, initiation, and course. With the exception of certain infectious diseases, one factor alone rarely explains a majority of the variance in the onset and course of a disorder, even where a causal relationship has been demonstrated. Furthermore, the dominance of an incorrect but popular etiologic theory can limit the field of investigation, thereby eliminating from study the very variables that will shed light on the etiology of a disorder.

Finally, there is often a lack of continuity across etiologic hypotheses, diagnostic formulations and procedures, and treatment approaches. For example, in the study on which we report in this book, senior therapists trained in psychoanalytic methods when interviewed presented psychoanalytic descriptions of the disorder and psychoanalytic approaches to its treatment; yet, when their sessions with the BPD study patients were analyzed, it was found that these therapists had used a variety of therapeutic strategies incorporating psychodynamic, cognitive-behavioral, and psychoeducational approaches.

Thus, although studies of causation may have an intuitive appeal to mental health practitioners, such studies have not demonstrated the link between etiologic hypotheses and the development of effective treatments. In fact, the reverse may be true; that is, the testing of models of treatment that prove to be effective may shed light on causal factors. For example, an overemphasis on etiologic hypotheses about phase-specific developmental factors for explaining the borderline disorder led to treatment models that ignore the potentially informative role of female gender dominance in patients with BPD. Feminist conceptualizations of the etiology, diagnosis, and treatment of borderline personality could provide fruitful contributions for developing effective treatments for these patients.

Clearly, the development of effective treatments for BPD cannot await the conclusive ascertainment of BPD etiology. Also, as has been shown, retrospective studies of early life experiences of BPD patients reveal a complex set of factors that contribute differentially to the onset and course of the disorder. Thus, it is unlikely that a specific developmental paradigm could account for the variation observed within this disorder.

Therapy Techniques and the Relational and Contextual Features of Treatment

Borderline personality disorder is a disorder that primarily affects women, whose strongest feature is a striking set of interpersonal problems, and that has been primarily studied, diagnosed, and treated in mental health service delivery systems. It stands to reason that new models of treatment might profit from a greater emphasis on the integration of therapy techniques with the treatment relationship and with contextual features of psychotherapy, in particular the treatment relationship and the manifestations of the disorder itself. For example, it is not unheard of (as was experienced in our study) for a person with BPD to appear at a hospital emergency room in a full-blown crisis, threatening suicide, and in all respects presenting as completely incompetent and to be seen only a few hours later at a local mall smiling and chatting with a group of friends. This example is not meant to question whether problems and serious distress were present in the first instance but, rather, to indicate the potential role that context (institution versus shopping mall) and relationship (doctor/therapist versus friend) play in the manifestation and even the experience of the problem. Incorporating relationship and contextual factors in the development and assessment of treatment necessitates the creation of a complex, multifactorial treatment model and of multidimensional and interconnected assessment procedures; however, the knowledge to be derived from the study and the potential effectiveness of the treatment are likely to be superior to those achieved through approaches that ignore these factors.

Interpersonal Group Psychotherapy: A New Approach

This book presents a new treatment strategy for BPD, interpersonal group psychotherapy (IGP). It describes the evolution of the treatment model as a response to the problems inherent in the diagnosis and in traditional approaches to BPD treatment, including the roles played by the therapeutic relationship and the contextual features of psychotherapy and, indeed, by the presentation of the disorder. The IGP treatment model is not a direct response to etiologic formulations. It arose out of clinical practice and observation. Nonetheless, traditional etiologic formulations and the research to date on the etiology of borderline disorder are reviewed, and a theoretical explanation for the effectiveness of the IGP strategy is presented.

The development of the IGP treatment closely paralleled the approach to treatment development advocated by the NIMH described earlier. The IGP treatment is based on the Relationship Management (RM) BPD treatment model developed by Dawson (1988) for individual treatment of BPD. The RM approach was developed in a community psychiatry outpatient clinic in the late 1970s and early 1980s at a time of emerging awareness of the limitations of traditional long-term individual treatment. A clinical team began to experiment with alternate responses to BPD. The aim was to shift the locus of authority away from the treatment providers to the patients; that is, the clinicians began to reflect the reality of the clinical outcomes for BPD patients. The uncertainty of a positive outcome following involvement in psychiatric treatment was a reality that both patient and therapist had to address. The RM model as it applies to individual treatment of BPD has now been presented in a recently published book (Dawson & MacMillan, 1993). Interpersonal group psychotherapy represents an adaptation of RM in a group psychotherapeutic context.

Simultaneously, Marziali (Munroe-Blum & Marziali, 1988) was testing a time-limited group treatment approach with patients with severe personality disorders. From this pilot research and the clinical experience of Dawson, Munroe-Blum, and others in the development of the RM approach, it was concluded that there would be merit in adapting the RM model to a group format. A group treatment manual was developed and refined (along with the treatment) over further research applications. A training procedure was developed by Marziali and tested on a pair of senior therapists, as described in detail in chapter 7.

Research Parameters

A full-scale randomized clinical trial was determined to be the only research design with sufficient rigor to address the treatment development problems identified and to test the IGP treatment appropriately. In 1986 a trial was undertaken with the support of provincial and, subsequently, national mental health funding agencies. Patients randomly assigned in five waves of the IGP treatment were compared with patients who received psychodynamically oriented "individual treatment as usual."

Over 6 years of research, 110 subjects who met the criteria for BPD diagnosis according to Gunderson's Diagnostic Interview for Borderlines

(DIB) (Gunderson et al., 1981) were randomly allocated to receive either the experimental IGP treatment or the control "individual treatment as usual." Thirty-one subjects refused treatment or dropped out of treatment very early, and 79 accepted treatment (individual treatment, $N = 41$; group treatment, $N = 38$).

Research procedures included a number of strategies to control for the limitations of prior BPD treatment research. Among methods used to enhance the research contributions were

1. Selection of subjects from consecutive referrals to psychiatry services in a broadly demarcated catchment area in a Canadian city (because of comprehensive health coverage, no person was excluded for economic reasons)
2. Random assignment of qualifying subjects to the two treatment conditions
3. Equal levels of experience for therapists in both treatments
4. Standardized process and outcome measures using trained assessors in addition to a "free-form" account of subjects' subjective experience of what factors they believed did or did not help; and follow-up at 6, 12, 18, and 24 months.

The major dependent variables of interest in the study included behaviors related to social performance and symptom status. The primary hypothesis in this study was that BPD patients treated with the experimental treatment (IGP) would make greater improvements than patients treated with the "individual treatment as usual" (individual dynamic psychotherapy) in the areas of problematic behaviors, symptoms, and social adjustment. Secondary objectives included the prospective investigation of the total study cohort.

With respect to compliance, the patients who accepted either treatment did not differ from refusers on any of the pretreatment assessments or on diagnosis or comorbid conditions. Illness scores in the severe range and comorbid Axis I and Axis II conditions were the norm in both groups. Outcome findings for the two treatment groups at 6 months (during treatment), at 12 months (end of treatment), and at 24 months (1-year posttreatment follow-up) on the major outcome variables indicated no statistically significant differences in outcome between the two treatment groups. Significant improvements occurred over time for subjects in both groups on behavioral indicators, social adjustment, global symptoms, and depression. These results are reported in table 1.1 as an analysis of the total cohort over time.

Table 1.1
Cohort Analysis of Variance
SCALE MEANS

	OBI	SAS	HSCL	BDI
Pretreatment	32.01	2.13	1.76	25.9
12 months	30.99	1.91	1.26	18.4
24 months	23.61	1.89	1.03	14.6
	$N = 48$	$N = 43$	$N = 45$	$N = 46$
	$F_{(2,094)} = 10.76^*$	$F_{(2,084)} = 7.04^*$	$F_{(2,088)} = 16.42^*$	$F_{(2,090)} = 17.93^*$

OBI: Objective Behaviors Index (Munroe-Blum & Marziali, 1986)

SAS: Social Adjustment Scale (Weissman & Bothwell, 1976)

HSCL: Hopkins Symptom Checklist (Derogatis, Lipman, & Covi, 1973)

BDI: Beck Depression Inventory (Beck et al., 1961)

Note: N values vary because of missing data.

$^*p = < 0.001.$

The rate of change across the three time points also varied for the total cohort. Raw scores for each of the outcome measures at each point of observation were used in individual regression models to generate slopes and intercepts for each outcome measure across three points in time, pretreatment, 12-month, and 24-month follow-ups. Following a procedure for standardizing the slopes, the weighted mean slopes for the different outcome measures were compared using analysis of variance (see table 1.2). The greatest rate of change was demonstrated on the measure of behavioral indicators, followed by the measure of depression. The rate of change on the general symptom index was approximately one-half of that for the behavioral indicators. The lowest rate of change for the cohort was on the general measure of social adjustment.

These results confirm the findings of several smaller studies; that is, when BPD patients experience change as a result of psychotherapy, these changes are primarily behavioral and symptomatic rather than characterological in nature.

Table 1.2
Absolute Differences in Change Rates among
Weighted Mean Slopes of Outcome Measures

	BDI	HSCL	SAS
BIS	0.065	0.095	0.139
BDI	—	0.030 (nonsignificant)	0.074
HSCL	—	—	0.044

BIS: Behavioral Indicators Scale (Munroe-Blum & Marziali, 1986)

BDI: Beck Depression Inventory (Beck et al., 1961)

HSCL: Hopkins Symptom Checklist (Derogatis, Lipman, & Covi, 1973)

SAS: Social Adjustment Scale (Weissman & Bothwell, 1976)

Note: Overall $F = 25.78$, corrected degrees of freedom = 2,131; $p < 6.001$; Fisher least-square difference $d = 0.049$; $p < 0.01$. BIS had the largest average change, followed by the BDI and HSCL; the smallest average change was on the SAS.

Although the statistically significant changes at outcome existed for the total study cohort, not for the treatment group comparisons, several points are worth noting about study findings in favor of the IGP treatment. Both therapists and patients reported increased satisfaction with the IGP treatment (IGP therapists valued the cotherapy and group structure of the treatment and the dilution of the intensity of patient demands; they reported increased empathic response to the patients and decreased anxiety in the early stages of treatment); the IGP treatment demonstrated increased cost-effectiveness over the comparison "individual treatment as usual"; last, the IGP treatment has the advantage of being a manual-guided treatment with established training procedures, easily utilized in a range of service contexts by multidisciplinary practitioners. These latter characteristics show that the IGP treatment model is in keeping with the current emphasis on the development of innovative service approaches for patients with personality disorders.

Unfortunately, randomized trials of treatments for BPD or other personality disorders are few. The rigorous investigation of the IGP treatment model and the demonstrated treatment and cost benefits warranted a detailed presentation of the model. That is the purpose of this book. We also provide an overview and analysis of prior clinical and research work on the etiology, diagnosis, and treatment of BPD to contextualize the IGP treatment approach.

Structure of the Book

This chapter has presented the rationale and development of the IGP model and related relevant research. Chapter 2 presents the diagnostic features of BPD, including a historical overview of the evolution of BPD definitions; a review of diagnostic approaches and related problems; a summary of a pilot study of diagnostic subgroups that was carried out within the context of the larger clinical trial; clinical case examples of patient diagnostic summaries categorized according to one diagnostic measure, the DIB; and a discussion of the clinical implications of various diagnostic approaches, of comorbid conditions, of severity, and of subgroup dimensions of the disorder. Chapter 3 provides a comprehensive review of etiologic formulations of BPD and presents a particular developmental model that can be used to understand the disorder and the subsequent effects of IGP. Chapters 4 and 5 present in detail the IGP model, related treatment philosophy, and key principles, and highlight the contrasts between the IGP approach and traditional treatments. Chapter 6 addresses problems in any treatment of BPD, especially intersubjectivity and therapeutic derailment and error and provides means of correcting for these within the context of the IGP approach. Clinical examples from the study are used to illustrate the main points. Chapter 7 offers a review of the IGP training procedures, their development, and numerous examples of training applications from the clinical trial and the within-study ministudy on IGP training procedures. Next, chapter 8 provides a detailed presentation of the phases of an IGP group. The final chapter, 9, reviews the unique features, strengths, and potential limitations of IGP and highlights the possibilities for extending IGP to treatment of other diagnostic groups and to different treatment contexts.

The appendix contains training materials that have been divided into three parts. Part I lists therapist statements, which trainees assess on their representativeness of IGP. By matching these therapist statements to those listed in chapter 7, the trainees learn to distinguish the interventions that are more typical of IGP. Part II provides a list of "tentative words," which is useful for ensuring that all interventions reflect uncertainty. Part III provides five "dialogues" taken from actual treatment sessions, which can be used to test the trainees' judgments about interventions that best reflect the style of IGP therapists.

As is clear from the chapter topics, this book can be used as a training manual. Each chapter contributes to an integrated understanding of the salient diagnostic, etiologic, and treatment issues that we believe are essential for the successful clinical management of patients with BPD.

2

Diagnosis of Borderline Personality Disorder

Borderline personality disorder eludes meaningful definition. Diagnostic questions abound. Is it a personality disorder? Does it comprise a group of syndromes? Is it a level of severity of psychopathology? Over the past fifty years clinicians and clinical investigators have addressed these questions. However, there remains little consensus on which sets of criteria are specific to describing patients with BPD and whether the classification is useful in clarifying prevention and treatment strategies.

Psychodynamic Approach to Borderline Personality Disorder Diagnosis

Historically psychoanalysts have made the major contributions to refining definitions of the disorder. A category of psychopathology referred to as the "borderline group" was first introduced by Stern (1938) to describe patients who fit neither psychotic nor neurotic forms of psychopathology. Stern noted that these patients were clinically challenging and "extremely difficult to handle effectively by any psychotherapeutic method." Although this definition still applies, subsequent psychoanalysts have attempted to describe more clearly metapsychological features of the disorder as well as its developmental precursors. What has evolved is a definition of the borderline disorder described as a level of psychopathology comprising diverse syndromes that are etiologically linked to early developmental conflicts or deficits in ego function (Knight, 1953) and in object relations (Adler, 1985; Gunderson, 1984; Kernberg, 1975). Viewed in this way BPD or borderline organization (Kernberg, 1975) is classified as a severe personality disorder and includes a heterogeneous group of patients (narcissistic, histrionic, dependent, and antisocial) characterized by

1. Identity diffusion
2. Primitive defenses (projective identification, splitting)
3. Intact reality testing.

To apply effectively this diagnostic system, considerable training in psychoanalytic theory and technique is needed. A high level of inference is required for assessing the meanings of patient dialogue in the context of the three dimensions described. Although trained clinicians are able to make the diagnosis of borderline personality organization reliably (Kernberg, Selzer, Koenigsberg, Carr, & Appelbaum, 1989) and the diagnostic theoretical model is closely linked to the recommended treatment (long-term, intensive psychoanalytic psychotherapy), the validity of the diagnostic procedure and the resulting label are difficult to establish. In this respect, a psychodynamic formulation shares with all other diagnostic systems the problem of establishing the specificity and validity of the BPD diagnosis.

Categorical Approach to Borderline Personality Disorder Diagnosis

The DSM categorical approach (APA, 1980, 1987; Spitzer & Williams, 1980) to the diagnosis of BPD is concerned with the application of a specific set of criteria that are considered to represent the disorder best. The original DSM-III (APA, 1980) criteria for BPD included the following:

1. Identity disturbance
2. Unstable, intense relationships
3. Impulsivity that is potentially self-damaging
4. Inappropriate, intense anger
5. Physically self-damaging acts
6. Affective instability
7. Chronic feelings of emptiness and boredom
8. Problems tolerating being alone.

A patient qualifies for the diagnosis on the basis of any five of the eight criteria. Revisions to the criteria for the proposed DSM-IV are in progress and include the following changes:

1. The "intolerance of being alone" criterion is changed to "frantic efforts to avoid real or imagined abandonment "
2. The retention of "chronic feelings of emptiness" but the deletion of "boredom"

3. Addition to the "identity disturbance" criterion of "persistent self-image distortions" (e.g., feeling that one embodies evil or does not exist)

4. Deletion of the "alternation between idealization and devaluation" from the unstable relationships item

5. Inclusion of "marked reactivity of mood" in the affective instability item

6. "Physically self-damaging acts" is expanded to "recurrent self-destructive threats, gestures, or behavior"

7. Addition of a new criterion concerned with cognitive or perceptual aberrations, "transient, stress-related dissociative or paranoid ideation" (Gunderson & Sabo, 1993).

Much of the research on the reliability and validity of the borderline diagnosis has been based on the DSM categorical method. Studies have focused on examining comorbidity of BPD with Axis I and other Axis II disorders. Between 40% and 60% of patients diagnosed with BPD have concomitant Axis I affective disorders (Akiskal, 1981; Frances, Clarkin, Gilmore, Hurt, & Brown, 1984; Gunderson & Elliott, 1985; Perry, 1985; Soloff, George, Nathan, & Schultz, 1987). However, when BPD and affective disorders co-exist, subjects with BPD tend to be more manipulative, suicidal, impulsive, and suffer from more substance abuse problems than depressed patients (Zanarini, Gunderson, & Frankenberg, 1989). Similarly, Westen and colleagues (1990) found that borderline depressives showed lower capacity than non-borderline depressives on the following four dimensions of object relations and social cognition:

1. Complexity of representations of other
2. Affect tone
3. Capacity for emotional investment
4. Understanding of social causality.

In contrast, studies on the possible overlap between BPD and schizophrenia show no diagnostic comorbidity—that is, the disorder is distinct from DSM-III Axis I psychotic disorders (Barasch, Frances, Hurt, Clarkin, & Cohen, 1985; Jonas & Pope, 1992; Pope, Jonas, Hudson, Cohen, & Gunderson, 1983). However, disturbed and quasi-psychotic thought is common among BPD patients (Links, Steiner, Offord, & Eppel, 1988; Silk, Lehr, Ogata, & Westen, 1990; Zanarini, Gunderson, & Frankenburg, 1990).

There is substantial overlap between the borderline diagnosis and other Axis II personality disorders (Fryer, Frances, Sullivan, Hurt, &

Clarkin, 1988; Nurnberg et al., 1991; Oldham et al., 1992; Zanarini, Gunderson, Frankenburg, & Chauncey, 1990); however, the prevalence of comorbidity for BPD does not differ from other Axis II disorders (Fryer, Frances, Sullivan, Hurt, & Clarkin, 1988). Many features of the BPD disorder are nondiscriminating from other Axis II disorders (Zanarini, Gunderson, Frankenburg, & Chauncey, 1990). Nurnberg et al. (1991) found that multiple personality disorders apply when BPD is present, but no specific pattern of overlap is evident. Similarly, Oldham (Oldham et al., 1992) found that substantial overlap occurred among the personality disorders and that the borderline group co-occurred more frequently with histrionic and dependent personality disorders. The histrionic disorder also co-occurred with narcissistic and antisocial diagnoses; thus, no consistent pairing of any two Axis II disorders was evident.

Challenges to both the psychoanalytic and the Axis II categorical approach to diagnosis of BPD have come from biological psychiatry. Klein (1973, 1977) has argued that borderlines should be included as a subcategory of patients with affective disorders. He has noted specific parallels between Grinker and associates' (1968) subgroups of borderlines and some categories of affective disorders. For example, he compares Grinker's hostile depressive subgroup to his hysteroid dysphoric group who responded favorably to monamine oxidase (MAO) inhibitors. Similarly, Grinker's emotionally unstable borderlines responded to lithium, and Grinker's more neurotic, phobic, anxious subgroup of borderlines responded well to imipramine. Like Klein, Akiskal (Akiskal et al., 1985, & Akiskal, 1992) has advocated the elimination of the BPD diagnosis because he views the affective components of the disorder as overriding all other diagnostic criteria; borderlines should be included in the affective disorder group of patients and therefore treated with pharmacological interventions.

In summary, the studies of comorbidity between BPD with Axis I disorders or other Axis II disorders show that

1. There is a relationship between BPD and affective disorders but the exact nature of the relationship is unknown
2. The consistency of overlap between BPD and other personality disorders is unknown.

The revisions to the DSM (DSM-III-R) have partially dealt with the problem of comorbidity among the Axis II disorders by proposing "clusters" of personality disorders; borderlines are included in a cluster of dramatic, emotionally unstable personality disorders (histrionic, narcissistic, and antisocial). Although this attempt at resolving the issue of comorbidity within the Axis II disorders acknowledges the sharing of criteria within the subgroups, diagnostic clarity essential for designing effective treatments has not been advanced.

Studies of the reliability, validity, specificity, and sensitivity of DSM criteria for diagnosing borderline personality disorder have used a series of semi-structured interview methods and self-report instruments. The one most frequently used, the Diagnostic Interview for Borderlines (DIB) (Gunderson, Kolb, & Austin, 1981) and its revised version the DIB-R (Zanarini, Gunderson, Frankenburg, & Chauncey, 1989) are specific to the borderline diagnosis. Other instruments have included diagnostic criteria for all 11 Axis II disorders. Examples include two self-report measures, the Millon Clinical Multiaxial Inventory (MCMI) (Millon, 1987) and the Personality Disorder Questionnaire (PDQ) (Hyler et al., 1989), and two coded interview schedules, the Personality Disorder Examination (PDE) (Loranger, Susman, Oldham, & Russakoff, 1985), and the Structured Clinical Interview for DSM-III-R (SCID-II) (Spitzer, Williams, & Gibbon, 1987). Each of these diagnostic systems has demonstrated good reliability but has added little to enhancing the discriminant validity of the BPD diagnosis.

Dimensional Approach to Borderline Personality Disorder Diagnosis

Investigators who have been concerned with enhancing the validity of the BPD diagnosis suggest that a precisely defined boundary for the disorder may not be found (Livesley & Jackson, 1992; Widiger & Frances, 1985). Frances (1982) suggests that "a dimensional approach will eventually become a standard method for personality diagnosis because personality disorders do not have the internal homogeneity and clear boundaries most suited for classification in a categorical system" (p. 526). With a dimensional approach certain personality factors other than behaviors and symptoms are included in the diagnostic description. For example, dimensions such as affective response, type of cognitive functioning, pattern of interpersonal behavior, self-concept (Millon, 1987), complexity of representations of self and others, regulation of affect, capacity for emotional investment, and social cognition (Westen, 1991) would provide important focal points for exploration. However, attempts to distinguish the unique and independent contributions of these dimensions within a system of diagnostic categories would be relinquished in favor of an approach that would integrate the relative contributions of all of the dimensions in explaining the pathological syndrome.

Several dimensional approaches have been proposed. Livesley and Schroeder (1991) used factor analysis of self-report measures of features that span the DSM-III-R Cluster B diagnoses (antisocial, borderline, histrionic, and narcissistic). For the BPD group, factor loadings for 14 theoretically derived criteria for identifying BPD were analyzed. The first factor was chosen to represent core features of borderline pathology. In addition to replicating several of the DSM criteria (diffuse self-concept, unstable moods, and unstable interpersonal relationships), the factor included two additional features not found in the DSM system (separation protestation and brief stress-related psychosis) that were both related to significant problems in attachment relationships.

Livesley and Jackson (1992) have debated whether personality disorders are best classified using categorical or dimensional models. Dimensional models assume a continuity between normal and abnormal personalities. The authors address three issues that need to be considered for determining factors that could enhance diagnostic reliability and validity:

1. Theoretical issues focus on defining for each disorder the disorder's unique features and their interrelatedness.

2. Measurement issues are concerned with determining how many criteria are relevant and whether these should be summed to the minimum required (e.g., five of eight DSM-III, Axis II criteria for BPD) or summed to yield a total score.

3. Issues that have to do with assigning meaning to the diagnostic system must be considered. For example, using the DSM system, how is one to interpret the significance of endorsing five rather than eight of the criteria for BPD or the differences about which five criteria are endorsed? Similarly, when a reliable diagnostic measure such as the DIB uses a cutoff score to assign the diagnosis, how is this to be interpreted (e.g., score range 7 to 10 for the DIB or 8 to 10 for the DIB-R)?

Perry (1990) argues that information from several domains is important to validate the diagnosis of personality disorders. These include DSM descriptive criteria, the psychological mechanisms that determine pathogenesis and maintenance of the disorder, the course of the disorder, and the response to treatment. Although this approach would be all-inclusive, there are problems in generating reliable and valid methods for appraising the significance of patient information in each of these domains. For example, the measurement of "psychological mechanisms" would involve a complex measurement enterprise with significant problems in terms of levels of inference and generalizability.

Additional data that would be useful for developing an effective diagnostic system include outcome predictors that have been derived from follow-up studies. For example, follow-up studies (McGlashan, 1986; Paris, Brown, & Nowlis, 1987; Plakun, Burkhardt, & Muller, 1986; Stone, 1993) of borderline patients have isolated the following positive predictors:

1. Higher IQ
2. Distractibility
3. Shorter length of hospitalization prior to index treatment
4. Talent and attractiveness
5. Absence of parental divorce.

Negative predictors include:

1. Substance abuse
2. Affective instability
3. Antisocial traits
4. Dysphoria
5. Narcissistic entitlement and traits
6. Chronic feelings of emptiness and boredom.

Integration of Categorical and Dimensional Diagnostic Systems

The DIB interview schedule (Gunderson, Kolb, & Austin, 1981; Zanarini, Gunderson, Frankenberg, & Chauncey, 1989) for diagnosing BPD can be viewed as including both a dimensional and categorical approach. Four dimensions present in both the original DIB and the revised DIB (DIB-R) identify specific areas for exploration:

1. Affective
2. Cognitive
3. Impulse
4. Interpersonal.

Each is weighted differently to reflect the special relevance of that dimension for identifying the disorder. Scores of 7 to 10 (DIB) or 8 to 10 (DIB-R) are used to assign the patient to the BPD category. For the DIB-R Zanarini (1989) changed the scoring algorithm to reflect the findings of previous diagnostic studies that supported higher weights for the interpersonal and impulse dimensions. Thus, both the dimensions and the scoring system of the DIB and DIB-R provide opportunities for assigning the diagnosis reliably and for examining clinically relevant dimensions that are important for designing treatment interventions and assessing treatment effects.

Oldham and colleagues (1992) have suggested that the DSM system could be used to study the specific nature of the overlap between BPD and other Axis II personality disorders. Because several diagnostic categories share similar criteria, it would be possible to isolate combinations of criteria that apply consistently when BPD patients qualify for a second Axis II diagnosis. For example, what are the overlapping criteria when both BPD and narcissistic personality disorder diagnoses are assigned? When these dual diagnoses apply, how can the overlapping criteria be used to design effective models of treatment?

Similarly, studies of comorbidity would be useful for understanding the distinction between BPD patients who have affective symptoms (e.g., depression) but do not qualify for an Axis I affective disorder diagnosis and patients who qualify for both the BPD diagnosis and Axis I major depressive disorder. After DSM categorization, a dimensional approach could be used to generate finer distinctions between these two groups of patients (Zimmerman, Pfohl, Coryell, Stangl, & Corenthal, 1988). For example, it would be possible to isolate dimensions that distinguish depressive disorders that occur in the context of significant pathology of object relations from those that occur in subjects who have a capacity for initiating and maintaining intimate relationships. Evidence for this approach has been provided by studies that have shown that borderline depressives display exaggerated feelings of loneliness and desperation in relation to important people in their lives and that they also differ qualitatively from non-borderline depressives in their expression of labile, diffuse negative affect (Westen, Lohr, Silk, Gold, & Kerber, 1990; Wixom, 1988).

The success of any system for diagnosing BPD largely depends on the dimensions chosen for study and the degree of inference required in assessing their independent and combined contributions to describing the disorder (Widiger, Mieler, & Tilly, 1992). The DIB and DIB-R instruments have good face validity, clinical sensitivity, and require low levels of inference for scoring the contribution of each dimension. In contrast, Kernberg's diagnostic dimensions for assessing borderline personality organization (identity diffusion, use of primitive defenses, intact reality testing) require complex levels of inference in that patient dialogue needs to be assessed within the context of psychoanalytic perspectives about early development and personality formation.

Alternate diagnostic systems could evolve from the use of measures that assess object relations and social cognition. Westen and colleagues (1990) have developed a measure for assessing phenomena that focus on two areas of functioning that are particularly relevant for identifying problems shared by severe personality disorders patients, the regulation of emotions and the cognitive attribution of cause in interpersonal contexts. However, the use of the measure in clinical settings is not currently feasible because the reliable application of the scales requires considerable training and the availability of extensive data (either transcribed responses to a Thematic Apperception Test, or transcribed interviews). However, this measure and other similar ones developed to assess core personality features (Bell, Billington, & Becker, 1986; Burke, Summers, Selinger, & Polonus, 1986; West, Sheldon, & Reiffer, 1987) could be tested so as to extract multiple dimensions related to the diagnosis of BPD and could be important for designing parsimonious and effective treatment models for BPD. The fit between salient dimensions of pathological forms of the BPD disorder, specific models of treatment, and predicted outcomes could be greatly enhanced. (See table 2.1.)

Table 2.1
Approaches to the Diagnosis of
Borderline Personality Disorder

Categorical Psychodynamic
Identity diffusion
Primitive defensive operations
Capacity for reality testing

Categorical DSM-III-R Axis II
Marked, persistent identity disturbance
Unstable intense relationships
Impulsivity
Inappropriate, intense anger
Recurrent suicidal threats/gestures
Affective instability
Chronic emptiness/boredom
Frantic efforts to avoid abandonment

Dimensional Multiple Factors
Affective response
Cognitive functioning
Pattern of interpersonal behavior
Complexity of representations of self and others
Psychological mechanisms that determine pathogenesis
Substance abuse
Response to treatment
Course of the disorder

Models for Isolating Subtypes of Borderline Personality Disorder: An Overview

Despite the diagnostic problems outlined, models for subclassifications of BPD have been proposed. Grinker (1966) outlined a typology of borderlines based on "functions of the ego." Four subgroups of borderlines were identified:

1. Lowest functioning group: borderline psychosis
2. Core borderline group
3. Adaptive, affectless "as if" group
4. Depressive group that bordered on neuroses

Gunderson (1984) has described levels of borderline functioning according to subjective experiences of the primary object; these span a continuum in which at the highest level the object is perceived as supportive, at the next level the object is perceived as frustrating, and at the lowest level of functioning the object is perceived as absent. Clarkin and colleagues (1991) used an agglomerative cluster analysis to generate subsets of DSM-III criteria used in the clinical diagnosis of a large cohort of borderline patients. Three clusters were identified:

1. Identity cluster
2. Affect cluster
3. Impulse cluster

In a subsequent publication Hurt (Hurt, Clarkin, Marziali, & Munroe-Blum, 1992) demonstrated how the three clusters form the basis for the development of specified treatment strategies for BPD.

The Random Control Trial Analyses of Borderline Personality Disorder Subtypes

Several methods for determining subtypes of BPD were developed in the Random Control Trial (RCT) that tested the effects of Interpersonal Group Psychotherapy (IGP) for borderline patients. The ultimate aim is to examine whether subgroups, once identified, differ in terms of response to treatment. The DIB was used as the primary screening instrument. A subset of qualifying patients were also interviewed with three other interview schedules: the DIB-R; the PDE (Loranger, Susman, Oldham, & Russakoff, 1985), which screens for all Axis II disorders; and the Schedule for Affective Disorders and Schizophrenia (SADS) (Endicott & Spitzer, 1978), which screens for Axis I disorders. In addition patients completed several measures of symptoms and problematic behaviors.

In terms of reliability of the BPD diagnosis, 77% of the patients referred with a clinical diagnosis of the disorder qualified on the DIB (scores of 7 or more); agreement between the original and revised version of the DIB (DIB-R) was only 71%, but there was adequate agreement between each version of the DIB and the PDE (77% for the DIB and 100% for the DIB-R). Approximately 55% of the DIB-diagnosed subjects also qualified for major depressive disorder.

In addition, the findings showed that the DIB and DIB-R scores when correlated separately with the symptom scores functioned as indices of severity. For example, subjects with the lowest DIB qualifying score of 7 were the least severe symptomatically. Conversely, DIB subjects with scores of 8 or more were more severely symptomatic and were more likely to be alcohol and drug dependent. From these analyses it was clear that BPD severity subgroups could be identified on the basis of their DIB scores.

A second strategy for isolating BPD subgroups was tested. A qualitative analysis of multiple assessment measures used in the treatment comparison trial was conducted. The aim was to examine whether subgroups that included a number of dimensions in addition to severity would evolve. Diagnostic criteria, DIB scores, individual item scores and total scale scores from the assessment measures were examined for 7 patients who participated in one of the groups treated in the treatment comparison trial. The aim was to locate diagnostic and clinical dimensions that appeared to distinguish subgroups and exclude dimensions that showed little to no variation across subjects. Ten data sets were examined in the analysis: three diagnostic systems (DIB [Gunderson, Kolb, & Austin, 1981]; SADS [Endicott & Spitzer, 1978]; PDE [Loranger et al., 1985]), six measures of symptoms and behaviors (HSCL 90 [Derogatis, Lipman, & Covi, 1973]; Beck Depression Inventory [Beck, Ward, Mendelsohn, Mock, & Erbaugh, 1961]; Objective Behaviors Index Scale [Munroe-Blum & Marziali, 1986]; Social Adjustment Scale [Weissman & Bothwell, 1976]; Inventory of Interpersonal Problems [Horowitz, Rosenburg, Baer, Ureno, & Villasenor, 1988]; Stress Events Scale [Marziali & Pilkonis, 1986]), information on family history, and previous therapeutic experiences.

Contrary to expectation, half of the data sets did not show sufficient contrast between patients to warrant subgroupings within the borderline disorder. These included the DSM III Axis-II-R criteria (PDE); the Inventory of Interpersonal Problems (Horowitz et al., 1988); the People in Your Life Scale (measure of social support, Marziali, 1987); a Stress Events Scale (Marziali & Pilkonis, 1986); and the Target Complaints measure (Battle et al., 1966).

From the analysis of the remaining 5 dimensions, three subgroups emerged: a Dependent group (3 patients), a Substance Abuse group (2 patients), and an Impulsive Angry group (2 patients). The DIB scores separated the three groups; the patients in the Dependent subgroup obtained scores in the 7–8 range (mean 7.3); the Substance Abuse group had scores of 8 and 10 (mean 9); and the Impulsive Angry group scored 9 and 10 (mean 9). If the DIB represents an index of overall severity, then the latter two groups could be classified in the more severe category.

The Beck Depression Inventory (Beck, Rush, Shaw, & Emery, 1979) distinguished the three groups, but the levels of severity did not parallel the DIB score levels. The Substance Abuse group had the lowest mean score on the BDI (mean 23); the Dependent group scored at the next highest level (mean 25), and the Impulsive Angry group scored in the severe range (mean 33.5).

On the Objective Behaviors Index scale (Munroe-Blum & Marziali, 1986) all of the patients reported problems with intimate relationships. All had been involved in a number of intimate relationships that had ended badly. Verbal and/or physical abuse occurred in all intimate relationships, but the frequency and intensity varied across groups. Some of the patients in both the Substance Abuse group and the Impulsive Angry group were verbally and physically abusive with both their mates and their children. However they were frequently the recipients of abuse. Because of problems with their children, these patients had contacts with school counseling services, child mental health agencies, and child welfare services. In contrast, the Dependent group was more apt to be the recipients of either verbal or physical abuse. For both the Impulsive Angry and the Substance Abuse groups control of anger was a major problem. These patients tended to develop rage reactions to what appeared to be daily routine events. The Dependent group reported the experience of anger but inhibition in its expression; several of these patients resorted to bouts of overeating or overdrinking in response to helplessness and frustration. Two of the patients in this group used various self-harming behaviors in response to anxiety and frustration.

In terms of family history, both the Dependent and Substance Abuse groups had experienced early childhood traumas, but for the majority, their parents had remained together despite severe marital difficulties. Although a number of the patients eventually witnessed their parents' separations, these tended to occur just prior to the onset of puberty or later.

All of the patients in the three groups suffered some form of early childhood trauma, but higher severity and longer duration applied to the Impulsive Angry group: physical and/or sexual abuse, periods of separation from the parents; and erratic and unpredictable affectionate caring juxtaposed with either a harsh or lax disciplinary regime. Many of the patients were well aware of the strategies they used as children to deal with their frustrations and helplessness. One patient dealt with the trauma of being abandoned by her father by clinging to her mother and complaining of physical ailments so as to gain her attention. Another patient was able to predict when another foster home placement might occur on the basis of her observations of the escalating violence between her parents. Many of the patients left home by mid-adolescence because of severe quarrels and unresolvable disagreements with their parents.

The patients varied in terms of their views of psychiatric treatments prior to the index treatment. The Dependent group tended to describe favorable prior experiences in psychotherapy; they spoke positively about their past therapists and felt that they had been helped despite the fact that their problems had not been entirely resolved. The patients in the Substance Abuse group had more varied responses to their prior experiences with therapy. One had had successful experiences with Alcoholics Anonymous and had managed to remain alcohol free. The other patient abused both alcohol and drugs and had not been as successful in curtailing these habits despite repeated periods of treatments with various mental health services. The patients in the Impulsive Angry group felt extremely angry with their previous experiences in therapy. They were critical of their therapists and of the health care system in general. They felt rejected and "turfed out" every time they showed up in emergency psychiatric services. Both had had a series of brief hospitalizations in conjunction with suicidal threats or attempts. One of these patients had made good connections with therapists during stays in hospital but felt rejected by them when at discharge a referral to an outpatient service had been made. It was clear that the mental health care system had failed to meet the therapeutic needs of this subgroup of patients.

The qualitative analysis of a comprehensive set of assessment data on a cohort of 7 patients provides some support for defining subgroups of the disorder. Thus, the question is no longer which treatment is more effective for BPD but, rather, which treatment is more effective with which subtype of the disorder. In the analyses of the IGP treatment, one of the groups treated in the trial was examined to explore how patients in each of the subgroups participated in the process of the group. (See table 2.2.) In chapter 8 patients from each of the subgroups are selected to highlight their unique responses to IGP. The aim is to illustrate the continuity between specific diagnostic features of the borderline disorder, specific treatment strategies, and patient responses both within and across the treatment sessions.

Table 2.2
Dimensions of Borderline Personality Disorder Subtypes

DIMENSIONS	SUBTYPES		
	Dependent	**Substance Abuse**	**Impulsive Angry**
DIB Mean Score	7.3	9	9
BDI Mean Score	25	23	33.5
OBI Dimensions	Recipient of verbal/physical abuse, self-harming behaviors and suicidal gestures/attempts	Recipient or perpetrator of verbal/physical abuse, alcohol/drug abuse	Verbal/physical abuse toward significant others, frequent loss of control over anger
Family History	Intact family of origin during early childhood, parent marital conflicts, verbal/physical abuse of children	Intact family of origin during early childhood, later separation/divorce of parents, verbal/physical abuse of children	Family breakdown during early childhood, frequent periods of separation from parents, verbal/physical abuse of children
Treatment Compliance	Positive about previous therapy experiences, high compliance to index therapy	Ambivalent about previous therapy experiences, moderate compliance to index therapy	Very negative about previous therapy experiences, high compliance to index therapy

Summary of Diagnostic Perspectives of Borderline Personality Disorder

It may be that a clear-cut method for isolating a single "pure type" of BPD cannot be found and that such a goal may be irrelevant in terms of clinical management and the study of the course of the illness. Although a system for describing subtypes of BPD may be useful, it may be more important to describe diagnostic features that are not only common to all subtypes but have special relevance for designing effective models of treatment. For example, all criteria systems developed to diagnose the borderline disorder include at least one interpersonal dimension among the following:

1. Identity diffusion (Kernberg, 1975)
2. Intense, unstable interpersonal relationships and an unstable sense of self (Gunderson, 1984)
3. Identity disturbance and unstable, intense relationships (DSM-III & III-R, Axis II, APA, 1980, 1987).

Furthermore, many of the remaining features used by each system to confirm the presence of the borderline disorder could be described as symptomatic and behavioral responses to core problems in the interpersonal domain:

1. Primitive defensive operations (Kernberg, 1975)
2. Manipulative suicide attempts, negative affects, and impulsivity (Gunderson, 1984)
3. Inappropriate intense anger, physically self-damaging acts, affective instability, impulsivity, chronic emptiness/boredom, and intolerance of being alone (DSM-III & III-R).

It is argued that the assessment of the interpersonal problem core of BPD provides the salient diagnostic elements essential for its effective management and treatment. There is considerable support for this perspective (Gunderson, 1984; Kernberg, 1975; Westen, 1990). In particular, Widiger and Frances (1985) state "an interpersonal nosology is particularly relevant to personality disorders. Each personality disorder has a characteristic and dysfunctional style that is often central to the disorder. There is also some empirical support for the hypothesis that a personality disorder is essentially a disorder of interpersonal relatedness" (p. 621).

Borderline patients report that their major disappointments and accompanying symptoms arise from conflicted, unstable relationships with important others. For example, the salient feature, consistent across the three subgroups of BPD described, was a history of repeated conflicts in managing important relationships. A patient in the Dependent group differed from a patient in the Impulsive Angry group in terms of external manifestations of the disorder, with the former resorting more to depression and isolation and the latter showing frequent angry or violent outbursts. Yet, what was most painful for both patients was their despair about securing and maintaining mutually gratifying relationships with significant people in their current life situations. There was much evidence to show that their patterned ways of interacting with significant others was replicated in all new relationships, including those with therapists. The style of interacting manifested by the Dependent subgroup had been more successful in sustaining previous therapeutic contacts, whereas that of the Impulsive Angry subgroup had resulted in many failed contacts with the helping professions.

It is postulated that each borderline patient's style of managing interpersonal conflicts is manifested in the initial diagnostic session and that the assessing therapist's responses vary according to overall philosophy of treatment approach with borderline patients. The therapist's understanding of interpersonal conflicts as they are transacted within the assessment session provides important indicators for the fit between salient diagnostic criteria and treatment approach. Various approaches to assessing BPD, concluding with the process and strategies recommended from the perspective of IGP, follow.

Clinical Formulation of Borderline Personality Disorder

PSYCHOANALYTIC ASSESSMENT PROCESS

Kernberg (1975; Kernberg, Selzer, Koenigsburg, Carr, & Appelbaum, 1989) and Silver and Rosenbluth (1992) discuss both the aims and process of assessment sessions with BPD. Their primary goal is to determine the borderline patient's capacity for engaging in intensive psychoanalytic psychotherapy. In approaching the assessment process Silver recommends that the therapist should have an open-minded and eclectic attitude; that is, he believes that a variety of social, biological, and psychodynamic theoretical models are applicable to understanding and treating the borderline patient. In contrast, Kernberg's approach to conceptualizing the borderline patient is concerned with assessing the presence of criteria for borderline personality organization that draw on an object relations perspective to explain the origins of borderline pathology.

Both Silver and Kernberg view the assessment process as requiring two to four sessions. In addition to taking an extensive early and current life history, they observe the patient's reactions to the therapist within the session, noting in particular transference demands that parallel patterns of interactions with significant others. Suicidal risk is assessed and discussed openly with the patient. Whereas Silver is prepared to hospitalize a patient who is suicidal, Kernberg recommends referral to a hospital and is clear about keeping separate the aims of psychotherapy and the management of suicidal risk. Silver assesses criteria for major depressive disorder and recommends pharmacological intervention when warranted as an adjunct to psychotherapy. A similar approach has been taken by Clarkin and colleagues (1992) who are investigating the reliability and validity of Kernberg's model of psychoanalytical psychotherapy.

Silver emphasizes the importance of assessing the patient's capacity for developing a therapeutic alliance with the therapist. An important diagnostic indicator is whether the patient has had at least one meaningful, not self-destructive relationship for a minimum of 1 year between adolescence and the current assessment (Silver, 1992). Silver also adds that the patient must demonstrate a capacity for empathy in order to make therapeutic progress.

An additional important diagnostic parameter is the assessment of the therapist's subjective reactions to the patient during the diagnostic interview. When extreme anxiety or negative feelings are evoked and the therapist has difficulty restoring balance in his or her communication with the patient, then the therapist should be alerted to the possibility of borderline interpersonal phenomena being played out in the diagnostic session. It may be that this is one of the most valid and reliable criteria for testing hypotheses about the possible presence of BPD.

For both Kernberg and Silver the assessment process inducts into therapy those patients who fit the criteria for borderline personality organization and who are able to contain acting-out impulses sufficiently to agree to the conditions presented in the form of a therapeutic contract. Responsibilities of both patient and therapist are discussed, and Silver is especially explicit about explaining to the patient the clinical realities, including what can be realistically achieved.

In summary, a psychoanalytically oriented assessment process is well suited to the structure and procedures of intensive psychoanalytic psychotherapy. Both the patient and the therapist experience within the diagnostic sessions their respective role functions as well as affective and attitudinal reactions. Thus, the assessment process represents an initial trial of the therapeutic process; a test of what can be expected once commitment to therapy has been mutually agreed on.

THE INTERPERSONAL GROUP THERAPY APPROACH

Patients were referred to the treatment comparison trial following a clinical DSM-III-R–based diagnosis of BPD. The initial screening took place in psychiatric outpatient clinics as part of standard procedures. Following referral to the study, additional screening procedures were used. In particular, standardized diagnostic interviews were used with referred patients. Although these procedures were essential to ensure the internal and external validity of the RCT, it is recommended that a diagnostic schedule such as the DIB or DIB-R be used routinely to confirm a clinical diagnosis of BPD, especially when a model of treatment designed to respond to specific features of the disorder is being used.

Interpersonal Group Psychotherapy was designed to integrate a definition of the borderline disorder that focuses on pervasive problems in interpersonal relationships with an empirically based method for defining the disorder. Diagnostically, the aim was to include patients who met DSM-III Axis II (APA, 1980) criteria for BPD. Patients qualify for IGP if they meet criteria for BPD on the basis of a reliably administered semi-structured diagnostic interview schedule such as the DIB (Gunderson, Kolb, & Austin, 1981), the DIB-R (Zanarini, Gunderson, Frankenburg, & Chauncey, 1989), the PDE (Loranger et al., 1985), or the SCID-II (Spitzer et al., 1987). All of these instruments include DSM-III, Axis II-R criteria for BPD. The original and revised versions of the DIB also include psychodynamic criteria and a section on nonpsychotic odd thought processes that the others exclude.

The BPD patients treated with IGP in the treatment comparison trial were selected for inclusion if they met the cutoff score (7 or more) on the original DIB, so that the outcome results could be generalized to patients selected on this instrument. When patients are identified reliably with instruments such as the DIB, it is possible subsequently to compare the results of a treatment trial with those obtained by other investigators using the same instrument for patient selection. Also, variability of treatment response can be understood only when patient factors are controlled and examined in relation to the effects of specific treatment strategies. In other words, the effects of a treatment program can only be understood and generalized when the patient population is carefully described and when the treatment methods are well articulated and reliably applied. For BPD there is sufficient heterogeneity within the disorder that still eludes precise definition; thus, it is imperative that reliable methods for identifying the disorder be used so that the interaction between specific diagnostic and treatment variables can be examined.

The recommended diagnostic schedules are easy to administer, and only a small amount of training is needed to achieve acceptable levels of reliability. From our experience with the various diagnostic instruments, it appears that the original version of the DIB- and DSM-based diagnostic systems such as the PDE and SCID includes a wider band of BPD patients who show greater variance in symptomatic severity and types of overlap with Axis I and Axis II disorders, whereas the revised version of the DIB, the DIB-R, seems to include a narrower band of BPD patients who may be somewhat closer to the criteria planned for DSM-IV. In addition, the suggested instruments do not exclude patients with co-occurring major depressive disorder and point to the need to screen for this Axis I disorder. When major depressive disorder is suspected, an interview schedule that screens for Axis I disorders needs to be used. The SCID (Spitzer, 1987) can serve this purpose, whereas the PDE screens personality disorders only and the two versions of the DIB are specific to BPD. With its focus on core personality features of the disorder (pervasive instability of interpersonal relationships), the IGP model of treatment was viewed as addressing the needs of both the dual-diagnosed patients (BPD and major affective disorder) and those with BPD only. However, in order to explore factors that might explain variations in response to treatment, it was important to identify, from the onset, the dual-diagnosed BPD patients.

Table 2.3

Characteristics of Measures of Borderline Personality Disorder

Characteristic	DIB	DIB-R	PDE	SCID	PDQ	MCMI
Interview	x	x	x	x		
Self-report					x	x
All DSM-III-R Axis II diagnoses	no	no	yes	yes	yes	yes
BPD diagnosis only	yes	yes	no	no	no	no
Number of items	165	136	126	120	155	175
Scoring system	x	x	x	x	x	x
Completion time	60 min.	60 min.	90 min.	90 min.	20 min.	20 min.

Note: For a complete list of instruments for measuring BPD, see Reich (1992).

Summary of Features Relevant to Interpersonal Group Therapy

If a continuum exists between diagnostic precision, treatment specificity, and predicted treatment effects, the linkages between diagnostic
criteria selected to represent BPD best, the application of IGP, and the
expected outcomes need to be made specific. Because IGP was
designed to respond to the interpersonal features of the borderline disorder, the interpersonal diagnostic dimensions have saliency over others. Similarly, symptoms and problematic behaviors were not viewed
as independent diagnostic criteria but as responses to interpersonal
conflicts; thus, treatment effects would be demonstrated by a reduction
in these response behaviors. A summary of the diagnostic features of
BPD that were particularly relevant in the design of an interpersonal
group psychotherapy treatment for BPD included the following:

1. Pervasive problems in distinguishing self-motivations from
those of significant others
2. Impulsive behaviors that are potentially harmful to self
and/or others and that are responses to intense disappointments in important relationships
3. Difficulty in managing emotions, especially anger that erupts
in disproportionate response to threats of rejection or abandonment by significant others
4. Multiple unsatisfactory experiences in all areas of functioning that reinforce low self-esteem and malevolent representations of others.

In summary, the review of diagnostic systems for describing patients
with BPD shows that diagnostic precision is best achieved when a reliable diagnostic schedule or measure is used. However, the issue of
diagnostic validity remains problematic. Within the BPD category there
is considerable variation in the style of presentation of each patient. As
was demonstrated in the qualitative, dimensional approach described,
each of the three subgroups (Dependent, Substance Abuse, and
Impulsive Angry) varied considerably in the manifestation of forms
and levels of severity of BPD psychopathology. Yet, consistent across
all three groups was the core problem of managing intimate relationships effectively. Thus, regardless of the external manifestations of the
anxiety, frustration, and despair associated with conflicted, painful
interpersonal issues, all BPD patients are engaged in a lifelong search
for more caring, gratifying, and secure relationships with significant
others. This primary patient focus converged with the central rationale
for designing the IGP treatment.

3

Etiology

There is considerable variation among clinicians about the etiologic and developmental precursors of BPD. Although most acknowledge the possible influence of genetic, constitutional, neurobehavioral, and early developmental factors, clinicians disagree on which of these features is more important in determining the presence of borderline pathology in adults. Historically, the best formulated and most persuasive postulates regarding the etiology of the borderline syndrome have come from psychodynamic models of personality development that infer from the adult patients' reconstructions of past experiences possible intra- and interpsychic models of separation-individuation and identity formation. Patients' memories of early childhood physical and sexual abuse have not been emphasized by psychoanalytic theorists, even though Stern (1938) in his seminal paper on borderline pathology noted that "actual cruelty, neglect and brutality by the parents of many years' duration are factors found in these patients" (p. 468). Only in the 1980s have clinical investigators begun to explore the relevance of early life experiences (physical and sexual abuse, neglect, separation, and loss) in explaining the onset of the disorder and its behavioral manifestations in the adult patient. Results of studies of the effects of neurological impairment in childhood have also been linked to the onset of BPD. It is likely that many etiologic hypotheses obtain and that there are multiple causes to the onset of BPD.

Not unique to BPD, yet equally important for understanding its salient symptomatic and behavioral features (intense, unstable interpersonal relationships, self-damaging behaviors, affective instability, and impulsivity) is the study of early childhood attachment and bonding, of stages of cognitive development, and of parallel stages of emotion processing. A growing empirical literature illustrates the relevance of these developmental factors in explaining maladaptive behavior in adults. In addition, studies of diagnostic groups of adult patients, including borderlines, provide some evidence for inferring associations between negative early life experiences and later onset of psychopathology.

Three perspectives on the etiology and pathogenesis of BPD are reviewed: psychodynamic, neurobehavioral, and familial. In addition, clinical and theoretical hypotheses generated from studies of early childhood attachment and of cognitive and emotional development, as well as studies of adult borderline perceptions of attachment and emotion processing are critiqued.

Psychodynamic Perspective

In psychoanalysis, developmental-diagnostic hypotheses are inferred from observations of the patient, reported symptoms, and interview material that includes patient recollections of early life experiences with caregivers. Although different psychoanalytic theorists disagree on the specific factors that contribute to the development of BPD, most locate the occurrence of developmental failures or conflicts in the first two years of life (Adler, 1985; Gunderson, 1984; Kernberg, 1975; Mahler, 1971; Masterson & Rinsley, 1975; Mahler, Pine & Bergman, 1975).

According to Kernberg (1975), certain constitutional phenomena combined with deficiencies in the environment contribute to the formation of early developmental conflicts that fail to be adequately resolved. An excessive aggressive drive coupled with a deficiency in the capacity to neutralize aggression or a lack of anxiety tolerance are associated with a failure to integrate good and bad self–other object representations. Primitive defenses (denial, projection, and splitting) are mobilized to keep separate the conflicted perceptions of self and other. Kernberg underemphasizes the role of the parent in determining the pathological outcome of the borderline's identity formation. Rather, his focus is on the progressively integrative aspects of ego development. His model presumes that in the borderline patient, the cognitive capacity for object constancy has been acquired and that borderline pathology evolves from a failure to acquire emotional object constancy. He outlines four stages for the development of integrated images of self as separate from other:

1. Undifferentiated self-object (first month)
2. Coalesced good and bad images of the self and of the object (12 to 18 months).

3. Emotional object constancy
4. Accompanying capacity for intimacy.

Kernberg's fourth developmental stage overlaps with the separation-individuation subphase of Mahler, Pine, and Bergman's (1975) rapprochement stage of early development.

Masterson and Rinsley (1975) believe that the etiology of BPD is associated with the mother's withdrawal of libidinal supplies at the developmental stage when the child attempts to separate from the mother in search of his or her own identity. Mahler's (1975) rapprochement subphase of separation-individuation is used to locate the developmental conflict. Masterson and Rinsley (1975) describe the mother of the borderline as having a pathological need to cling to her child to perpetuate the gratification experienced earlier when the infant's survival was symbiotically bound to her. According to this paradigm, the mother is available if the child clings and behaves regressively and withdraws if the child attempts to separate and individuate. Masterson and Rinsley describe the child's response to the mother's withdrawal as "abandonment depression" that results from the attempt to keep separate the positive and negative affective states experienced in relation to the mother. Reality is distorted, and ego development is arrested.

Buie and Adler (1982; Adler, 1985) also draw on Mahler's developmental thesis and add elements of Kohut's (1977) self-psychology for explaining the etiology of borderline personality. They believe that the borderline patient has not experienced an environment that could support the development of a stable self-identity in relation to the perception of an independent other. Adler (1985) suggests that the aloneness experienced by borderlines may be associated with the absence of good-enough mothering during the phases of separation-individuation. Because of the mother's emotional unavailability the child borderline fails to achieve "evocative memory" represented in Piaget's (1954) theory about the function of memory in cognitive development at age 18 months. Thus, the borderline, in the face of certain stresses, is unable to restore a solid integrated memory of the object and regresses to the earlier stage of "recognition memory" (age 8 months). Even though Adler agrees with other theorists in locating the developmental failure in Mahler's rapprochement and separation-individuation subphase, he believes that borderlines experience a primary emptiness due to the absence of stable images of positive introjects; that is, in the absence of these positive introjects, a holding, soothing sense of self does not develop.

Although most psychodynamic hypotheses about borderline

pathology draw on Mahler's observational longitudinal studies of mothers and their children, Mahler (1971) cautioned against drawing inferences about adult psychopathology from observations of childhood developmental phenomena. She suggested some link between the ego fixation problems of the borderline and developmental conflicts during the rapprochement subphase of separation-individuation; but she also believed that this hypothesis was not specific to BPD. Similarly, Kernberg's dynamic perspective of the etiology of borderline organization is not unique to borderline personality disorder but applies as well to schizotypal, narcissistic, histrionic, and antisocial personality disorders.

In summary, psychoanalytic hypotheses about the precursors of BPD emphasize intrapersonal, developmental dimensions concerned with identity formation. Borderline pathology is a manifestation of early childhood developmental failures that result in unresolved self-conflicts (Kernberg, 1975; Masterson & Rinsley, 1975) or self deficits (Adler, 1985). From these perspectives the BPD patient is viewed as either salvaging fragments of a self-identity by keeping separate good-versus-bad images of self and significant others (Kernberg, 1975) or needing to substitute a primary emptiness with new, more stable images of positive self-objects (Adler, 1985). Empirically, it would be extremely difficult, if not impossible, to test whether these hypotheses apply to all BPD patients. Yet, experienced clinicians would agree that many (but not all) BPD patients manifest difficulties in processing negative affects; that some (but not all) report feeling empty and rudderless; and that some (but not all) have difficulty in controlling high levels of anxiety and rage.

The problem with linear, unidirectional models of causation of a disorder is that alternate explanations are potentially ignored, and observed behavior is interpreted to fit the model, even if it is incorrect. For example, one of the patients screened for the random control trial (RCT) qualified for the BPD diagnosis on all eight of the DSM-III, Axis II criteria. However, the premorbid history provided by the patient, her husband, and chart reports supported a diagnosis of major affective disorder and the absence of BPD. The year before she was included in the study the patient had thrown herself in front of a moving bus and had sustained severe head injuries. Although she had recovered physically and had fully regained her memory and speech, she manifested many of the symptoms and behaviors typical of BPD patients. Clearly a neurobehavioral perspective was needed for understanding the meanings of this patient's behavior. As will be illustrated, neurological trauma sustained at any time in the life cycle, particularly in early childhood, challenge etiologic perspectives that fail to incorporate a range of factors that predispose to a disorder. Similarly, it will be demonstrated that studies of cognitive development, childhood regulation of affect, and early life psychological trauma provide a rich and complex set of factors for revising hypotheses about the developmental precursors of BPD.

Neurobehavioral Perspective

The neurobehavioral model suggests a connection between the negative developmental effects of childhood brain dysfunction and the development of borderline symptomatology. For the neurologically impaired child, developmental symptoms appear in the form of hyperactivity, short attention span, distractibility, mood oscillation, and high impulsivity. The resultant behavioral syndrome includes problematic social interactions, academic difficulties, and low levels of achievement. Several authors (Hartocollis, 1968; Murray, 1979) postulate an association between the distorting effects of minimal brain dysfunction (MBD) and the child's perceptions of his or her own behaviors and interactions with caregivers. The outcome is one of confused cognition, affect regulation, and impulse control that ultimately leads to borderline ego development and behavior. Some studies have explored empirically the MBD and adult psychopathology hypotheses (Milman, 1979; Quitkin, Rifkin, & Klein, 1976; Weiss, Hechtman, Perlman, Hopkins, & Wener, 1979; Wender, Reimher, & Wood, 1981). Only a few have examined factors specific to the development of borderline pathology (Andrulonis et al., 1981; Andrulonis & Vogel, 1984; Akiskal et al., 1981; Soloff & Millward, 1983). Overall, the findings are equivocal.

A frequently quoted study by Andrulonis et al. (1981) was the first of a series that examined neurological factors specific to the development of BPD. A retrospective chart review was conducted on 91 subjects meeting DSM-III criteria for the borderline diagnosis. Andrulonis was able to subdivide the subjects into three groups: a nonorganic group, a minimal brain dysfunction (MBD) group with a history of attention deficit disorder or learning disabilities, and an organic pathology group comprising subjects with a history of traumatic brain injury, encephalitis, or epilepsy. Overall, 38% of the subjects had a history of organicity, either MBD or organic pathology. The group with the history of organicity differed from the nonorganic group on several dimensions; they had earlier onset of illness, acted out more frequently, and were more apt to report family histories of drug and alcohol abuse.

In a subsequent study Andrulonis identified four subcategories of BPD, two of which included organicity factors, attention deficit or learning disabled, and organic. Of particular interest were the results that showed differences between male and female borderlines. Forty percent of the males compared with only 14% of the females suffered from an attention deficit disorder or learning disabilities. Also, 52% of the males compared with 28% of the females has either a current or past history of organic assaults, such as head trauma, encephalitis, or epilepsy. Andrulonis concluded that borderlines with minimal brain dysfunction are predominantly male and have an earlier onset of emotional and functional difficulties based in part on a constitutional deficit.

Akiskal (1981; Akiskal et al., 1985) conducted several studies to demonstrate the association between borderlines and affective disorders. Even though his primary focus was not on the exploration of specific neurological factors in borderlines, Akiskal's study of 100 borderline patients showed that in addition to overlapping affective diagnoses for almost half of the group, 11% had organic, epileptic, or attention deficit disorders. The discrepancy between Andrulonis's findings (38% of the subjects had histories of organicity) and Akiskal's findings (11% diagnosed as having neurological problems) can be explained by differences in both the aims and methods of the two studies. Andrulonis used chart reviews to obtain "histories" of organicity in borderlines. In contrast, Akiskal interviewed subjects to explore comorbidity between the borderline diagnosis and other psychiatric disorders that included organic syndromes; the subjects' past histories of organicity were not explored.

Soloff and Millward (1983) tested several etiologic hypotheses in a cohort of borderline patients. Included was a test of a neurobehavioral model of borderline personality style that was a partial replication of Andrulonis's study. Forty-five patients who met the criteria for borderline personality diagnosis on the Diagnostic Interview for Borderlines (DIB, Gunderson, Kolb, & Austin, 1981) were compared with 32 patients meeting research diagnostic criteria (RDC) for major depressive disorder and 42 patients meeting the RDC for schizophrenia. Information was obtained from the subjects and, for 43% of the cases, from family members as well. A neurobehavioral checklist was used. The results showed that more complications of pregnancy were reported in the prebirth histories of borderlines than in the other two groups. The borderlines had more childhood psychopathology, including temper tantrums, rocking and head banging, but learning difficulties were more prevalent in the schizophrenic group. Because Soloff excluded subjects with any known central nervous system (CNS) abnormality, CNS subjects who also may have qualified for the borderline diagnosis were excluded. The use of retrospective historical methods to infer neurobehavioral factors in both the Soloff and Andrulonis studies may explain the discrepancies in their findings. On the other hand, the consistencies in their findings lend some support for developmentally based neurobehavioral hypotheses for explaining the onset and course of BPD.

Family Studies

In the 1980s the results of a series of studies have provided some support for etiologic hypotheses that link early childhood separations, losses, neglect, and physical and sexual abuse with the development of borderline personality disorder in adults. These studies can be viewed as partial attempts to test psychodynamic, developmental theories about borderline pathology; that is, what associations, if any, exist between children's early experiences with their caregivers and later onset of the borderline disorder. Studies of early childhood experiences have relied on retrospective reports of developmental histories gleaned from chart reviews or reported by adult borderline patients. The results across studies are consistent.

SEPARATION AND LOSS

Bradley (1979) obtained histories of early maternal separations from the mothers or significant caregivers of 14 young adolescent borderlines and matched groups of 12 psychotic, 33 nonpsychotic psychiatric patients, and 23 nonpsychiatric, delinquent controls. Separation was defined as removal of the child from the home for more than 3 to 4 weeks. The results showed that the borderlines experienced significantly more early separations than the other groups. Soloff and Millward (1983) used a similar retrospective historical method to compare the early life separation experiences of borderlines with those experienced by schizophrenics and patients with major depressive disorders. The borderline group experienced more parental loss due to death and divorce, but there were no between-group differences for separations experienced due to either parent or child illnesses. The borderlines reported more problems in coping with normal separations such as attending school, transferring to a different school, and normal school transitions (elementary to high school). Both Bradley (1979) and

Soloff and Millward (1983) view their findings as supporting psychoanalytic theories that associate borderline pathology in the adult with an arrest during the separation-individuation phase of development in childhood.

PARENTAL CARE

Several investigators (Goldberg, Mann, Wise, & Segall, 1985; Paris & Frank, 1989) have examined qualities of parental care experienced by borderlines. Paris and Frank (1989) assessed subjects' recollections of the quality of care and protection received from parents during early childhood. Eighteen borderline (DIB score of 7 or more) and 29 nonborderline (DIB scores of 4 or less) female patients completed Parker's Parental Bonding Instrument (PBI; Parker, Tupling, & Brown, 1979). The PBI yields scores on two dimensions, parental care and parental protection. The results showed that only the degree of perceived maternal care significantly differentiated the two groups. In an earlier study, Goldberg, Mann, Wise, and Segall (1985) used the PBI to compare the responses of hospitalized borderline patients with two control groups; 24 had a clinical diagnosis of borderline, 22 had assorted psychiatric disorders, and 10 were nonclinical normal subjects. The borderlines perceived their parents to care less than the two control groups. The borderlines also perceived their parents to be more overprotective than the nonclinical control group but did not differ on this dimension from the psychiatric controls. Despite the sampling differences in the Paris and Frank (1989) and the Goldberg (1985) studies, the results could be viewed as supporting an association between the quality of early parental care and the development of borderline disorder. Alternately, the disorder itself may have influenced the responses to the instrument.

PHYSICAL AND SEXUAL ABUSE

There is increasing evidence for associating abuse trauma in childhood with psychological difficulties in adults (Bryer, Nelson, Miller, & Krol, 1987; Gelinas, 1983). Bryer, Nelson, Miller, and Krol (1987) obtained sexual and physical abuse histories from 68 female psychiatric patients who had been admitted to a private psychiatric hospital. The subjects completed a symptom checklist and received the Millon Clinical Multiaxial Inventory (MCMI). Overall, 72% of the subjects reported a history of early abuse by family members. The physically abused group contained a higher proportion of borderline patients; these patients had also experienced sexual abuse.

In a similar study, Briere and Zaidi (1989) reviewed 100 charts of female patients seen in a psychiatric emergency service for histories of sexual abuse. Fifty of the charts were selected randomly from files where the clinician had not been directed to inquire about sexual abuse. These were compared with 50 charts selected randomly from files written by a clinician who had been instructed to inquire about early childhood sexual abuse. The charts were coded for demographic variables, incidence of sexual abuse, and for the presence or absence of three personality disorder clusters (DSM-III-R). The most revealing finding was the very large discrepancy in the rate of reported abuse between subjects who had not been specifically asked about experiences of sexual abuse (6%) and those who had been asked (70%). For the latter, associations with clinical variables are similar to those reported by Bryer et al. (1987). Three times as many abused versus nonabused subjects had been given diagnoses of personality disorder. Also, five times as many of the abused patients had received specific diagnoses of BPD or borderline traits.

Three recent studies (Herman, Perry, & van der Kolk, 1989; Shearer Peters, Quaytman, & Ogden, 1990; Zanarini et al., 1989) compared reports of childhood trauma provided by borderline patients with those provided by several cohorts of patients with other psychiatric disorders. Zanarini (1989) used the revised version of the DIB to select 50 borderlines. Another interview schedule, the Diagnostic Interview for Personality Disorders (DIPD), was used to select 29 antisocial personality disorder controls. A second control group consisted of 26 patients who met the criteria for dysthymic disorder on the Structured Clinical Interview for DSM-III-R (SCID-II; Spitzer et al., 1987). Two semi-structured interviews were used to obtain histories of family pathology and early separation experiences. The reported neglect and abuse experiences were segmented into three childhood periods, early (0–5 years), latency (6–12 years), and adolescence (13–18 years). A significantly higher percentage of borderlines than controls (antisocial and dysthymic) reported being abused (verbal, physical, or sexual) during all three childhood periods. The borderlines were more likely than the dysthymic group to have been sexually abused during latency and adolescence and to have been physically abused during early childhood. A history of neglect, emotional withdrawal, and disturbed caretaker behavior discriminated the borderlines from the antisocial controls in each of the childhood phases. More borderlines than dysthymics reported early childhood prolonged separations, but they did not differ from the antisocial group on this dimension. The authors conclude that although their results lend support to hypotheses that link the development of borderline disorders with early life experiences of abuse, neglect, and loss, there is insufficient evidence to suggest that any one type of childhood experience predicts the development of the disorder.

In a similar study of BPD (Herman, Perry, & van der Kolk, 1989), childhood trauma reported by 21 subjects was compared with reports provided by subjects with related diagnoses (schizotypal and antisocial personality disorders and bipolar II affective disorders; $N = 23$). A 100-item, semi-structured interview was used to obtain childhood histories. The interview data were scored for positive indexes of trauma in three areas: physical abuse, sexual abuse, and witnessing of domestic violence. The frequency of occurrence of each type of trauma was segmented into three childhood stages; childhood (0–6 years), latency (7–12 years), and adolescence (13–18 years). Eighty-one percent of the borderline patients gave histories of major childhood trauma: 17% had been physically abused, 67% had been sexually abused, and 62% had witnessed domestic violence. The borderlines also reported more types of trauma that lasted longer. Women had significantly higher total trauma scores, and they reported more physical and sexual abuse in childhood. For the borderline group, when gender differences were controlled, the total childhood trauma score remained significant when compared with the other two groups.

In a study of suicidal behavior in 40 female inpatients with a BPD diagnosis, Shearer (Shearer, Peters, Quaytman, & Ogden, 1990) obtained histories of childhood sexual and physical abuse. The patients who reported sexual abuse were more likely to have a concomitant diagnosis of "suspected complex partial seizure disorder," an eating disorder, or a drug abuse disorder. A history of physical abuse was associated with early family disruption, more psychiatric hospital admissions, and a concurrent diagnosis of antisocial personality disorder. Because of the small sample size the authors were cautious in interpreting the significance of their findings. However, they hypothesized that the subjects may have had neurological problems at birth and that the accompanying deficits made them more vulnerable to family neglect, abuse, and disruption.

In summary, the results of these studies were well supported in our observations of the BPD patients who qualified for the RCT. As a group, every form of negative childhood experience was reported, but the nature and intensity of the experience varied for each patient. Some had sustained truly horrible experiences in which they had been both physically and sexually abused, whereas others had not sustained either form of abuse but had experienced a see-saw relationship with one or both parents. As one patient put it, "one day they loved me, and the next I was stupid and useless." The ongoing wish for a reunion with parents who would acknowledge their earlier failures as protective caregivers was of clinical significance. For example, many of the female patients who had been sexually abused wanted their mothers to admit that they had known at the time but had failed to rescue them. For many, this awareness was more painful than the actual experience of the abuse. Some patients wanted to gain acknowledgment and approval from parents whom they perceived as either unavailable or hypercritical. One patient who was 38 years old when he entered the study talked about his wishes for approval from his father whom he remembered as having consistently rejected him no matter how hard he tried to please him. In contrast, one of the female patients had been abandoned by her father in early childhood. She was an only child and remembered having enjoyed her privileged position in relation to her mother. However, as an adult she continued to have a morbid attachment to her mother despite the fact that her mother was very demanding, intrusive, and perpetually critical.

Each patient's early childhood traumatic experiences were "packaged" differently and held different meanings for each patient. Loss of a parent, sexual or physical abuse, or neglecting parents did not affect in equally damaging ways the patients who shared these experiences. Thus, the arena for observation of the effects of the patient's early life experiences was not so much in their portrayals of specific childhood trauma but, rather, in their narratives about the meanings of current adult intimate relationships, including their ongoing relationships with one or both parents.

Developmental Hypotheses from Normative Studies of Early Life Experience

Theoretical and clinical hypotheses about the pathogenesis of BPD must be interpreted in the context of empirical investigations of normative patterns of early life development. This is particularly important as theoretical and clinical propositions about the dynamic precursors of BPD have not been empirically validated. A number of authors (Bowlby, 1979, 1988; Stern, 1985; Westen, 1990) have critiqued a psychoanalytic theoretical approach that assumes that there is a parallel association between a continuum of early development and of psychopathology. However, no empirical findings support clinical inferences about children's intrapsychic experiences from the reports of adult patients. The notion that phase-specific trauma or fixations in early childhood lead to adult pathology has not been supported empirically. In fact, studies of early child development challenge psychoanalytic formulations about psychological development. Given the weight of this evidence, etiologic hypotheses about personality formation, including maladaptive versions, must include the study of the following:

1. Attachment and relationships
2. The nature of cognitive processing
3. The function of emotion processing.

Parallel emphasis needs to be placed on the study of contextual factors, in particular of genetic endowment and environmental variables. There is evidence to support the validity of each of these areas of personality development, but their respective contributions to an integrated model of personality function remain untested. Nonetheless, a review of the empirical literature on child development elucidates variables that may be important for understanding characteristics of borderline behavior. Studies of attachment, cognitive, and emotional response behaviors in adult borderline patients are also reviewed. A synthesis of these approaches may support hypotheses for linking features in the psychopathology of borderlines with early developmental experiences.

ATTACHMENT AND RELATIONSHIPS

Influenced by the work of ethnologists and by his own observations of children's reactions to separations from their mothers, Bowlby (1973, 1979, 1980, 1982, 1988) proposed a model for understanding the development and function of attachment behaviors. He arrived at the following conclusions:

1. Attachments between individuals serve basic survival functions.
2. Attachments operate as cybernetic systems; that is, each partner is attuned to maintaining accessibility to the other.
3. Attachment systems operate efficiently because in the mind of each partner working models of self in relation to other are learned and retained in memory; these working models contain the patterns of interaction that have developed between them.
4. Internal working models of relationships shape later relationships.
5. In turn, later relationships serve to modify working models of relationships.

Bowlby's paradigm about the function of attachment is logically and intuitively plausible. It proposes a developmental pathway that reflects coherence, flexibility, and the possibility for progressive change over time.

Bowlby's work has found considerable support from Mary Ainsworth's (Ainsworth, Blehar, Waters, & Wall, 1978; Ainsworth, 1985, 1989) pioneering studies of infants' experiences in "stranger situations" and in those of subsequent investigators who advanced her work (Bretherton & Waters, 1985; Rutter & Quinton, 1984a, 1984b; Stroufe & Fleeson, 1986). Ainsworth's work illustrates three qualities of attachment:

1. Secure attachment is associated with being raised by sensitive, caring parents
2. Anxious avoidant attachment is associated with intrusive parenting
3. Anxious ambivalent attachment is associated with inconsistent parenting (Ainsworth et al., 1978).

Other investigators (Bretherton & Waters, 1985; Bretherton, Ridgeway, & Cassidy, 1990; Cohn, 1990; Kobak & Sceery, 1988; Main & Cassidy, 1988) have shown that attachment classifications in infancy are associated with specific patterns of relationships with peers at later ages. Similarly, parental caregiving has been shown to have characteristics analogous to the quality of attachment (Bretherton, Biringen, Ridgeway, Meslin, & Sherman, 1989; George & Solomon, 1989). Thus, there is mounting evidence indicating that the attachment history of an individual may affect profoundly self–other behaviors in new relationships. Motivations and expectations derived from early relationships generate expectations about new relationships and about patterns of behaviors that reflect those expectations. These in turn affect the behavior of the new attachment figure. Because all relationships are reciprocal, the expectations and behaviors of the new attachment figure play a role in the evolving dynamic interactions. The resulting interpersonal transactions reflect both converging and diverging expectations of the partners in the relationship. Their respective capacities for modifying and reshaping divergent expectations determine the outcome of the attachment.

Although there is some support for hypotheses that associate the quality of past attachments with the quality of future relationships (Cohn, 1990; Crittenden, 1990; Main, Kaplan, & Cassidy, 1985), the exact function of internal working models of self in relation to other is unknown. For example, the BPD patients who qualified for the RCT spanned a continuum of perceived satisfaction with intimate others. Despite having conflicted perceptions of intimate others (friends, family members, or partners) they viewed these relationships as providing important sources of support. In fact, it was surprising to find that the mean response on satisfaction with intimate others on a measure of the adequacy of social support was not dissimilar to that reported for a cohort of neurotic patients. Thus, it would appear that BPD patients have experienced and retained both positive and negative images of self in relation to other. The proportion of negative over positive determines their expectations in new relationships, including the therapeutic relationship. For example, one of the patients had withdrawn from relationships with the exception of her husband and son. She felt that her expectations of others had been consistently thwarted in the past to an extent that she had given up engaging with others, including leaving a job because it required "too much communication with co-workers." In the group sessions this patient observed others and revealed little of herself. The therapists and the other group members were not to be trusted because, as with others in the past, her expectations would be frustrated. In contrast, another patient had sustained several friendships of long duration, had good rapport with her sister, an ambivalent relationship with her father, but had experienced a series of volatile, mutually violent relationships with men. This patient readily engaged with the group but wanted "answers" from the therapists and other group members. They were to tell her how to disengage from a current, abusive relationship with a man that she seemed unable to control.

COGNITIVE PROCESSING

The notion of self-schema has been proposed as a theoretical paradigm for the cognitive processes involved in coordinating perceptions of self and other in a relational context. The term is frequently interchanged with self and object mental representations and was derived from Piaget's (1952, 1954) studies of children's cognitive development. Piaget's work generated the concepts of mental schemas, representation, assimilation, and accommodation. These constructs provide theoretical structures for understanding mental contents that have to do with processing information about relationships. Of importance are the consistencies across three approaches to understanding relationship formation: Piaget's description of the function of assimilation and accommodation in the construction of schemas, Ainsworth's findings about specific qualities of attachment, and Bowlby's idea of internal representational models of attachment relationships. In all three models, cognitive and affective information is processed and utilized for defining a sense of self in relation to the external world. According to Bowlby, internal working models are important because they guide the individual's processing of relationship information, as for example, perception, encoding, memory retrieval, regulation of affect, assessment of information, and selection of suitable responses.

Different representational models contain different types of information derived from different memory systems and processed differently. Three types of memory systems have been identified (Bowlby, 1980; Crittenden, 1990; Tulving, 1983, 1985, 1989) in terms of relationships:

1. Semantic memory consists of generalizations about relationships.
2. Episodic memory contains information about events experienced between self and other.
3. Procedural memory carries information about patterns of behavior that represent learned feelings and expectations regarding the interaction of behaviors between self and other (Crittenden, Partridge, & Claussen, 1992).

Because memory systems develop at different ages (Tulving, 1989), the actual interplay between each memory system for encoding, retrieving, and expressing information about relationships is unknown. However, there is agreement that when a mismatch between learned expectations and perceptions of a new relationship occurs, the potential attachment may be too threatening and is abandoned. When expectations and behaviors exactly match, or are not too dissimilar (differences between expectations stored in memory and those observed), the new relationship can be assimilated to existing mental schemas, requiring only small accommodation of adjusted expectations. In this paradigm the internal representational model is revised, or, put in another way, new learning about self and other has been acquired and assimilated.

When these concepts are applied to the understanding of personality development, it is possible to infer a continuity between learned quality of attachment in early childhood and the quality of relationships in adulthood (Crittenden et al., 1992). For example, secure individuals have ready access to attachment-relevant information stored in memory, are able to integrate affect with cognition, accommodate discrepancies, and select appropriate actions. Anxious avoidant individuals appear to block or defend against awareness of attachment-relevant information, seem to have less access to memories, and are unable to integrate information about affect with cognition. Anxious ambivalent individuals appear to have access to attachment-relevant information, including affect tone; however affect is not regulated in a useful way; thus, relationship information perceived as threatening cannot be distinguished from nonthreatening information (Crittenden et al., 1992).

In maladaptive personality formation, extreme forms of early attachment experiences that were either anxious avoidant or anxious ambivalent seem to apply. The internalized self-schemas resulting from these models of attachment inhibit openness to new information and flexibility of response to others' behaviors. In these cases, there may exist a limited repertoire of schemas, and those which are available are inflexible and preclude a fit between self-expectations and perceptions of the external environment. Both self and other are perceived within a restricted range of expected behaviors and affects; also the restricted sense of self may exert a powerful distorting influence on the other person in the relationship (Crittenden et al., 1992). It may be that the significant difference between maladaptive and adaptive personalities rests on the fact that the former have a limited repertoire of enduring schemas (Horowitz, 1991) to call upon when presented with new interpersonal situations.

Enduring schemas contain generalized formats of knowledge about people and relationships that affect perceptual processes. They seem to draw on all three memory systems (semantic, episodic, and procedural) and influence in important ways the processing of new interpersonal situations. In maladaptive personalities what appears as blocked access to attachment information may possibly reflect a paucity of enduring schemas; thus attempts at processing new meanings are curtailed by the absence of person knowledge, including the absence of information for appraising aroused emotions. In contrast, adaptive personalities have access to a wide range of enduring schemas that are processed more flexibly; there is an openness to new information, and affective responses are integrated with stored information about previous affect-laden experiences.

An example from the IGP group treatment study illustrates the limitations and the rigidity of expectations contained in self–other schemas. At the first session of one of the groups a patient announced that she did not want to be in the group but was going to "stick it out" because that was all that the referring hospital could offer her. Although she told fragments of her story in ensuing sessions, she was very persistent in conveying to the other group members and the therapists that she did not want to talk to them. Yet, she showed up for every session. When other group members were rejected by her after repeated attempts to involve her, they started to attack her, saying, for example, "you needn't come, no one is forcing you." The patient's responses were counterdefensive; it seemed that, regardless of the quality of the other group members' communications, this patient was unable to alter her expectations. Either her feelings toward a group of strangers overpowered her judgments about their trustworthiness or she had a paucity of positive self-schemas to guide her wishes to engage with them in a good way. This patient's mental schemas seemed to be restricted to anxious ambivalent views of self in relation to others. She communicated a wish to engage with the group by being present at each session and by talking about her problems but simultaneously rejected the group members' and therapists' overtures to connect with them. The schemas were often played out through subtle manipulations during which the patient would first allude to feelings of hopelessness and suicidal ideation and then punish anyone who attempted to come to her rescue. She preserved these rigid and limited versions of self–other expectations for three-quarters of the scheduled group sessions. Only after several open and hostile confrontations with two of the other group members was she able to observe and begin to alter her perceptions of herself and others. The patient's routine pattern of simultaneously engaging and rejecting others were tolerated by the group members and by the therapists. They challenged the patient, let her know how her behaviors were frustrating and hurtful, but did not reject her.

Because borderline patients have persistent difficulties in maintaining social relationships, possibly the cognitive-processing problems described for maladaptive personalities in general are relevant to BPD. Integrating psychoanalytic and cognitive theories of developmental processes, Fonagy and Higgitt (1990) offer parallel hypotheses about cognitive deficits in adult BPD patients. They posit that a developmental paradigm in which the child has accurately perceived the caregiver as hostile and rejecting is at the root of the disorder; but in order to protect herself or himself from the awareness of the violent intent of the caregiver, the child defensively blocks cognitive processing of the mental states of others. Thus, the borderline patients' self-object schemas and their external relationships with others are profoundly constrained by a failure to conceptualize others as thinking, feeling, and needing emotional supplies. Fonagy and Higgitt (1990) suggest that this failure in cognitive processing can take place anytime during early development, but they speculate that it most likely occurs between the ages of 2 and 4 when cognitive development advances rapidly. Support for these hypotheses can be found in clinical situations in which the borderline patient projects on to others (including the therapist) the expectation of harm and abandonment. These expectations are not surprising; as Westen (1990) points out, "patients may expect and elicit much abuse in relationships in part because that is precisely what they learned to expect and became motivated to induce from relationships in childhood" (p. 684). Thus, change in the borderline patient's expectations would require the development of new ways of thinking and feeling about self and other in an interpersonal context that is tolerant, empathic, and supportive.

Emotion Processing and Temperament

As is clear, the processing of emotions occurs in conjunction with cognitive processing of other forms of information. Despite this fact, a separate review of the literature on developmental stages of emotion processing and the development of temperament is provided to highlight the importance of understanding emotion processing in BPD.

The process of affect regulation central to distinguishing maladaptive from adaptive emotion expression can only be understood in the context of how information about emotions is acquired. Developmental psychologists have studied the parallels between Piaget's stages of cognitive operations and developmental pathways through which emotions are processed. In these studies, emotions are defined as primary motivational forces in all human interaction. They provide the organizing principles for interpersonal relating and determine the quality of attachments and the conditions for separations (Lewis & Michelson, 1988). Emotion elicitation and regulation are concerned with three components:

1. The appreciation of the significance of important events
2. The appraisal of individual feelings and coping potential in relation to the event
3. The actions taken to deal with the external environment (Campos, Campos, & Barrett, 1989).

Emotion regulation begins in the neonatal period (Kopp, 1989). Studies have shown that infants' facial movements correspond to expected patterns of expression of basic emotions (joy, fear, anger) (Demos, 1986). In response to painful stimulation, infants show facial signals and instrumental manifestations of a pain state, including withdrawal from social interaction and a decreased ability to self-soothe (Campos, 1988). Fitzpatrick (1985) and Harris (1989) have shown that during the preoperational and operational stages of cognitive development (ages 2 to 7 years) children develop a logical system of emotion constructs. Feelings are external to the self and are bound to events. For example, happiness "arrives" with a gift and "leaves" when the gift is taken away. Children in this age group appear to externalize the stimulus for their experienced emotions. Also they are unable to process simultaneously positive and negative emotions (Gnepp, 1987; Harter, 1987). Between the ages of 7 and 12 years (concrete operational stage of cognitive development) children are able to provide more refined definitions of feelings, both their own and those of others. They are able to distinguish feelings arising from internal states from feelings associated with external events. Also, feelings within the self are differentiated from feelings in others, even when they are discrepant (Selman, 1980). By the age of 10, children are able to recognize the experience of opposite valenced emotions toward the same event, but true capacity for the processing of mixed emotions is not integrated until adolescence (Harter, 1987).

Studies of emotion processing in children from disturbed families show that these children are less accurate in deciphering the feelings of peers, and they recognize anger more frequently than happiness (Camras, Grow, & Ribordy, 1983; Reichenbach & Master, 1983). Camras speculates that the study children were impaired in their capacity to decode feelings expressed by peers because of the inconsistent manner in which feelings were expressed in their own families.

Studies of the processing of emotion are closely linked to studies of child temperament. Emotions expressed through temperamental dispositions provide the core of continuity in the development of the self throughout the life span (Campos, Barrett, Lamb, Goldsmith, & Steinberg, 1983; Emde, 1981, 1983; Izard & Malatesta, 1987). Temperament can be defined as the characteristic manner in which emotions are expressed and processed by each individual. A major study of childhood temperament (Chess & Thomas, 1984; Thomas & Chess, 1977) showed that

1. Children raised in the same environment manifest individual differences in emotional and behavioral development.
2. Children are active agents in shaping their own environments.
3. Neurobehavioral and genetic factors combined with environmental variables contribute to child behavioral and emotional attributes.

Other studies have shown that

1. Temperament emerges early in life and shows high heritability (Buss & Plomin, 1986; Rushton, Fulker, Neale, Nias, & Eysenck, 1986).
2. Temperamental disposition is stable over time (Fox, 1989; Gunnar Mangelsdorf, Larson, & Hertsgaard, 1989), but its behavioral manifes-

tations change over the course of development (Kagan, Reznick, & Snidman, 1986; Reznick et al., 1986).

3. Two categories of temperamental states, irritability (Korner Hutchinson, Koperski, Kraemer, Schneider, 1981; Matheny, Riese, & Wilson, 1985; Riese, 1987) and inhibition (Kagan, Reznick & Snidman, 1988) show impressive levels of continuity over time.

4. Children's temperamental features influence the ways other people respond to them (Rutter, 1978).

This latter point is especially relevant for understanding psychological risk factors attributed to temperamental disposition. For example, Lee and Bates (1985) found that temperamentally difficult infants elicited more conflicted confrontations from their mothers. Stevenson-Hinde & Hinde (1986) showed that children with negative emotionality were more likely to have mothers who were irritable and teachers who responded with hostility. Huttenden and Nyman (1982) and Carey (1986) found an association between difficult temperamental disposition and an increased rate of accidents, sleep difficulties, and infantile colic.

Although temperament has been studied as a variable separate from cognition and emotion, all three variables play significant roles in explaining personality development. More important, these factors influence the organization of intrapersonal and interpersonal processes. In particular, the studies of temperament underline the reciprocal influences of interpersonal transactions and support both the nature *and* nurture hypotheses on personality development. From this perspective, personality can be seen as an amalgam of cognitions about affective and behavioral attributes of the self in interaction with the environment. These cognitions define the self system and determine how change occurs.

The BPD patients who qualified for the study varied enormously in temperamental style. The angry, aggressive, and provocative style most often associated with BPD was certainly evident in a number of patients. When coupled with some paranoid thinking, this patient style of behavior results in alienation of others. One man in his late twenties was very resentful when patients did not attend group sessions regularly. Why were they not there? Their absence affected the quality of the treatment he expected. He attacked the therapists for their failure to enforce rules that would require consistent attendance. Because the "rules" that this patient wished to invoke were entirely reasonable he could not understand the concept that each patient needed to decide for herself or himself whether or not to attend a session. In contrast, some patients portrayed primarily a compliant, dependent style. They

wanted to please others, particularly the therapists. Many had difficulty expressing angry thoughts and feelings and expected conflict and
chaos if feelings (their own and others') got out of hand. One patient
perceived herself to be a "nice person" who was generous, sensitive,
and helpful to others; however, she had little awareness of the meanings of her punitive behavior toward her husband. She had several
male friends with whom she spent time, excluding her husband but
later telling him how much more affectionate they were than him. All
of this was recounted in the group in a jolly, humorous manner.

Studies of Attachment, Cognitive Processing, and Emotion Responses in Adult Borderline Patients

In the 1980s increasing attention has been given to the study of borderline patients' responses to measures of attachment behaviors, mental
representations of self in relation to others, and processing of emotions.
These empirical studies, although few in number, are reviewed. They
demonstrate new directions for exploring etiologic hypotheses about
BPD.

STUDIES OF ATTACHMENT

The quality of attachment experienced by borderlines can be inferred
from studies of adult patients' ratings of their parents. Gunderson,
Kerr, and Englund (1980) compared borderline patients' perceptions of
their parents with those of a group of paranoid schizophrenics and a
group of neurotics. The BPD subjects reported more paternal psychopathology and more maternal ineffectiveness. As reported in the
Family Studies section, other investigators have found that, when compared with other psychiatric groups of patients and nonclinical groups,
borderlines perceived their fathers as less interested and less approv-
ing (Frank & Paris, 1981); perceived both parents as less nurturing and
less affectionate (Frank & Hoffman, 1986); rated both parents as more
overprotective and less caring (Goldberg et al., 1985); and rated their
mothers as significantly less caring (Paris & Frank, 1989).

A recent study (Stalker, 1993) used Main's Adult Attachment
Interview (AAI) (Main & Goldwyn, 1990) to assess internal working
models of attachment in a cohort of 41 adult women who had been
sexually abused as children. The AAI instrument uses extensive interview data to rate the quality of attachment of the subject during early
childhood. Each category (secure, preoccupied, dismissing) are con-
ceptualized as parallel forms of Ainsworth's (1985) qualities of attach-

ment in young children (secure, anxious avoidant, and anxious ambivalent). Thirty-six subjects met criteria for one or more personality disorders on the SCID (Spitzer et al., 1987); all were classified as either preoccupied or dismissing. Eight subjects met criteria for BPD; one-half were classified as preoccupied, and the other half as dismissing. Most of the borderlines (7 out of 8) were also classified as "unresolved," indicating that issues concerned with childhood loss and trauma remained problematic. These results challenge theoretical models that posit either "conflict" or "deficit" models of early childhood development for borderlines; rather, borderlines have complex, problematic internal working models of self in relation to other that are manifested through different patterns of interpersonal transactions, as for example, "preoccupied" and "dismissing."

In a study of attachment pathology West and colleagues (1993) used the Reciprocal Attachment Questionnaire (West, Sheldon, & Reiffer, 1987) to assess the responses of borderline patients compared with nonborderlines. On four of eleven scales (feared loss, secure base, compulsive careseeking, and angry withdrawal), the borderline subjects had significantly higher mean scores. According to the authors two of the scales that differentiated the two groups (feared loss and secure base) are related to attachment anxiety, that is, the degree to which the subject fails to experience security in an attachment relationship. The other two scales (compulsive care seeking and angry withdrawal) identify patterns of dysfunctional attachment relationships. These results parallel those of Stalker (1993) and underscore the importance of attachment phenomena for understanding the effects of specific relationship dimensions on the development and course of borderline pathology.

STUDIES OF COGNITIVE PROCESSING

Using a model of social behavior built on two axes, Structural Analysis of Social Behavior (SASB), Lorna Smith-Benjamin (1992) has shown differences in the perceptions of interpersonal patterns of behavior of several patient groups, including BPD patients. Three interpersonal surfaces reflect perceptions of other, the self, and the introject. An individual's perceptions can be described on the basis of self ratings or of objective coding by observers. Compared with antisocial personality disorders borderlines represented themselves as less self-loving, more self-attacking, less autonomous, and engaged in less loving relationships. In contrast the antisocial personality group represented themselves as more autonomous, more controlling, and had more alienated significant others.

Burke, Summers, Selinger, and Polonus (1986) devised a semi-structured projective test, the Comprehensive Object Relations Profile (CORP) to measure three separate dimensions of a subject's capacity to relate to others: object constancy, object integration, and empathic capacity, which was divided into two subdimensions, subjectivity and appreciation. The authors found that object constancy, object integration, and empathy as measured by the CORP were lower for inpatient schizophrenics than for inpatient borderlines, whose scores in turn were lower than those of an inpatient neurotic group. The overall composite score significantly differentiated the three diagnostic groups; thus, the level of object representation appears to vary with degree of pathology.

Bell and colleagues (1986, 1988) developed the Bell Object Relations Inventory from which four subscale scores can be generated: Alienation, Insecure Attachment, Egocentricity, and Social Incompetence. When compared with a group of schizophrenic subjects, borderline patients had significantly higher mean scores on the first three subscales. Both groups had higher mean scores on all four subscales when compared with a nonpsychiatric group of subjects. In particular, the alienation subscale was the most successful for differentiating the borderlines from the other two groups.

Marziali and Oleniuk (1990) developed a measure for assessing levels of object representation on the basis of spontaneous descriptions of significant others. The measure, Descriptions of Significant Others (DSO), was derived from a method devised by Blatt and Lerner (1983). The capacity to differentiate perceptions of self from perceptions of other is defined on a continuum of high to low object differentiation. A preliminary study that compared the descriptions of borderlines with those of a nonpsychiatric group showed that the overall level of object differentiation generated by the borderline patients was significantly lower. In a subsequent study Oleniuk (1992) was able to demonstrate that the DSO borderline patients had significantly lower mean scores (the lowest level of object differentiation) than both a schizophrenic and nonpsychiatric group of subjects. This means that the borderlines were the least able to describe self as separate from other.

The Core Conflictual Relationship Theme (CCRT) method developed by Luborsky (Luborsky & Crits-Christoph, 1990) provides a systematic procedure for evaluating patients' patterned ways of perceiving self in relation to other. Narratives about relationship episodes involving patients and other people in their lives provide the unit of analysis. Within each object narrative, the patient's wishes, needs, and intentions toward the other person can be inferred. Similarly, the expected responses from the other person as well as self-reactions to those responses can be rated. Schleffer (Schleffer, Selzer, Clarkin, Yoemans, & Luborsky, 1989) applied the CCRT method to relationship episodes extracted from treatment sessions of borderline patients. The most prevalent themes included:

1. Borderline patients' most frequent wishes were to avoid conflict and to be close to others.
2. Their most frequent responses from others were rejecting and oppositional.
3. Their most frequent responses from self were anger and being out of control.

Furthermore, the CCRTs of the borderline patients were characterized by confusion between self and other, between negative and positive impulses, and between wish and action.

Westen and colleagues (1990) developed a method for scoring dimensions of object relations from responses to the Thematic Apperception Test (TAT). Four dimensions of object relations can be reliably and validly assessed:

1. Complexity of representations of people
2. Affect tone of relationship paradigms
3. Capacity for emotional investment in relationships
4. Understanding of social causality.

With the exception of affect tone, each dimension is assessed on scales which span high and low levels of developmental functioning. In a study comparing the responses of borderline subjects with those of major depressives and normals, Westen, Lohr, Silk, Gold, & Kerber (1990) found that the borderline group did not differ from the depressive group on the two cognitive dimensions (complexity and social causality) but had lower mean scores on affect tone and emotional investment. The borderlines also produced more pathological responses than either of the other two groups. Of interest was the fact that nearly half of the borderlines produced representations at the higher levels of complexity. This finding shows the variability of cognitive functioning in borderline patients; at times their representations are cognitively quite primitive, whereas at other times they are able to represent others in complex ways and sometimes in overly complex ways. Westen (1990) suggests that "the cognitive structure of borderline object representations may be characterized by two opposite forms of pathology: a tendency to represent people in ways that are too shallow and develop-

mentally primitive, and a tendency to represent people in overelabo-
rated ways that are not shallow enough in the face of limited data" (p.
680).

The results of the studies of borderline patients' processing of information about relationships show considerable congruence. Borderlines
have difficulty in distinguishing perceptions and emotions related to
themselves from those related to significant others. They tend to experience others in need-gratifying ways. They represent themselves as
negatively as they represent others. They expect to be alienated,
rejected, and criticized. Of importance is the variation both within and
between borderline patients in their capacities for representing self in
relation to other. These findings challenge psychodynamic hypotheses
that associate the development of borderline personality disorder with
preoedipal developmental arrests, and support a perspective that
views object-relational development as continuing throughout childhood, adolescence, and adulthood.

The study patients' narratives about important people in their lives
revealed their negative expectations of themselves and others. Most
hoped for rescue by a fantasized caring and trustworthy love object,
but few actually believed that their life situations would change. One
patient said that she knew what she needed: love from a caring man,
marriage, and a family but had given up hope that her wishes would
be fulfilled. She alternated between taking good care of herself, initiating social contacts, and maintaining a positive attitude, with ignoring
her appearance (did not bathe or wash her clothes), isolating herself,
overeating, overdrinking, and thinking of killing herself. Many of the
patients had similar self–other narratives. A young male patient
engaged in relationships with positive expectations. For example, he
had allowed a friend who was "down and out" to share his apartment
until he was able to "get it together again." After a few days the
"friend" had taken money from his wallet, had damaged furniture
with burning cigarette butts, and had seduced the patient's girlfriend.
The patient was hurt and angry but had no awareness of the type of
interpersonal information he would need to process to make more
accurate predictions about others' behaviors. Rather, he was driven by
the need to hold on to the relationship.

STUDIES OF EMOTION PROCESSING

Although the problems that borderline patients experience in the regulation of affect have been well described, there has been little empirical
work directed at understanding how emotions are perceived and

processed. In a recent study, Levine (1992) selected four measures of emotion processing and compared the responses of borderlines to those of a cohort of nonpsychiatric subjects. The measures included:

1. Levels of awareness of emotions in self and in other, which included an empathy subscale
2. Capacity to coordinate mixed valence emotions
3. Accuracy with which pictures of facial expressions of emotions are distinguished
4. Intensity of emotion responses to daily life events.

Compared to the control group the borderline subjects showed lower levels of awareness of their own and others' emotions, gave fewer empathic responses, provided fewer mixed valence responses, were less accurate in recognizing facial expression of emotions, and showed a significantly greater intensity of negative affects. The results of this study confirm clinical observation and have implications for the technical management of borderline patient's exaggerated emotions witnessed in any therapeutic encounter.

In the study by Westen and colleagues (1990) two of the dimensions included in their measures of object relations focus on isolating specific emotions in an interpersonal context. "Affect tone of relationship paradigms" is concerned with the affective quality of the object world or interpersonal expectancies, from malevolent to benevolent. The second dimension, "capacity for emotional investment in relationships and moral standards," defines a continuum between need-gratifying interpersonal orientation versus investment in values, ideals, and committed relationships. As predicted, Westen found that the responses from borderline patients were rated at the lowest end of a five-level scale for each dimension. For the Affect Tone scale, representations of others reflected violence or negligence from significant others, or of others as hostile, capricious, although not profoundly malevolent. Ratings of the Capacity for Emotional Investment scale showed that borderlines emotional investment in others is ruled by their own needs and preoccupations. Moral standards are immature or adhered to so as to avoid punishment. Given these findings, the results of both studies (Levine, 1992; Westen et al., 1990) might be understood as showing that borderline patients' views of others' emotions are inaccurate or negatively skewed because their judgments are very much colored by their own cognitive-emotional states. Psychodynamic hypotheses would suggest that a primitive defensive structure (projection, splitting, denial) developed in response to unresolved early childhood conflicts or deficits prevents adaptive processing of emotions, especially negatively valenced affects. But, what is less clear is the interaction between the processing of emotions and of other sectors of information about self in relation to others. There is an obvious connection between these two components of identity formation and psychological functioning, but its exact nature is not fully understood.

Summary

Recent and current research studies point to a multidimensional model for explaining the etiology of borderline pathology. The important elements under study include assessments of the interactions between genetic, biological, and environmental factors that converge, diverge, and evolve over time to yield significant variations in the development of the adult personality. Infant studies that have postdated the work of Mahler and colleagues (1975) observational studies fail to confirm her conclusions about the phases of separation-individuation and identity formation. For every patient who reconstructs a history that confirms the problematic separation-individuation hypothesis, there is a patient or individual with a comparable early history who did not develop the disorder. Chess and Thomas's (1984) longitudinal study of childhood temperament, Werner and Smith's (1982) longitudinal study of children in Hawaii, Rutter's (1980) epidemiological studies of children and their families, and the Harvard Grant longitudinal study (Vaillant, 1977) all have shown that although some children and adolescents experienced highly conflicted interactions with their caregivers, they did not develop behavior disorders as adults. Thus, a clear linear association between phase-specific developmental "deficits" or "conflicts" and the onset of borderline personality disorder in adults cannot be supported.

The developmental etiologic hypotheses that arise from early childhood studies and studies of adult borderline patients suggest alternate paradigms for understanding borderline pathology. It may be useful to think of the development of BPD in the context of factors that predispose to the disorder; that is, which factors sustain or alleviate the possibility for developing the disorder. The results of the neurological studies of borderline behavior suggest that there may be a subset of borderlines who share diagnoses with attention deficit disorders and other disorders of the CNS. The studies of bonding, attachment, and object relations are congruent in showing that borderline patients form and perpetuate anxious avoidant or dismissing attachments. The reason for this persistent and debilitating form of interpersonal relating may be linked to the existence of mental representations of self in relation to others that are governed by expectations of malevolent, rejecting responses from others. As West, Keller, Links, & Patrick (1993) suggest the behavioral consequences of the constant fear of rejection and loss may reflect lifelong attachment patterns that oscillate between care seeking, disappointment, and angry withdrawal.

The borderline patient's difficulty with perceiving and processing emotions can be understood only in the context of the meanings emotions carry in important relationships. In other words, the borderline patient's attempts to understand others' motivations are much influenced by experienced emotions, especially anxiety and rage. From a social-cognitive perspective, borderline patients may be restricted in their capacity to process information about emotions in an interpersonal context because of self-schemas that persevere despite inherent inaccuracies and distortions. As stated, borderline patients' difficulties with the regulation of affect are readily observable in clinical situations. However, etiologic explanations of which early or later life factors contributed to this incapacity are not well studied or understood.

Self-object schemas that contain cognitive-emotional elements connected to early life trauma with caregivers are reflected in the way information and emotions are acknowledged and processed in the treatment relationship. It may be that the most therapeutic factor in any treatment encounter with a borderline patient is the therapist's understanding of the affective components of the patient's self-object schemas. When these are understood in the context of the treatment relationship, the therapist is better equipped to avoid therapeutic error and disruption of the treatment—a frequent outcome with borderline patients. For example, when confronted with a "yes but" patient, one of the study therapists failed to understand the meanings of these qualifying statements when the patient described a series of conflicted relationships with previous therapists. She described therapeutic relationships that she had found initially helpful but that inevitably disappointed her. When the therapist focused on the positive aspects of these previous therapeutic encounters the patient would inevitably answer angrily, "yes but." The therapy had not been good enough, long enough, and so on. The therapist had been unable to identify with the patient's anger and frustration at losing her previous therapists regardless of the reasons for the loss and had failed to understand the patient's enormous anxiety about engaging in yet another therapeutic encounter that might end badly. The patient dropped out of therapy. What was needed was a response that showed the therapist's capacity for identifying with these negative affective states and tolerating the patient's loss of control over strong feelings of anxiety and rage. In this way the therapist models for the patient appropriate regulation of powerful affects and is able to promote more effectively the curative function of the therapeutic interaction.

Among the etiologic hypotheses about the development of BPD in adult patients the developmental antecedents of the capacity in adults to regulate affects may have the greatest importance for designing effective models of treatment. For example, if, during early development, adaptive models for recognizing and processing emotions are not portrayed by adults in the child's social environment, then problems in regulating intense emotion may be the outcome. If the treatment model, including the training of therapists, fails to include theoretical and technical responses to borderline patients' problems with the management of intensely experienced emotions, especially in the context of interpersonal relationships, the therapy could be in jeopardy from the onset. It may be that the documented high dropout rate from psychotherapy typical of borderline patients is associated with the failure of the treatment model to address adequately the patients' ubiquitous problems with regulating affects, especially as they emerge in new interpersonal encounters. This hypothesis underlies the development and testing of an interpersonal group psychotherapy for BPD.

4

The Design and Structure of Interpersonal Group Psychotherapy

The structural and strategic format of Interpersonal Group Psychotherapy is similar to traditional forms of psychodynamic group psychotherapy, but it also differs in several important ways. The design of the IGP method responds to an integration of diagnostic and etiologic factors specific to the borderline disorder. The aim of this chapter is to illustrate the process of change within the context of group interactions and to describe the phases of the treatment.

Theoretical Hypotheses: Historical Overview

Despite the lack of clinical and empirical consensus on the diagnostic and etiologic factors that distinguish patients with BPD from patients suffering from other forms of pathological disturbance, clinicians make choices about conceptualizations of the disorder that best support the treatment strategies they use. For example, Kernberg (1975) and colleagues (1989) focus on a psychoanalytic, confrontational, interpretive model of intervention that addresses the primitive defenses used by borderline patients to ward off intrapsychic conflict. He hypothesizes that during early development these patients failed to develop adequate psychic mechanisms for dealing with contradictory images of self and other; primitive defenses are substituted to protect positive images from being overwhelmed by negative ones. These unresolved infantile conflicts are expressed in adult interpersonal relationships, including the treatment relationship; thus their interpretation is assumed to have therapeutic value.

Buie and Adler (1982), Adler (1985), and others (Brandchaft & Stolorow, 1987; Palombo, 1987; Toplin & Kohut, 1980) suggest a trauma-arrest theory for explaining early developmental deficits experienced by borderline patients. These clinical theorists hypothesize that during early development patients experienced an environment that was lacking in sufficient emotional and behavioral supplies to ensure the development of positive, empathic self-objects; thus, the child is fixated at an archaic level, and in its adult form is expressed in the demanding, hostile, and self-destructive expressions of borderline patients. From this theoretical perspective the treatment must provide initially a holding, soothing, and empathic environment in which the patient can experience an emerging self-identity. Confrontation and interpretation are used only at later stages of the treatment when the patient has begun to accommodate the trauma of early developmental deficits through identification with a caring, empathic therapist.

Other psychoanalytic therapists (Grinker, Werble, & Prye, 1968; Knight, 1953; Zetzel, 1971) endorse psychodynamic developmental perspectives about the etiology of borderline personality disorder but oppose the use of an interpretive treatment approach. They recommend a supportive stance that includes suggestions, education, and a facilitating relationship with the therapist; their aim is to provide the patient with new information about the connections between painful feeling states and self-destructive behavior. Linehan (1993) adopts similar therapeutic strategies in her cognitive-behavioral approach to the treatment of borderlines; she uses behavioral skill acquisition techniques, problem-solving procedures, and empathic, supportive responses to help patients relinquish parasuicidal behaviors in favor of more gratifying current life experiences. Despite the differences in their etiologic perspective of BPD, some psychoanalytic and cognitive-behavioral therapists share a supportive approach to the treatment of BPD patients.

In general, supportive therapists view change as dependent on the experience shared between patient and therapist that Alexander (1957) has described as the "corrective emotional experience." A therapist who communicates warmth, concern, and empathic understanding coupled with consistent availability and the absence of retaliation is considered to be more helpful to the borderline patient than explanatory statements about the genetic or transference meanings of maladaptive behaviors. In this regard, Higgitt and Fonagy (1992) quote Frieda Fromm-Reichmann as saying about borderlines, "What these patients need is an experience, not an explanation" (p. 33).

Psychoanalytic approaches to the treatment of borderline personality disorder are intended to address etiologic rather than diagnostic issues attributed to the disorder; as, for example, the presence of primitive defense mechanisms, identity diffusion, and intact reality testing (Kernberg, 1975). Put in another way, the inadequate defenses and the confused sense of self witnessed in the adult borderline patient are seen as manifestations of unresolved early childhood conflicts. Because the same hypotheses can be applied broadly, the recommended treatment strategies can be employed with a mixed group of patients including borderlines, narcissistic, histrionic, schizotypal, antisocial, and dependent personality disorders. Thus psychoanalytically oriented psychotherapists ignore attempts at achieving diagnostic specificity as exemplified in the DSM-III-R approach to psychiatric diagnosis, especially as the DSM system eschews etiologic criteria and disregards the relevance of etiologic hypotheses for selecting specific treatment strategies.

In addition to the diagnostic confusion concerning BPD, there is no evidence to support the use of a particular set of therapeutic strategies with this group of patients. Specifically, should the treatment approach take into account the type of overlap between the borderline disorder and other Axis II disorders? The same question could be addressed with respect to overlap with Axis I disorders. For example, should BPD patients who also qualify for the Axis II dependent personality disorder be treated with a combination of psychotherapy and assertiveness training? Should BPD patients with major affective disorder be treated with pharmacotherapy and psychotherapy? Given the lack of data to support continuity between etiologic hypotheses, diagnostic factors, and treatment approaches, the clinician continually tests the optimal fit between an assumed belief system and selected therapeutic behaviors. The IGP approach to the treatment of BPD was designed to address the linkages between etiologic and diagnostic perspectives of BPD and their associations with specific intervention strategies. In addition, an important component of the treatment design is the examination and management of the therapist's subjective reactions to therapeutic work with borderline patients.

The Interpersonal Group Psychotherapy Treatment Model

The IGP treatment model is based on a definition of personality that specifically emphasizes understanding the meanings of interpersonal relationships for explaining maladaptive behavior. Developmental hypotheses that link cognitive representations of early life attachments to cognitive interpersonal schemas in the adult borderline patient are combined with an approach to treatment that values experiential learning as necessary for change. Borderline patients are better able to make shifts in their expectations of themselves and others when they have had the opportunity to replicate in new relationships (as within an IGP group) their anxieties, angry reactions, and disruptive behaviors without the risk of rejection or retaliation. When their worst fears are not confirmed, new information about self and other can be processed more effectively. We believe that the repetition of these new learning experiences across the various phases of the IGP process promote change within each patient.

The most impressive diagnostic feature of borderline patients is the dramatic changes in mood and behavior when, in an interpersonal context, their wishes for understanding and gratification are frustrated. There is a considerable range in intensity of response to disappointments with significant others; some patients become depressed and withdraw from social contact, whereas others resort immediately to angry outbursts and/or self-destructive behaviors. Stone (1993) encapsulates the borderline patient's exaggerated responses as follows: "More so than most other personality disordered patients, those with BPD are exquisitely sensitive to initial conditions. Minor events lead to major upsets; major events that most people take in their stride lead to catastrophe" (p. 304). These "overreactions" to stressful life events represent the borderline patient's patterned ways of interacting with others and can be expected to be replicated in most new relationships including the treatment relationship. The developmental inference to be drawn is that these patterns of relating were learned at some earlier time in response to familial trauma; subsequent efforts to alter negative interactions between self and other have not been successful. Thus, it is to be expected that in the context of important relationships the borderline patient will express disillusionment, anger, and depression.

Interpersonal Group Psychotherapy was designed to support a therapeutic context in which the borderline patient is able to replicate problematic interpersonal behaviors without having to resort to "fight" or "flight." The group therapists avoid a "fight" by affirming the patient's view of the world and by optimizing the patient's choices as to whether that view can be changed. In particular, they value all of the patient's attempts to manage past and current life stresses. For example, when at a first group session a patient states, "I'm not going to like this, I don't think coming here will do much good," the therapist confirms the patient's viewpoint by replying, "You may be right, you may not like this; the group may help, but then it may not." The therapists avoid patient "flights" by tolerating patient demands, attacks, and threats without retaliation; that is, they anticipate therapeutic derailments in response to these provocations, attempt to avoid them, but are prepared to address the derailments when they do occur. For example, when a patient accuses the therapists of being inept and useless (as frequently occurred in all of the groups treated in the trial), the therapists accept the criticisms; often, they do not need to respond directly as other patients intervene with more or less intensive criticism. If needed, the therapists make an empathic statement to the effect that they understand the patients' disappointment in not having their expectations met. In contrast, a derailment or disjunction in the group process occurs whenever the therapists respond to patient attacks by attempting to explore their meanings or with rationalizations about the utility of certain therapeutic behaviors. The aim of IGP is to provide a new learning experience in which, contrary to the patient's expectations, negative self-schemas are not confirmed. When this learning experience is sufficiently reinforced and consolidated, the patient is able to accommodate relational information that was previously blocked, and an altered self-schema emerges.

Interpersonal Group Psychotherapy is provided in a time-limited, group format. The very issues that would seem to preclude the use of a group model of treatment for borderline patients, such as demands for exclusive attention, repeated interpersonal difficulties, and impulsivity, are addressed rapidly in a group because the members readily identify with each other's problems and needs. The group context provides liberal doses of understanding and support ("we are in this together"); these help the patients both to express and contain anger and despair that have frequently overwhelmed important others in their lives, including previous therapists with whom they have been in individual psychotherapy. By setting at the onset a time boundary (30 sessions) on the limits of the therapy, the patients are assured of a predictable, safe, time structure. This factor has particular therapeutic value for those with BPD because they have had repeated experiences with unpredictable, unsafe interpersonal encounters in which the testing of boundaries frequently led to rupture. In addition to time limits, the patients benefit from other forms of group structure, such as the invariability of the meeting time and place, the fixed duration of each session, and the dependability of the therapists.

RATIONALE FOR GROUP FORMAT

The provision of group psychotherapy for patients with borderline personality disorder is not new. Typically, borderline patients have been included in groups of patients with other diagnoses, and the treatment approaches have varied widely. Some clinicians suggest that group treatment may be more effective than individual treatment for BPD patients (Horwitz, 1977, 1980, 1987; Stone & Gustafson, 1982; Wong, 1980b). Certain characteristics of group psychotherapy are particularly relevant. Group therapy can be helpful in diluting the intensity of the transference relationship that typically occurs in individual psychotherapy by providing multiple targets of emotional investment. For example, in individual psychotherapy the therapist becomes the focus for powerful omnipotent projections, such as "savior," "rescuer," or "protector," and thus is vulnerable to taking up these projections, especially as one of the therapist's functions is to help the patient preserve control over destructive impulses. In the group, patient projections are directed to the therapists and other group members and thus are diluted in the power they exert on any one person in the group.

The multiple and varied member-to-member interactions provide the opportunity for a range of identifications and help the borderline patient to shift away from the polarized interactions that are more apt to occur in one-to-one psychotherapy. Opportunities for changing maladaptive patterns of behavior are best tested by borderline patients in an environment that supports multiple perspectives. Within a group, borderline patients can more readily process feedback from peers with whom they share the same intensity of anxiety about self-destructive behaviors. Group members serve as interpersonal buffers for borderline patients, who typically exaggerate their subjective reactions toward therapists. Borderline patients with schizoid features may benefit especially from group stimulation and interaction. Peer pressure is especially useful for setting limits for borderline patients who have severe problems with impulse control. Group treatment may provide a more benign and safe holding environment in which borderline patients can find support for coping with extreme shifts in affect.

Three conceptual issues dominate the literature on group psychotherapy for BPD patients:

1. Should treatment groups include only patients with borderline personality disorder, or are borderlines best treated in mixed-diagnosis groups?
2. Should group therapy be an adjunct to other treatments, in particular individual psychotherapy, or should it be the sole therapeutic intervention?
3. Is it necessary to modify psychotherapeutic technique in groups with borderline members?

The responses to these questions are varied, and there is no consensus on the optimal management of borderlines in group psychotherapy. Although most clinicians advocate that borderline patients be included in mixed-diagnosis groups (Horwitz, 1987; Leszcz, 1992; Pines, 1990), Chatham (1985) supports the use of psychotherapy groups made up exclusively of borderlines. Slavinska-Holy (1983) and Battegay and Klaui (1986) also support the use of homogeneous borderline groups but only when the group intervention is combined with concurrent individual psychotherapy and the same therapist is involved in each mode of intervention. Slavinska-Holy believes that the two treatments work well in managing the transference and in promoting self-learning. For similar reasons other clinicians have supported the use of simultaneous individual and group treatments for BPD patients (Kibel, 1980; Linehan, Armstrong, Suarez, Allmon, & Heard, 1991; Tabachnick, 1965; Wong, 1980a). Both Tabachnick and Kibel suggest that in the combined treatments the transference is split; negative features are more likely to be enacted in the group, and the positive aspects of the transference may enhance the productivity of the individual treatment. Within a cognitive-behavioral perspective Linehan combines individual and group approaches but assigns different treatment tasks to each form of intervention. For example, the individual treatment therapists reinforce the individual patient's learning of self-control whereas the group is used to process the educational component of the treatment. Horwitz (1980) has suggested sequencing group and individual psychotherapy, in that order, so that the group experience can be used to prepare the borderline patient to make more productive use of individual psychotherapy.

In the pilot developmental phase of IGP, several formats of sequencing individual and group treatment, versus group treatment alone, were tested. We found that the patients responded well when the group intervention was the singular mode of treatment, and less well to a sequencing format, which offered individual sessions followed by group. We also tested the effects of varying the intensity of the treatment by offering the group sessions twice a week for the first four weeks as an "inductive" phase, and then reducing the sessions to once a week for the duration of the time-limited treatment. This format was also problematic because a number of patients found the transition in frequency of the sessions at the onset of therapy too stressful and dropped out of the group. Following these experiences we designed the structure and duration of IGP as it was tested subsequently in the treatment comparison trial. In fact, the invariance of the format of IGP provided an important therapeutic component especially during the initial phase of the group when the patients needed the security of the group's predictable structure in order to test their ambivalence about engaging in the process.

Stone and Gustafson (1982) stress the importance of noninterpretive activity for developing and maintaining a therapeutic alliance in group psychotherapy with groups that have some borderline patient members. The working alliance is viewed as a goal rather than an intermediate step, and the importance of the therapist's empathic responses to each group member is emphasized. Leszcz (1992) suggests that the group member here-and-now feedback addresses the typical distortions of borderline patients in mixed diagnosis groups and thus reduces the need for therapist interpretations. Macaskill (1982) found that group therapy for borderline patients was effective in increasing self-understanding. Also contrary to expectations, borderline patients were able to respond altruistically to one another; patients' insights and altruistic responses tended to follow therapists' empathic feedback to a maltreated group member.

A noninterpretive, empathic feedback approach is central to IGP. From our experience, this approach was essential during the initial phase of each group treated in the study and contributed to the development of positive working relationships between the group members and therapists and among the group members. We also found that as the patients tested, challenged, and altered the nature of their relationships in the group, their capacities for empathic responses to one another increased in tandem with an expanded tolerance for sadness and despair when expectations of others could not be met. As one patient put it, "I keep hoping that my mom will be able to apologize and say that she treated me badly as a kid, but I know that she probably won't."

In summary there is considerable support for the use of group models of psychotherapy with borderline patients. Both Bellak (1980) and Vaillant (1992) have suggested that group models of treatment may be necessary adjuncts for the effective treatment of severe personality disorders. Vaillant believes that these patients can only identify with other individuals who feel as they do. Also, as suggested, the group is better able to absorb the assault of the borderline's immature projections that frequently overwhelm the efforts of individual therapists. Finally, a group format provides patients with the opportunity to give and receive empathic feedback, an opportunity that is unavailable in individual psychotherapy where empathic feedback is unidirectional, from therapist to patient.

RATIONALE FOR TIME BOUNDARIES

A time limit was set for the group; 25 weekly sessions followed by 5 sessions spaced at 2-week intervals. This form of a short-term group intervention was chosen for the following reasons:

1. Although long-term intensive psychoanalytic psychotherapy has been the treatment of choice for borderline personality disorder, there is growing concern over the efficacy and availability of this form of treatment (Gunderson, 1984; Perry, 1989; Silver 1985; Waldinger & Gunderson, 1987). High patient drop out and moderate levels of improvement typify most intensive treatment approaches with borderlines. Furthermore, only patients in the socioeconomic middle to upper-middle classes can afford to pay for long-term, intensive treatments that are provided primarily in the private mental health sector. Publicly supported mental health clinics rarely have the resources (human and economic) to provide intensive long-term psychotherapy.

2. Focused short-term psychotherapy is sufficient for achieving more modest outcome goals, such as cessation of self-destructive behaviors (Linehan, 1992), the acceptance of the limits and frustrations experienced in daily living (Leibovitch, 1983), and the management of crises (Bellak & Small, 1978; Perry, 1989; Silver, 1985).

3. Individual, intensive, psychoanalytic psychotherapy for borderline patients requires a level of expertise (psychoanalytic training and a personal analysis) beyond the training of most therapists. Therapists with less training who attempt this form of intervention may be at greater risk of committing therapeutic errors.

4. Briefer forms of therapy, especially in a group format, protect against severe therapeutic regressions that are more apt to occur when the borderline patient becomes exclusively dependent for survival on one therapist and the therapy (Friedman, 1975; Silver, 1985).

5. A time boundary, set prior to treatment, provides a secure and reassuring structure, especially for borderline patients whose expectations about the constancy of persons of trust have been frequently frustrated.

6. The combination of duration of treatment (30 sessions) and group format accelerates the achievement of important changes in maladaptive behaviors.

7. The time boundary and the group format of IGP make the achievement of treatment goals more cost-effective.

GROUP MEMBER SELECTION

From the literature on clinical models of group psychotherapy for BPD it is difficult to discern which selection criteria are used to determine inclusion versus exclusion. It appears that clinical diagnoses of the disorder are made on the basis of a broad set of criteria, more akin to Kernberg's (1975) criteria for "borderline organization" and Silver and Rosenbluth's (1992) criteria for "characterologically difficult patients"; both include a cluster of Axis II disorders. There is some indication that narcissistically vulnerable patients should be excluded from group treatment (Horner, 1975). Only in experimental treatment trials has there been an attempt to specify selection criteria with more precision through the use of structured interview schedules. Linehan (Linehan et al., 1991) included in her study of cognitive-behavioral treatment borderline patients who qualified for the diagnosis on the basis of the Diagnostic Interview for Borderlines (DIB) (Gunderson, Kolb, & Austin, 1981). In his study of time-limited group psychotherapy for severe personality disorders, Budman (1989) used the Structured Clinical Interview for Personality Disorders (SCID-II, Spitzer, Williams, & Gibbon, 1987). Despite these attempts to ensure diagnostic homogeneity, overlap with Axis I and other Axis II disorders is likely even when structured interview schedules are used (Oldham et al., 1992).

Of importance is not the exactness of the borderline diagnosis; rather, the selection criteria should provide a comprehensive clinical description that can be matched with reliable and specific intervention strategies that lead to specific treatment effects.

The selection criteria for the study of IGP included males and females between the ages 18 and 65 who met the DIB diagnostic criterion score of 7 or more. Exclusion criteria were mental retardation, neurological impairment, a primary diagnosis of alcohol or drug addiction, and physical disorders with known psychiatric consequence. Once patients had been selected for the study, randomization was used to assign them to either IGP or the comparison treatment (individual psychodynamic psychotherapy).

Five groups of patients were treated during the trial. From this experience we were able to make the following clinical observations about the optimal mix of borderline subtypes to be included in groups treated with IGP. The proposed additional selection criteria parallel those used for selecting members for most forms of group psychotherapy:

1. The group membership should be balanced in terms of patient DIB scores because they correlate with levels of symptomatic and

behavioral severity. By selecting a balanced distribution of patients across the DIB scoring levels (scores 7 through 10), the severity of symptoms and impulsive behavior is also more likely to be balanced.

2. Although our initial selection criteria included patients between 18 and 65, within each group a more limited age range is preferable; for example, in one group two patients in their late teen years did not share much in common (other than their diagnosis) with most of the other group members who were in their late thirties and who were dealing with different life issues.

3. Groups probably function more effectively when the members share similar levels of education and socioeconomic status.

4. It is rarely possible to achieve a balanced mix between male and female group members because the largest proportion of borderline patients (75% to 85%) are female. In the trial, groups with one male member functioned well, and the distribution of members by sex within a group was not an issue.

5. We concur with Silver and Rosenbluth's (1992) recommendations to exclude patients who are extremely paranoid, who resort to suicide attempts as the only dependable care-eliciting behavior, who have a concomitant diagnosis of severe antisocial personality disorder, or who are "forced" to attend therapy against their own wishes; these patients are amongst the most difficult to treat in any form of psychotherapy and probably require multiple forms of intervention, including intermittent hospitalization.

INTERVENTION TECHNIQUES

The primary techniques used in IGP were adapted from a model of individual psychotherapy for borderlines developed by Dawson (1989, 1993). The treatment strategy focuses on observing and processing the meanings of the contextual features of the patient–therapist interactions. The borderline patient is perceived as possessing a self system that contains conflicting attitudes. The patient seeks to resolve the resulting state of instability and ambiguity in the context of interpersonal relationships, including the therapeutic relationship. As in other relationships, the borderline patient externalizes his or her conflict in the therapeutic dialogue. For example, if the therapist takes up one side of a dialogue by being supportive and optimistic, the patient will assume the other side by being argumentative and pessimistic. A patient in one of the groups felt that she had failed at most things she had tried to accomplish and was of "no use to anyone"; the therapist failed to "read" accurately the message, that is, the possible presence of suicidal ideation with the potential for self-harming behaviors. However, he was aware of a surge in feelings of anxiety to which he responded by attempting to reassure the patient, telling her that she was doing well at a college course in which she was currently enrolled. The patient undermined this supportive attempt by saying, "It's a Mickey Mouse course that any dummy could ace!" This illustration shows that as long as the patient and therapist replicate the conflict, no resolution takes place. Because the patient has little knowledge of how internalized conflict is externalized in the therapeutic interaction, it is the therapist who must behave in a manner that will alter the dialogue and disconfirm the patient's negative expectations. The therapist's primary stance is that of a concerned, impartial observer who demonstrates an unwavering interest in the patient's dialogue. The therapist's therapeutic responses (especially during the initial phases of therapy) consist of acknowledgment, reflection, and affirmation of the patient's propositions. A supportive attitude is communicated in the therapist's acknowledgment of the patient's perceptions and attempts to manage past and current trauma. For example, in the above illustration of polarized patient-therapist dialogue, what was needed from the therapist was an empathic statement such as, "I guess you despair that anything will change and sometimes may even think of giving up entirely."

Most therapists' statements are tentatively phrased and communicate uncertainty and confusion. In reality, the therapist knows neither the exact causes nor the ideal solutions to the patients' dilemmas. Therefore, a confused response is an honest response and is more likely to resonate with the patient's own internal state. For example when a patient demands a solution to a current dilemma, such as, "Should I let my mother know how angry she makes me feel all of the time?" the therapist's response is "I don't know, it might help or it might not." In fact, the therapist does not know the outcome regardless of which approach the patient takes; he or she models for the patient tolerance for anxiety and ambiguity while various solutions to the dilemma are considered. In this model of treatment, it is the patient who has control over the dialogue, and it is the therapist who communicates uncertainty and confusion while maintaining a sharp interest in each patient's narrative.

The important contextual feature that sustains the group member–therapist connections is the therapist's ability to model regulation of intense affects that, if left unmanaged, reinforce the patient's vulnerability and risk of flight from the group. A considerable amount of the training and supervision of IGP therapists revolves around helping the therapists to monitor their feeling reactions to each patient. The aim is to understand the contextual meanings of the interaction—meanings that are very much governed by the patient's affective state and the therapist's response. In other words, the assessment of therapists' subjective reactions is paramount in the selection and timing of IGP interventions. As was illustrated, when a therapist is unaware that the source of her or his anxiety has to do with a patient being at risk of self-harm, she or he is more apt to resort to a supportive response that is, more often than not, rejected by the patient. If the polarized dialogue persists, the therapist's anxiety escalates and signals the possibility of a therapeutic derailment and, thus, the need for corrective therapeutic action. This process is described in greater detail in subsequent chapters.

The primary difference between the IGP model of therapy for borderlines and a psychoanalytic approach such as Kernberg's (1975) and Klienian analysts' such as Rosenfeld (1978, 1987) is the avoidance of the traditional techniques of interpretation and confrontation, especially during the early phase of treatment. In the classical psychoanalytic situation the self-system is addressed when the therapist initially explores or confronts and then interprets the nature of the conflict, its developmental antecedents and its manifestations in the treatment relationship. When used early in the treatment of borderline patients these strategies have the potential of disrupting the treatment. Gunderson and Sabo (1993) suggest that the frequency with which BPD patients drop out of psychotherapy may be due to negative reactions to early interpretations or confrontations. Early transference interpretations may perpetuate conflict in the therapeutic relationship because they reinforce the patient's role as "helpless and hopeless," maintain the therapist in the " healthy, responsible" role, and potentially exacerbate the patient's anxiety and frustration. Furthermore, the use of interpretations early in the treatment, which formulates the patient's current conflict, presumes an accurate fit between psychodynamic hypotheses (e.g., type and function of certain defensive behaviors) and the patient's actual experiences. The risk of an inaccurate fit is high and, not surprisingly, can result in a patient response that is either passively obtuse or angrily defensive. In either case, the patient's feelings of self-worth, control, and autonomy are not advanced.

The avoidance of genetic and transference interpretations, especially during the early phases of psychotherapy with borderline patients, has long been recommended by psychoanalysts who have believed that modification of psychoanalytic technique was necessary for the treatment of patients with borderline personality disorder (Knight, 1953; Zetzel, 1971). Other analysts, particularly those with a self-psychology orientation, refrain from using interpretive interventions in the early phase of treatment and emphasize the merits of experiential learning. Gunderson (1984), Giovacchini (1987), Brandchaft and Stolorow (1987), and Adler (1985) believe that borderline patients are not able to make use of interpretations until some shifts in internal structures have taken place. For example, Giovacchini (1987), in contrast to Kernberg, believes that early interpretation of the negative transference is likely to be heard by the patient as criticism. Searles (1986) also cautions against using transference interpretations early in the treatment because the patient's projections are frequently accurate. Pines (1990) concurs that interpretations are not real or meaningful for borderline patients; instead, the reactions (anxiety, hostility, and criticism) the patients engender in their therapists are experienced by the patients as real and genuine. It is through these troubled interactions between patient and therapist that a valid therapeutic connection is made. In this paradigm the therapist acts as a "container" (Bion, 1961) for the patient's confusion and distorted projections. Therapeutic change is due to the fact that the therapist remains stable, consistent, caring, and nonpunitive, notwithstanding the patient's rage and destructive impulses. This stance is not dissimilar to that advocated by Carl Rogers (1957); however, IGP differs from client-centered theory by placing considerable emphasis on monitoring the therapist's subjective reactions to the therapeutic transactions. Also, IGP holds that all therapeutic encounters risk derailment and that strategies for recognizing and recovering from these disjunctions to the process are paramount to ensuring a positive course for the therapy.

Once a secure bond with the patient has been established, most psychoanalysts concur that clarifications and interpretations can be used in the later phases of treatment with borderline patients. However, interpretations that reflect the context of the current therapeutic relationship are considered to be the most helpful. Higgitt & Fonagy (1992; Fonagy, 1991) advocate the use of interpretations that link current affects with confused thinking about self and other. They believe that explorations of borderline patients' early childhood experiences to explain current behavior are not helpful and most likely distract from the task of understanding current emotions and mental states. Gunderson (1984) and Masterson (1981) recommend using a combination of interpretations and supportive techniques during the later phases of therapy. These include discussions about the patient's new feelings, thoughts, and behaviors about themselves and important people in their lives. Supportive reinforcement of changes in self-identity helps the patient to master powerful emotions that previously led to self-destructive behaviors.

In large measure IGP replicates many noninterpretive techniques. Exploratory questions and explanatory open-ended statements, both of which are phrased tentatively, are used in the IGP model of treatment. However, only in the later phases of the therapy does the therapist test with each patient tentative connections between motivation, emotion, and self–other destructive behaviors. These interventions are intended to stimulate group member thinking about here-and-now interactions within the group. Because the interpretations are phrased tentatively and are syntactically open, the content and direction of the subsequent responses are determined by the patients. For example, an IGP therapist speaking to a specific patient *would not* say: "Your silence is a way of avoiding connection with the other group members and is not dissimilar from your reluctance to connect with your colleagues at work." An IGP therapist *would* make the following statement, addressing the whole group: "I wonder if maybe being quiet in this group has something to do with being afraid that no one really cares about what you have to say." Another difference between IGP and supportive models of treatment is that education and advice are avoided. In a group environment, the members frequently educate and give advice. This blocks the progress of therapeutic work because frequently the patient who persists in giving advice is communicating the need for control and the concomitant fear of addressing her or his own sense of confusion and uncertainty. Several patients whose input to the group was primarily that of advice giving were subsequently described as being "pseudo-competent"; that is, they appeared to have the "answers" to everyone else's problems but had difficulty in acknowledging their own vulnerabilities. These also posed the most severe challenges to the therapists' management of the therapeutic process.

In summary, the strategic difference between IGP technique and psychoanalytic interpretive technique is that the former focuses primarily on the acquisition of new learning by observing and experiencing the "here and now" context of the interpersonal dialogue whereas the latter emphasizes the acquisition of new knowledge through understanding and integrating the content of what is communicated. In the IGP model of treatment, change is more due to the experience of interactions in the group and less to the acquisition of insights about the genesis of internalized conflicts. Thus, the context of knowing is more important than the content of what is known. This reflects the belief that for the borderline patient the context has been historically imbued with debilitating levels of painful emotions that block effective cognitive processing of new information; thus when the context (member-to-member and member-to-therapist transactions) are well understood and adequately managed by the therapists, the borderline patient's inherent capacity for information processing is enhanced.

5

Phases of Group Process

The psychoanalytic literature on the treatment of borderline patients in individual psychotherapy emphasizes several stages or phases of the treatment process. Otto Kernberg (1975) stresses the importance of initially testing the patient's capacity and commitment to intensive psychotherapy. The aim is to establish a contract that communicates clearly the respective roles of patient and therapist. The patient's resistance in the context of the transference is confronted and interpreted. This initial phase may span many sessions as the patient may persist in challenging her or his commitment to the therapeutic process. The aim is to engage the patient as a working partner for the duration of the treatment while fully expecting the therapeutic endeavor to be challenged by subsequent disruptive maneuvers on the part of the patient. When the patient becomes a working partner, the therapist works on enhancing the patient's insight into maladaptive defenses and their role in blocking healthy identity formation. The patient's development of insight into intrapsychic processes is paramount for testing the success of this model of treatment.

John Gunderson (1984) outlines four stages of psychotherapeutic process with borderlines:

1. The first phase is concerned with the patient's search for a secure, caring relationship and is sustained by therapist interventions that are empathically supportive and tolerant of the patient's worldview.
2. The initial connection overlaps with the patient's expressions of negativity and struggle for control. The important therapist response is tolerance of the patient's anger and criticisms, along with actions that set limits on the patient's demands and expectations. The parameters and constraints of psychotherapy and of the psychotherapist are clearly articulated.

3. In the subsequent, attenuated phase of the therapy the meanings of the patient's maladaptive responses to distorted perceptions of self in relation to others, including the transference relationship, are interpreted.

4. The ending phase occurs when the patient is able to sustain adaptive responses to daily life stresses without resorting to self-incriminating or destructive behaviors.

The stages of psychodynamic group psychotherapies for borderline patients are not well articulated. Battergay and Klaui (1986) outline five stages of group process with borderline patients: exploratory contact, regression, catharsis, insight development, and social learning. These are not dissimilar from those observed in psychotherapy groups comprised of neurotic psychiatric patients. Roth (1980) has observed that groups with borderline patients spend considerable time managing defensive and impulsive behavior and that only in the final stages of the process are the patients able to develop care and concern for one another. The achievement of this transition from defensiveness to mutual concern and care initiates the termination phase of the treatment.

The Process of Interpersonal Group Therapy

In developing the IGP model of treatment emphasis was placed on clearly describing the therapeutic strategies perceived to respond most effectively to borderline patients' confused representations of self in relation to important others in the context of group interactions. Definitions of phases of group development resulted from observations of the processes that evolved with each of the five groups treated in the trial. The use of the word *phase* does not mean that the treatment foci were well demarcated within the group process. Rather, focal themes were introduced, and each took precedence over others at different points in the group. Some consistent themes of group development were identified. The first was a pregroup process during which the patient can experience the strategies that typify the IGP model of treatment. This was followed by four more themes: search for boundaries, attack and despair, mourning and repair, and integration of self-control. These themes describe the aims, focus, and actual experience of the IGP process. Group themes function as organizing principles. The initiation of each theme was signaled by the introduction of a core group issue. Of importance is the fact that all but one of the themes were introduced in the first three to six group sessions; each theme (search for boundaries, attack and despair, mourning and repair) was initiated and remained a core group theme for the duration of the treatment, but its form and intensity shifted over time. The last theme, integration of self-control, became evident late in the process and paralleled the anticipation of the ending of the group. The spacing of the sessions to every second week for the last five sessions reinforced the meaning of this theme for the group members.

PREGROUP PROCESS

At the time of referral qualifying patients are told about the time and place for the first group meeting, the length of each group session, the weekly format of the first 25 sessions followed by meetings every second week for the remaining 5 sessions, and the overall length of the therapy (30 sessions over a period of 10 months). The decision to attend the group is left to the patient. In response to questions about the group therapists, the other patients, or how the group works, the referring clinician offers the patient the opportunity to meet with the co-therapists prior to the first group session. The decision to meet with the co-therapists is left up to the patient. The purpose of the pregroup session is to experience with the patient the essential ingredients of the IGP model of treatment. The session is not intended to induct the patient to the group, but a "fact sheet" with some guidelines for participating in groups is available if the patient wishes to take it. Rather, the patient decides whether to use the time to inquire about group treatment or to share doubts about attending the group. The therapists' responses are neutral; for example, in response to questions about what will happen in the group, one of the therapists might state that he or she cannot be entirely certain because each group is different and what happens depends on how the patients want to participate. At this point the therapists might give the fact sheet to the patient and might state, "Here are some guidelines for participating in a group that sometimes people find helpful to look over before starting the group. It seems you've had some experience [in groups] so you might not be interested in it. If you would like it you are welcome to take it." The decision to attend the group is left up to each individual patient, and a commitment to attend is not exacted during the pre-group sessions. A typical pregroup session illustrates the process.

After checking on some of the structural issues concerned with the time and the place of the first group meeting, the patient, referring to the group, engages in the following dialogue:

PATIENT: I know what it's like. I mean, before I used to be in a group, and I just sat there and said nothing. I was too scared because I didn't have anything to say.

THERAPIST: This could be the same. The group might not have anything to offer you. It might not be of help.

PATIENT: I know. I've talked to a lot of people about being nuts. I mean you wonder who is going to help. I don't get anywhere and I'm sort of stuck now. I'm having a hard time making a decision whether I should leave this guy I live with. He has beat me up a lot. I don't know whether I should leave him, and nobody has helped me. Everybody says just do what you want. I know that if I throw him out, I'll probably end up letting him come back. I don't know, I'm pulled every which way.

THERAPIST: The advice you get from a group like this might be wrong. It might be the wrong advice.

PATIENT: My friends don't say what to do; they are afraid to say. They say, "well you'll have to decide." See, I'm not worried about being hurt; we've been through a lot together. I don't care what other people think or anything like that. I'm more worried about me and him.

THERAPIST: Sounds like a difficult position you are in.

This approach to the initiation of treatment is different from those proposed by most other models of intervention for borderline patients. As discussed, Kernberg, Selzer, Koenigsburg, Carr, and Appelbaum (1989) and others (Linehan, 1993) focus the initial treatment consultations on the negotiation and establishment of a treatment contract. The aim is to clarify how the treatment works and to develop a structure for the management of impulsive behavior that could result in the disruption of the treatment. Setting limits early in treatment is a theme that permeates most psychoanalytic approaches to the treatment of borderline personality disorder (Adler, 1985; Gunderson, 1984; Kernberg et al., 1989).

Impulsive, potentially destructive behavior toward self or others is also a concern in IGP, but its management depends on communicating to the patient from the onset that only she or he has power over her or his own behavior. This approach stems from the belief that the borderline patient, by definition, will have difficulty in complying with any "rules" that specify expected responses at the beginning of therapy. A contract may represent for the patient an injunction to relinquish or to correct expectations of the treatment relationship on the basis of externally imposed limits. To demand that a borderline patient alter at the onset of treatment distorted expectations of the therapist or therapy may remove any possibility for connection. The IGP model of treatment posits that only through the experience of the entire treatment will the patient be able to alter distorted representations of self and other. The patient's initial negatively valenced expectations of the therapist require a therapeutic process that allows the patient to test and survive undamaged, the anticipated consequences of hateful projections. The IGP presession is intended to enable the patient to experience future patient–therapist interactions and help her or him make a decision about joining the group.

FOUR THEMES OF GROUP PROCESS

The therapists involve themselves in the group process in the following manner. They function from the premise that every group transaction carries a message about a current relationship issue between the patient(s) and therapist(s). Each patient communication, in whatever form (verbal, nonverbal, direct, indirect), is transacting some patient expectation and some anticipated therapist response, or both. Thus, it is not the content per se that is important, or who is speaking to whom, but rather what is being demanded of the therapists. Borderline patients' persistent wishes for care, comfort, and love, while expecting abuse, rejection, and abandonment, are well documented in the literature (Adler, 1985; Gunderson, 1984). For effective therapy to occur, the therapist cannot assume roles that would confirm either side of the patient's conflict. In a traditional psychoanalytic psychotherapy group these transference wishes and fears could be interpreted in terms of their meanings in both the treatment relationship and current and past relationships. In IGP the therapists observe the group member interactions, noting whether the intensity of the transference demand is being adequately managed by the group or whether it is escalating and requires an intervention from one of the therapists. The patterns of interaction among group members and between members and therapists are the focus of observation and intervention throughout all treatment phases.

Search for Boundaries

The objectives of the initial group sessions are similar to those established for any psychotherapy group: engagement, testing group parameters, developing connections, and forming some commitment to group membership. However, the process with a group of borderline patients differs in some important ways from the more typical process of psychoanalytic group psychotherapy (Yalom, 1975). In the very first IGP group session borderline patients are apt rapidly to reveal, verbally and behaviorally, the intensity of their problems with intimate relationships. They recount a series of significant interpersonal disappointments and losses and their hopelessness about altering the course of their lives. In contrast, in groups that include patients at more neurotic levels of functioning the members are more likely to be initially guarded about revealing significant life experiences to a group of strangers. In the IGP groups many of the patients revealed too much too soon. It was not atypical in a first group session for several of the group members to talk about their most painful and intimate life experiences. For example, the patient (Donna) quoted in the example of a pregroup session told the following story in the first group meeting:

> I met this guy about a year and a half ago. He met me when I was doing a lot of drugs and drinking. He was interested in me and wanted to help me. Instead we both ended up doing a lot of drugs and stuff; we had sort of a wild relationship. He drank a lot, and I tried to help him with his drinking. As the drinking went on I turned more to drugs. Things got worse, started to go sour. I really hurt him. He's hit me and kicked me. Then later he pulled a knife on me. But he's nothing compared to what I've been through. I still have feelings for him. First person I've felt like this about for a long time.

In the same session several of the other patients begin to tell their "stories" but in a more guarded fashion. Following Donna's disclosure, several other patients talk about painful life experiences. One said, "I've been raped a couple of times, and now I live with a man who puts me down all the time; I can't take it anymore." In contrast to these patients who reveal too much too soon, there were some patients who could not speak about their own problem situations. They engaged with the group but spent their time commenting on other patients' stories or remaining on the periphery of their own stories.

For example in one of the groups, a patient (Elise) says little about herself throughout the early sessions. In the seventh session when another patient asks directly why she is in the group, she says, "I can't talk about what really bothers me." When challenged Elise replies, "I just can't, it's too hard." Not until the 21st session, and only after much probing by another patient, is the patient able to disclose her despair at not having made any progress. "I have to come up with a solution soon; will I never work again; will I never have a friend I can talk to?" Elise goes on to talk about her near-panic attacks when her son or husband are away from the house. She imagines the worst catastrophes happening. She is convinced that the odds in life are not in her favor. With much support from another patient she is finally able to talk about an important loss. Although her daughter had died during delivery 12 years previously, she sobs as she tells her story about never getting over the feeling of loss. She is embarrassed about her unresolved grief: "You get older, you have a husband and a healthy child so the death of a child you never got to know should eventually be okay; why is it still so important?" In response to a patient's injunction that she should talk to a good friend, Elise says that having a friend to talk to does not seem to be a solution for her; she doesn't have any close friends. She adds, "I can't get into a relationship like that anymore. It takes too long to figure out if you can trust."

These examples of patients' search for boundaries illustrate two very different modes of response to the same source of anxiety (Who can you trust?). Donna shows her overly permeable self-boundaries both by telling her very revealing story to a group of strangers and by the content of the story of her relationship with her boyfriend. She hurdles herself into the group in the same precipitous way she opens herself to her boyfriend without knowing if the group or the boyfriend are worthy of her trust; even when her boyfriend violates her trust, she is unable to extricate herself from the relationship and adds, "I still have feelings for him." Although Elise's boundaries are also overly permeable, she guards against the risk of hurt and disillusionment in relationships by not engaging in them. She also reveals the price she pays for her morbid concerns about her son and husband; she lives in constant fear of their demise.

Regardless of the form in which the search for boundaries is revealed, the message to the therapists is the same: Will the therapists rescue or reject? Are they worthy of trust? Can they tolerate the intensity of the anxiety, despair, and rage as the patients process the inevitable risks associated with new beginnings. Although Elise states that she does not want to have any close friends, she in fact engages with several group members, and their empathic support is valued. Similarly, the patients do not criticize Donna for still having feelings for a man who has abused her. The risk for the therapists is that they will confirm the patient's expectations either by initiating rescue responses or by ignoring or rejecting the patient's pleas for rescue. Patient opportunities for processing alternate expectations of significant others arise from the group interactions; the task for the therapists is to support group dialogue that advances the development of possible new "stories" about relationships. An intervention is needed only when patients' responses reinforce the polarized expectations; that is, they all engage in idealized solutions, or, alternately, all comments are negative, critical, helpless, and hopeless. In most of the groups the patients were more apt to be unrealistically hopeful (rescue is possible) or despairingly hopeless (the only escapes are substance abuse and/or suicide). When the group members joined together to reinforce either one or the other of these modes of interaction, the therapy risked derailing. The therapists' subjective processing of the affect tone of the group served as a signal that an intervention was needed. If the intervention adequately conveyed neither rescue nor rejection, the derailment was avoided. However, usually a series of interventions were needed to restore balance to the interpersonal dialogue. In other words, the patients needed to confront the dilemma: "If suicide is not the answer, what is"? Only over time were the patients able to relinquish their wishes for what could not be.

ATTACK AND DESPAIR

The attack and despair theme was evident within the first three sessions of each IGP group treated in the trial. The message to the therapists was consistent: The therapy was inadequate; nothing would change; and, what were the therapists going to do about it? Although this response early in a therapy group is not atypical, the intensity of the demands and the quality of the despair are more powerful with a group of borderline patients. These are patients who come to therapy because of numerous experiences with "not getting enough" from relationships, including previous therapeutic relationships. Furthermore, in a group situation their anxieties are heightened by the high ratio of patients to therapists; will there be enough caring to go around? will they be overlooked? will some patients attract more favor than others? These anxieties are expressed through demands on the therapists. However, a parallel process is evident that consists of important identifications between group members. Borderline patients know that the therapists, in all probability, have not had experiences similar to theirs; thus, the meaningfulness of therapists' empathic responses is limited. In contrast, feedback from other borderline patients resonates more closely with their own feelings and experiences. Thus the group structure both contains and provokes powerful affective reactions that the therapists are expected to regulate.

The attack and despair theme appears in many different versions. The important therapeutic stance is one in which the therapists tolerate the demands and the intense accompanying affects (anxiety, hopelessness, and rage) while affirming the patients' shared dilemma: "Will this therapy be enough? Will it help? Will the therapists survive the attacks undiminished?" When the therapists acknowledge the dilemma openly without resorting to defensive responses, the group dialogue shifts from despairing confrontations to discussions of alternate versions of the group process and what it might achieve. An example of a third group session illustrates this process.

A patient (Diane) starts the dialogue in an angry, demanding tone of voice:

DIANE: What are we to do between sessions? Should we call you or should we call our GPs?

SALLY: Yeah, it's not so good not being in one-to-one therapy; then you have someone all the time. You only have the group once a week; what do you do the rest of the time?

DIANE: I can relate to what Sally is saying. I thought I was making some progress, but now I feel I'm back at square one again. It's more superficial. The progress I had made with my previous therapist has been obliterated. There's no direction, I have to flounder on my own; I don't know what avenue to take; I don't know what to do.

THERAPIST: You both seem to be saying that the group is not enough; it's not providing the help you need.

DIANE: Yeah.

THERAPIST: Maybe it isn't enough.

[Pause]

SALLY: Perhaps we will see some perspective here that you don't see in one-to-one therapy. With a group you get different feedback. But with individual therapy I felt I had a safety net; now I feel I've lost it.

THERAPIST: I guess it's hard to see the group as a safety net.

DIANE: I would agree. A therapist in one-to-one therapy has more knowledge about you. Here it's a matter of logistics; with five of us you can't get to know us well.

THERAPIST: You mean you would get more talk time?

DIANE: Yeah. What I said in six months will take three years here. It will be slower in group.

NANCY: When I was in group at the day treatment center the group
leaders gave each of us goals to talk about. We each met with the
leaders, were given our goals, and then we talked about them in
the group.

THERAPIST: Would setting goals help?

The dialogue begins to shift when Sally asks Nancy about her goals in
the group. Nancy wants to stop the fights with her parents and says,
"They're angry at me because I'm a disgrace to the family; trying to kill
yourself is not a good thing." The group as a whole engages around
this new material and each patient begins to focus on specific frustrations with intimate others.

This vignette illustrates how the patients vacillate between wishes for
immediate relief and talk about life situations that they despair about
being able to change. The therapists avoided derailment by empathic
reflection of the patient's concerns in combination with affirmation of
the patients' fears. "Maybe it (the group) isn't enough." This constitutes the work of the therapy. When the group members are able to
reinforce this balance, no intervention is needed. When, on the other
hand, they become stuck in a polarized view of themselves and the
therapists, then an intervention is needed. The therapists walk a fine
line between not providing the answers (which they do not have in
reality) and providing empathic, confirming responses of the patient's
view of their life circumstances both within and outside the group.

MOURNING AND REPAIR

The primary aim of IGP is to provide a context in which the patients
are able to process the meanings of their unattainable wishes and
expectations. This includes acknowledging that relationships from the
past cannot be relived in the present. Neither the quality nor the quantity of emotional supplies longed for from early life caregivers can be
found in current adult relationships. The patients' task is to mourn the
loss of these unattainable childhood wishes as they are manifested in
current relationships, including therapeutic relationships. True mourning cannot be achieved until the representations of self in relation to
other are altered to accommodate different versions of the self-system.
Repair occurs when the wounded, abandoned, despairing representations of the self are recast into versions of the self characterized by
greater control over self-motivation and positive self-esteem. The
group provides a natural laboratory for testing numerous hypotheses

about the self in relation to others. The ready feedback from group members and the therapists' unwavering interest and affirmation provide secure boundaries within which the opportunity for experimentation and new learning is maximized and the risk of being criticized, shamed, or abandoned is minimized. The theme of mourning frequently appears in dialogue that shows shifting expectations of others or of the self, as seen in the following illustration.

In the sixth group session several patients begin by asking the therapists about their qualifications and whether or not they are going to be of any help in the group. The therapists answer specific questions about their professional training and experiences with groups. All but two group members join in the attack, which goes on for several minutes. One of the two then says in an angry tone of voice "this is the third time we've done this. I don't want to have to talk about this again for a long time." One of the therapists asks the patient if she may be feeling angry because she hasn't been listened to. (This question addresses the anger of all of the group members who have been saying to the therapists that they haven't been heard.) The patient agrees and adds that when the same issues were discussed in the past the therapists did nothing. The therapist acknowledges the disappointment and states, "We don't have the answers. We wish we did." Here the therapists focus on the patients' loss of their idealized expectation of the therapy and the therapists. The therapists have and will disappoint them (as have important people in their lives). The task for the patients is to tolerate the lost expectation while continuing the work of therapy, which in fact they were able to do.

The group interaction begins to shift and although several members continue to demand answers from the therapists, several others demonstrate that they had not been "listening" the previous week to one of the patients. One group member begins to focus on what happened the previous week when she felt that another member seemed unhappy but no one asked "whether you really wanted to talk about it or whether you just wanted to be left alone." The "unhappy" group member responds to this invitation and starts to talk about the recent loss of a close friend who had left the city. The remainder of the session focused on loss, disappointment, and anger and how to express the anger in a nondestructive manner. Several group members talked about parents who were critical and uncaring when they were children and who continue to reject them as adults.

This dialogue contributes to the work of mourning; that is, the patients describe real losses and emotional losses in early childhood while focusing on strategies for expressing intense feelings of disappointment and anger. For example, one patient kept insisting that anger should be expressed openly, regardless of the person at whom it was directed. In contrast, several other patients felt that the expression of anger currently toward parents would not alter the pain experienced in early childhood. They could not relive these early experiences; the lost wishes could not be denied.

In addition to demonstrating the therapist's response to the group transference demand, this group vignette illustrates the overall therapeutic goal of IGP, mourning what cannot be attained and searching for alternate and more adaptive ways of dealing with life's harsh realities. This goal is not dissimilar to that proposed by Leibovitch (1983) for "short-term integrative psychotherapy" for borderline patients. Leibovitch's therapy stresses "an acceptance of the separateness, distinctiveness and aloneness of the self, of separations and losses that need to be faced and deprivations that must be felt and endured" (p. 97). These issues need not be introduced by the group leaders because they represent the core problems of every borderline patient and are thus raised for discussion by most patients in most sessions. Within the group context each patient confronts personal fantasies and wishes that cannot be fulfilled, including the disillusionment with what therapy can and cannot achieve. The concomitant feelings of bitterness, inadequacy, and rage are acknowledged and tested within the group. The salient mutative factor is the patients' accumulative experience of the therapists' willingness and ability to absorb frustration, tension, and anger as it arises in the group. The therapists neither punish nor abandon the group; rather, they affirm the patients' capacities for similarly absorbing intense anger and anxiety without seeking immediate relief. The group members are also mutually affirming and tolerant of the anger and frustration expressed toward one another. The lost wishes can be mourned adequately when the patients feel that their intensely experienced emotions can be expressed without the risk of more loss and disillusionment. The mourning process helps the patients reflect on ways of mending negative and punitive representations of themselves and intimate others as illustrated by the following repairing transaction.

Enid had frequently talked about her disappointment and rage toward her mother whom she felt had not protected her during childhood when she had been sexually abused by an uncle. She had recently visited her mother in the hopes that she could talk to her about what had happened in the past. Her report of the experience reveals her achieved level of mourning.

> I never got to talk to mom about it. She had arranged everything so that we never got a chance to be alone, to go for coffee, to talk. So I said to myself, "Okay, on some level she knows what's going on and she's not ready to deal with it. Then I'm going to deal with it with my uncle and maybe that's where I should have been starting." So I went and I had about a three-hour talk at my uncle's grave. When I left there I felt I had gotten rid of a big burden. Then it wasn't so urgent to talk to mom, and I realized that it was really weird because I thought I hated the woman, but now I was feeling good about her. I just accepted the fact that maybe she wasn't ready to deal with it, and maybe what I was supposed to be dealing with was this uncle thing, and down the road maybe me and mom can come together and deal with it then; but right now I've let go of a lot of anger and a lot of hurt and a lot of hate.

Integration of Self-Control

As IGP therapy draws to an end, the patients begin to talk about which aspects of themselves they feel they can control and which self-ideas continue to impinge on the enhancement of self-esteem. Although fragments of this theme are introduced earlier in the group sessions, the time-limited structure of the group brings into sharp focus for each patient the gains made and the disappointments about what has not changed. The final five sessions are designed to occur bi-weekly so that the eventual loss of the group could be experienced in "doses." During this period the patients remount attacks on the therapists for being unhelpful and for having failed in relieving all of their life disappointments. However, in all of the groups treated in the trial, the patients also consistently used the final sessions to review gains made and to remourn the loss of fantasized wishes. A segment taken from the 27th session illustrates the process:

PATIENT 1: [Referring to the group] I'm going to be lost without this.

THERAPIST: So that's a disappointment and a loss?

PATIENT 1: Definitely a loss.

PATIENT 2: Like I don't have a hard time when I miss a session or there is a break of two weeks; it becomes a gauge for me, to see how I can handle my own problems and get through it. I mean, I've fallen apart, but I always make it through, and it gives me a boost knowing that if I was alone in this world, somehow or other I would be able to make it through because I got through that week we missed a session even though all kinds of shit was falling down around me. So, I use it as a gauge for my progress. Otherwise, I become too dependent on my support system and I really fall apart.

PATIENT 1: That's my whole problem. I am too dependent on everything and everybody around me. I trust other people. At least I'm starting to trust other people. But I have a hard time trusting myself.

PATIENT 2: But there is no right or wrong way to do any of it. It's just an action. And I think that's the most important thing. Like, I understand what you are saying. It's like, what if I fuck up this decision?

[In the discussion that ensues both patients go on to talk about the meaning of friendships.]

PATIENT 1: You don't count your friends by numbers, you count them by years. How long they've been there.

PATIENT 2: You have to acknowledge the positive side of yourself and the weak stuff that you can't change. You've got to accept that. But you got to at least try to change that, and when you try to change and you can't change, then you got to accept it.

In this segment the integration of self-control has to do with affirming the self while processing the limitations of self and others. Both patients acknowledge that there will be problems in the future and wonder if they will be able to manage them more effectively. The enhanced sense of self is reflected in the recognition that the duration of friendships is more important than the number of friends. Also the injunction to accept what cannot be changed shows how the risk to vulnerable exposure and loss of self-esteem can be contained.

Typical Group Events and Their Management

Discussed below are four group events that typify the kinds of special issues that need to be managed when working psychotherapeutically with a group of borderline patients. They include risks of self-harm, advice giving, silent group members, and the management of institutional problems. While some of these events (such as the response to silent group members) do not occur uniquely in psychotherapy groups with borderline patient members, the strategies specified for their management are consistent with the IGP model of treatment. Emphasis is placed on interventions that reinforce each patient's autonomy and control.

RISKS OF SELF-HARM

Issues of self-harm, especially reports of suicidal attempts in the past, are introduced by one or more patients at every group session. Patient transactions, including those that have to do with suicidal threats, carry an expectation that the therapist will initiate "rescue" procedures. Therefore, the needed therapeutic response is neutrality. In a group, the therapist is protected from assuming an anxious rescuing stance because one or more of the group members will play out this role in response to the patient's projected wishes. The patients offer other responses as well, modulated, problem-solving strategies when feeling suicidal, such as talking to a friend, going to a hospital, and so on. As long as the dialogue continues in a balanced fashion (a balance between despair and hopefulness), the therapist does not intervene.

If asked whether the patients can call the therapists when in crises the therapists tell them that they can but that this might be an exercise in frustration because it might be very difficult to reach them; they add that the help of emergency services of mental health clinics are available 24 hours a day. Repeatedly, control over the consequences of impulsive behavior is given to the patient. The therapists respond empathically to self-harm issues by stating that they do not want any patient to hurt herself or himself but realize that in reality they cannot stop the patient; they reiterate the availability of mental health emergency services, as illustrated in one of the group sessions.

Several group members have been talking about situations associated with suicidal ideation.

THERAPIST: I hear people struggling with ideas about suicide. Does the group want to deal with some alternatives for dealing with it. Is that something you want to get into now?"

[Several patients respond by talking about suicide ("hating it when I think of suicide," "what's another option besides suicide?"). One patient (Jill) becomes the focus of concern.]

JILL: I don't know [about other options] right now. I'm trying to find another option.

OTHER THERAPIST: Jill, are you saying that you have been having suicidal thoughts?

JILL: Yeah, lately.

OTHER PATIENT: Scary, because I have for about three weeks now.
That's why I keep freaking out when we talk about it here; I'm
fighting so hard not to.

THERAPISTS: It's certainly one way of dealing with the hurt and the
anger inside; none of us would like you to take that option.

Group members then talk about how they can reach out to one
another when they are feeling suicidal. They had exchanged their
phone numbers at a previous session and one of the members reminds
the group that they had agreed to call one another, especially when
they were having suicidal thoughts. Later in the discussion one of the
therapists asks Jill, "Do you have any warning that leads up to those
feelings?" Jill knows what triggered her most recent suicidal wishes.
She had seen her ex-boyfriend and contrary to her better judgment had
spent some time with him. She said, "I was afraid to let him in, but I
did and now I just feel really rejected and used again [boyfriend left
again]." The group members focus on giving Jill much support, both in
terms of managing suicidal ideation (calling a suicide hotline) and of
boosting her self-esteem (she's attractive, capable, and can meet men
who will appreciate her).

Suicidal wishes, thoughts, and previous attempts are discussed in most
group sessions. The therapists' response consistently communicates
that they would not wish the patient(s) to choose this option. What
were the precipitants of suicidal thoughts? How might they be managed? What meanings were conveyed by self-harming actions? All of
the patients experience suicidal ideation, and most have attempted to
commit suicide at least once. Some patients persist in using suicidal
talk to ensure the group's attention and care, but they are eventually
able to take increasing responsibility for their own behavior. Talking
with someone (within and outside the group) when flooded with feelings of self-harm functions as an important form of control.

ADVICE GIVING

The IGP model of treatment does not endorse advice giving as a useful
therapeutic strategy. If therapists are asked for information, they give it
as directly and succinctly as possible; no attempt is made to explore the
motivation behind the request because this is either apparent or

becomes apparent in the subsequent group member dialogue. However, advice giving among the patients occurs frequently and could be interpreted as reflecting individual patient competence. The IGP model of treatment is based on the premise that borderline patients are competent and that through the therapeutic experience a sense of self-control and competence is integrated into altered versions of the self. However, a pseudo-form of competence is not productive for either the advice giving patient or the group as a whole. In individual psychotherapy there are few, if any, opportunities for a patient to give advice to the therapist. However, in a group advice giving occurs frequently, and depending on the context of specific group member interactions it may reflect avoidance of involvement in the form of "pseudo-competence," the term we have applied when advice giving is used by the patient to avoid experiencing anxiety and the potential loss of control over anger and frustration. Several group vignettes illustrate how intervention is used to deal with patient-to-patient advice giving.

> During a negatively escalating dialogue around one patient's reluctance to express anger toward her mother and another patient's proffering of advice about the benefits of getting "those feelings of anger out," one of the therapists asks the "reluctant" patient, "Is that something that would be helpful to you? " and adds, "It seems that different people deal with things in different ways." Other patients respond by talking about their own experiences with processing anger.

The therapist's question, followed by a neutral statement, shifts the focus away from advice giving by one patient and defensive reaction from another. It also opens the possibility for both patients (and the group as a whole) to reflect on alternate ways of expressing negative feelings (there is not just one way). These shifts in dialogue diffuse the intensity of affects that escalate when polarized positions are played out in the group; each patient's experience of personal autonomy is also reinforced.

A second illustration of advice giving demonstrates how this form of communication reflects a pervasive personality trait. One of the patients seemed unable to engage in any dialogue with other group members without giving advice. Frequently, the advice contained heavy doses of "moralizing."

A patient (Jennifer) had been talking about how depressed she had been about her angry outbursts toward her children.

JENNIFER: I don't want to feel hurt anymore. I don't want any rage anymore. I'm fed up with it.

LESLIE: Right, you have every reason to be, but have you tried. . . . You see the thing is . . . that when you're hurting you need to be good to yourself . . . what you don't need is a kick in the butt. You need to say to yourself . . . "I'm sorry that you're hurting; you don't deserve to be hurting this much."

JENNIFER: I told my mother that I feel like I'm no good, and you know what she says to me? "You are." . . . But you know, she was the one who did it to me. Like how can the person that actually did it to me tell me that I'm . . .

TANYA: Maybe she realizes now, but she didn't realize then, the same as you do. You know what you are doing to hurt your kids, but you can't stop it.

JENNIFER: Oh, I know what I'm doing.

LESLIE: Maybe what you need, Jennifer, is to talk to yourself. Even though you don't feel it, but that's what you need.

JENNIFER: I don't feel it.

LESLIE: You need somebody to say, "Jennifer you are good, you're okay, you're special." You need someone to hold you until the hurt goes away. . . . You need some comforting, Jennifer, that's what you need.

After several similar exchanges, Jennifer asks, "Are you the therapist?" to which Leslie responds, "No, I just know from experience." The dialogue then shifts when another patient (Tanya) asks Jennifer if she thinks about her kids needing her when she contemplates suicide as an escape. Leslie immediately interjects saying that Jennifer can't handle the burden of thinking about her children because she needs to think about herself. One of the therapists asks whether maybe the members think of suicide as the only option when they feel depressed. Is it something they wanted to talk about? Several patients respond. From the dialogue that ensued, it is clear that the "message" behind the talk of hopelessness about changing behavior is in fact a communication about loss of control and suicidal thoughts. Both Tanya and the therapist have accurately processed the meaning of the message. However, Leslie subsequently persists in giving advice on how to handle suicidal thoughts.

This group vignette illustrates both the process and function of advice giving. Jennifer wants to talk about "giving up," which is later picked up by Tanya as suicidal wishes. Leslie's intolerance of her own anxieties about helplessness and hopelessness is converted into giving advice. Even though Jennifer lets her know that the advice is not help-ful, Leslie persists. To shift the dialogue away from advice giving from one patient and despairing responses from another, an intervention was needed. It came initially in the form of Tanya's question to Jennifer about her thoughts about her children when she feels suicidal and was reinforced by one of the therapists. The group process was advanced as other patients joined in the discussion of strategies for dealing with suicidal ideation. Leslie's advice-giving mode of communication did not shift significantly but was contained within the context of the core group theme, mourning and repair. Some of their wishes would not be realized, but there were options other than suicide.

MANAGEMENT OF SILENT GROUP MEMBERS

During the development and testing of the IGP model of treatment the importance of engaging all group members in every session became evident. Each patient was given the opportunity to contribute to the interaction but was also left free to decline the offer. The rationale for this approach to dealing with silent members evolved from the convic-tion that it was important to distinguish a patient's choice to remain silent from silences that harbored a patient's fear of emotions. If the group failed to engage silent members, then the therapists intervened, as illustrated by some case examples.

In a pregroup session a patient describes her hesitation about being in a group.

PATIENT: Eye contact means a lot to me. I like to look at the person I'm speaking to and vice versa. How am I going to do that, talking to a whole bunch of people?

THERAPIST: Do you think you will have difficulty talking?

PATIENT: I do think I'm going to have a problem with that. I might get use to it, but then again I might not. What happens then, where do I go from there?

THERAPIST: If you are having some difficulty talking, would you like us to help you with it? Would you like us to ask questions?

PATIENT: Fine, just don't center me out.

Frequently in the pregroup sessions the patients revealed their anxi-eties about joining the group. Would they feel free to talk. The thera-pists offered help, and in most cases the patients responded that they wanted to be called on but did not wish to become the focus of attention.

Several within-therapy examples of the management of silent members illustrate both the strategies used and the patient's responses.

THERAPIST: [Addressing the patient just quoted during the pregroup session] Is this a time to ask you a question?

PATIENT: No.

THERAPIST: [addressing another silent member] What about you Donna? Your head was nodding.

PATIENT: [Referring to earlier group discussion about how men treat women] I'm having trouble with how men at my job behave. They have big egos. That's why I quit.

[Donna then talks about her anger at these men and her own frustration at not being able to persist in her job despite them.]

This vignette illustrates how one patient chose to continue to remain silent whereas the other accepted the therapist's offer to contribute to the discussion.

Another example demonstrates how silences frequently mask suicidal ideation. The group has been talking about broken relationships and managing the loss. Samantha has been silent throughout. One of the therapists addresses her: "Samantha, is there something that you connect to? You've been kind of quiet." The patient accepts the offer to engage and begins talking about suicidal thoughts connected to a recent decision to leave an abusive boyfriend. The patient states, "I loved him but I knew I had to leave him; I hate being alone so I think about giving up." In the subsequent exchange the group members identify with the patient's dilemma and talk about managing suicidal ideation.

With borderline patients the meanings of silence need to be explored. If the silence means that a patient is guarding intense and potentially explosive emotions, and if the patient is ignored by the group, the patient may be at risk of engaging in harmful behaviors after leaving the sessions. Our observations of the management of silent group members showed that a therapist's empathic attempt to engage a silent patient was often followed by supportive comments from other group members. However, when silence is perceived as being used in a manipulative manner, both therapists and group members alter their responses, as shown in the following exchange.

In the ninth session of one of the groups treated in the trial a heated exchange occurs between several group members and a silent patient who has been viewed as being deliberately withholding. After many attempts to engage the silent member who frequently needed to be prodded to participate, the following dialogue developed.

PATIENT 1: We keep asking questions because every now and then we see that crack when you come out and share some emotions with us.

SILENT PATIENT: Things aren't good with me right now, and I just don't feel like I want to share it with six people. But I'm here even though I don't want to be.

PATIENT 2: No, you choose to be here.

SILENT PATIENT: No, I force myself to come.

PATIENT 2: You're here. Nobody is dragging you.

SILENT PATIENT: If I didn't come here, then I would end up in a very bad situation.

PATIENT 2: But nobody is dragging you into this room. It's still your choice to come through that door.

SILENT PATIENT: I don't want to talk to you about it.

PATIENT 2: Why, did I step on your toes?

SILENT PATIENT: Yes, you did.

PATIENT 2: Makes you uncomfortable, so you can't talk about it, or won't talk about it? That's how you make us feel, at least from my point of view.

SILENT PATIENT: Well, I apologize.

THERAPIST: Is it okay to give each other feedback as to how you are coming across?

This comment by the therapist is picked up by several group members who use it to explain their attacks of the silent patient. The group gradually and empathically lets the silent member know that she is perceived as rejecting them when she chooses not to talk about what's bothering her when clearly something is bothering her:

GROUP PATIENT: What's wrong was not that you weren't able to say something in front of six people, but that you constantly remind us that you can't talk to us.

SILENT PATIENT: I didn't know that I was even doing it.

The discussion in the group then focuses on the meaning of member behaviors in the group interaction and the importance of giving and receiving feedback.

MANAGEMENT OF INSTITUTIONAL PROBLEMS

Dawson (1988, 1993) has argued that the staff of mental health institutions frequently conspire to reinforce the borderline patient's difficulties with using and benefiting from treatment. They become involved in "rescue" responses, thereby reinforcing the patient's helpless and hopeless image of self. More important, institutional responses frequently ignore the patient's capacity for engaging in a collaborative process in which he or she has control over management of self-harming behaviors. In his book (1993) Dawson provides many examples of mental health institutions' responses that contaminate the treatment of borderline patients. An instance from one of the IGP groups illustrates his point.

At the 22nd session of one of the groups the therapists report that one of the members (Carol) had called to say that she could not return. This was surprising because she had attended all previous sessions and was a committed group member. Three days before the session Carol had gone to one of the hospital psychiatric emergency services because she was frightened by her suicidal thoughts. The assessing psychiatrist admitted her. Subsequently, a consultant for self-harming patients recommended that Carol leave the IGP group and attend instead a group in a day treatment program. The IGP co-therapists were not contacted by the hospital. The therapists were forthright with the group in expressing their dismay about Carol's management by the emergency staff at the psychiatric outpatient service and subsequently queried the decision by the consultant psychiatrist, but to no avail. Carol did not return to the group.

This is an example of poor clinical management of a psychiatric patient. Of importance is the fact that poor clinical management is more apt to occur with borderline patients than with any other patient group. It is true that borderline patients are at risk of carrying out their suicidal wishes, and their pleas for help cannot be ignored. However, the therapeutic response needs to value the contribution that the patient can make to ensure her or his own well-being. A patient who has attended 21 sessions of treatment has made a convincing commitment to try to manage her life in a different way. The group therapists had in part contributed to Carol's escalating anxiety and depression because they had not understood that her apparently competent behavior in the group masked increasing despair about her loneliness. The pending termination of the group (9 sessions remained), and the focus of the group discussions on concerns about ending the group escalated Carol's anxiety. Carol had responded appropriately by going to the emergency service when she was afraid of harming herself. The appropriate institutional response should have involved an assessment of the suicidal risk, temporary hospitalization if needed, consultation with the group therapists, and referral back to the IGP group. Instead, the hospital staff chose not to associate the patient's heightened anxiety with her experiences in the group. Nor did they support the need for continuity in the patient's clinical management; that is, referral back to the group.

Summary

Interpersonal group psychotherapy was designed to respond specifically to borderline patients' internalized and expressed dialogues about self in relation to significant others. Regardless of which group member is speaking or to whom, the therapists are the targets of the internalized dialogue. They must absorb and tolerate the confusion, uncertainty, and ambiguity of the dialogue as it is manifested in group member transactions. They must also model adaptive modes of affect regulation in a therapeutic context that sustain the patients' disregulation of powerful emotions.

The therapeutic strategies of IGP are in part similar to those used in most forms of psychodynamic group psychotherapy. However, there are some important differences. Most interventions are phrased in a tentative way to allow the patient to control whether or how to respond. Especially important is the tentative phrasing of explanatory statements (interpretation) and the fact that interpretive statements are located in the here and now of group member dialogue and interactions. Distinguishing group dialogue that is "stuck" from dialogue that advances the work of the group is another important approach with IGP. For example, when patient dialogue becomes polarized, the therapists are alert to the fact that an intervention is needed. Their aim is to restore the balance of a give-and-take dialogue that advances interpersonal process within the group. When the meanings of the "stuck" dialogue are misunderstood by the therapists, derailment occurs. The therapists are again alerted that an intervention is needed. Mending the derailment may have the greatest therapeutic impact on the patients because they witness the effects of the therapists' confusion and suspended capacity for processing both their own and the patients' emotions. However, contrary to the patients' experiences with managing explosive emotions, the therapists are able to produce a balanced response and process the meanings of the derailment. As the therapy progresses, the patients are increasingly able to address the derailments in the interpersonal dialogue. These patient "interventions" are manifestations of the integration of self-control that is the ultimate aim of IGP.

In addition to the unique technical features of IGP, both the group format and the time-limited boundary provide important therapeutic structures that are especially relevant for the optimal treatment of BPD patients. By preventing the therapist from being the sole target of the patient's demands, as is the case in individual psychotherapy, a co-therapist approach in a group context reduces the risk of therapeutic derailments. The patients provide targets for one another's demands, and an additional therapist provides support for processing the many confusing communications occurring in any group but that are particularly perplexing in a group composed entirely of borderline patients.

To be practiced effectively, IGP presumes a co-therapy model and consultation with colleagues during the treatment process so as to maintain the specified therapeutic attitudes and techniques. In the IGP treatment model, consultation advances the therapeutic work by acknowledging the fact that therapeutic errors or deviations from the recommended therapeutic attitudes are inevitable when treating borderline patients. For the IGP therapists, the most important task is to recognize and manage their subjective reactions to the treatment dialogue. When this is adequately managed, treatment progresses; when it is ignored or badly managed, treatment derailments and eventual failure are the result.

6

Intersubjectivity and the Management of Group Derailments

Therapeutic derailment occurs when a therapist action or inaction results from a failure to understand the contextual features of patient–therapist transactions. The therapist makes an error; the therapeutic process is derailed. For example, when a patient states that the evening before the session she took five sleeping pills, what is being transacted is "I'm out of control; I could kill myself; are you going to rescue me?" A typical therapist response is to show concern, such as "you must have been pretty upset." If further patient talk conveys the message, "I'm truly alone; I've given up; I will kill myself," then the reality of that injunction is dealt with.

An exaggerated therapist response is to launch immediately into questions about the type, dose, and effects of the sleeping pills, followed by the threat of hospitalization if the patient plans to do this again. The precipitant of an exaggerated therapist response, that is, therapeutic error, is the therapist's subjective reaction to the transaction.

The IGP model of treatment views all therapist subjective reactions as human, normal, and expected. Subjective reactions provide important sources of information and serve as cues for understanding the meanings of the patient–therapist dialogue. Because of the interpersonal nature of therapy transactions, therapists must decipher both their own contributions and the patients'. The possibilities for distortion are many. Given the ubiquitous occurrence of complex and confusing transactions in all forms of psychotherapy, especially with borderline patients, IGP's aim is to focus on understanding the precipitants, manifestations, and management of therapeutic derailments.

Theoretical Assumptions

In his book *My Work with Borderline Patients,* Harold Searles (1986) makes the following observation: "It develops on rare occasions that the transference-countertransference emotions in my work with borderline patients become so intense that it feels to me it is all I can do simply to stay in the same room with the patient throughout the session—whether because I am finding him so infuriating, or insufferable, or disturbing in various other ways" (p. 282). It is hypothesized that every therapist who has ever treated a borderline patient has had similar experiences and perhaps not just on "rare occasions."

Traditionally, the constructs of transference and countertransference have been used to conceptualize the intersubjective nature of the therapeutic dialogue with borderline patients. Psychoanalytic writings about the treatment of these patients have described the effects of transference demands on therapists; they activate in the therapist exaggerated emotional responses, counteraggression, and fears of losing control over the therapeutic process (Adler 1985; Gunderson, 1984; Kernberg et al., 1989). Emphasis has been placed on maintaining a therapeutic attitude of "abstinence," which according to Kernberg (1975) means not giving in to the patient's demands for transference gratification. Gunderson states that therapists who work with borderline patients must adopt ways of responding to their transference demands. Other clinicians have recommended specific therapist attitudes, such as therapist consistency and reliability, attunement to the patients' affects and needs, acceptance of the patient's worldview, and refraining from retaliation (Wells & Glickauf-Hughes, 1986). Higgitt and Fonagy (1992) stress the importance of a nonanxious, calm attitude and that perhaps only therapists with phlegmatic personalities are suited in character to work with BPD patients. The literature is well supplied with these therapeutic injunctions, but there is a paucity of procedures and strategies for assuming a "proper" therapeutic stance when working with borderline patients. In contrast, the IGP model of treatment places special emphasis on the ubiquitous occurrence of therapeutic derailments when working with BPD patients and furthermore specifies criteria for recognizing when derailments have occurred and the recovery actions to be taken. In IGP, the detection of and recovery from therapeutic derailment forms the central strategic core of the therapeutic model and is directly linked to the maintenance of positive group process. In addition, therapist subjective reactions during the group process provide the cues for detecting threats to the maintenance of therapeutic direction and continuity.

Meaning of Therapists' Subjective Reactions

The IGP model of treatment presumes that therapist subjective reactions are intrinsic to understanding and managing the borderline patients' projected expectations. This approach is based on the integration of two theoretical paradigms that are especially pertinent for the treatment of borderlines and that emphasize the interpersonal focus of IGP:

1. Ogden's (1979) formulation of the function of projective identification in the treatment relationship
2. Wachtel's (1980) application of the cognitive processes of assimilation and accommodation (Piaget, 1954) for understanding the
patient's projected self–other representation in the transference.

According to Ogden (1979), projective identification is useful for understanding the meanings attributed by the treatment partners to their interactions. Ogden provides a clear definition of this process and suggests that, schematically, projective identification consists of a three-part sequence:

1. The patient rids herself or himself of unwanted aspects of the self
by depositing them into another person.
2. The patient exerts pressure on the recipient of the projection to
behave in a way that confirms the projection.
3. The patient introjects or reinternalizes the projection whether or
not it has been psychologically processed by the recipient.

In the therapeutic relationship, through projection the patient expects the therapist to resolve the patient's internal polarized view of the world as either hostile and rejecting or caring and protective. In the projective process the patient feels united with the recipient of the projection, and this is to be distinguished from projection as a defensive function, in which the patient disassociates herself or himself from the projected fantasy.

Projective identification provides a parsimonious model for understanding interpersonal transactions, in particular the therapeutic relationship (Marziali & Munroe-Blum, 1987). Psychological growth for the patient is dependent on the quantity and quality of "psychological processing" by the therapist of the patient's projected, negative fantasies. With BPD patients, four outcomes are possible:

1. Withdrawal
2. Rejection
3. Rescue
4. Acceptance and tolerance.

The first three reinforce the patient's negative views of self and others and have the potential of making the therapeutic process derail. Case illustrations of each of the negative outcomes are presented.

WITHDRAWAL

In the first example, the therapist fails to process adequately the projection and withdraws from the patient, thereby confirming the patient's fears that her or his negative and destructive self merits rejection and abandonment. In this instance, the identification with the therapist involves the re-internalization of unaltered negative aspects of the self accompanied by deepening feelings of anger and despair.

Tiffany was a 22-year-old woman who had been hospitalized extensively over a 6-year period for self-mutilating behaviors that entailed burning patterns on her arm with a cigarette, refusing to eat, or purging. She had been successful in obtaining employment on many occasions but never maintained a position beyond 1 or 2 months. While in hospital, Tiffany would refuse to engage in any meaningful discussions regarding her experiences, feelings, or the reasons behind her self-destructive actions. What was evident from the history provided by her mother was that Tiffany had been raised by unhappy and self-absorbed parents who spent the majority of their marriage threatening to separate and divorce and who pressured her to take sides in their many arguments. Although her mother described Tiffany as having always been a moody and difficult child, her self-destructive behavior and related hospitalizations began when her father suffered a heart attack at home in the midst of a particularly bitter family dispute and died shortly thereafter. Tiffany had never before agreed to participate in any outpatient treatment program, so it was somewhat surprising that she agreed to participate in a group experience when released from hospital. Although Tiffany attended the group regularly, during sessions she withdrew to a corner of the room at the outside perimeter of the group circle, kept her eyes to the floor, and never spoke, even when directly addressed. The other group members expressed frustration about her lack of active participation. They, along with the co-therapists, commented on her withdrawal and encouraged her to express herself verbally. In supervision, the co-therapists voiced their own frustrations about their sense of failure to elicit her involvement and their anger at her disruptive presence. During a subsequent session, following several group members' comments regarding Tiffany's lack of verbal participation, one of the therapists in a state of frustration stated, "Perhaps Tiffany's silence is her way of controlling the group, we certainly do spend a lot of group time talking about her. Perhaps we should get on with topics of concern to the active participants." Tiffany fled the session and was rehospitalized in the subsequent week.

REJECTION

In the second outcome the therapist not only fails to endure and integrate the patient's warded-off negative projections but also behaves in an actively negative and punitive manner. The therapist's inability to reflect on his own rejecting behaviors toward a patient results in the use of hospitalization as a form of punishment rather than protection for the patient.

Patricia was a 28-year-old vivacious woman with excellent superficial social skills and an engaging manner. She was unhappy in her relationships with men, routinely meeting someone new, becoming infatuated and overinvolved, and suffering acute distress when in the face of her excessive demands and intense attention, the man would withdraw from the relationship. This series of relational crises led to equally frequent suicidal gestures of a serious nature and related emergency room visits and hospitalizations. At the time of her referral to group, Patricia had had 32 hospitalizations in the preceding 3 years. In spite of this, she maintained employment as a child care worker, a broad network of social contacts, and a busy social schedule. In group, Patricia assumed a pseudo-competent, co-therapist role. She used extensive psychiatric jargon in her many interpretations of the problems of the other group members. She rarely made any reference to her own difficulties, although she hinted at her experiences through her many negative comments about mental health professionals, their incompetence and ineptitude, and the ease with which a "smart person" could manipulate the hospital system. The efforts of the therapists to engage Patricia in more personally reflective activity only led to an escalation of her pseudo-competent contributions. In one session, in the face of mounting frustration, one therapist commented, "your description of Ted's [a group member] problem is interesting Patricia, but you might get more out of the group personally if you focused on your own problems rather than those of the other group members." Following this session, as the therapist was locking up the building and leaving, he found Patricia sitting on the front steps waiting for him. Patricia stated that she was very upset following the session and that she felt the same way as when she had ingested cleaning fluid the previous year. The therapist responded, "Well, we are right across the street from the Emergency Department, I'll walk you over." Patricia was hospitalized and did not return to group.

Rescue

In the third outcome, the therapist gives in to rescue fantasies in the face of the patient's self-presentation of helplessness and hopelessness and projections of the therapist's omnipotence. Tony was a 30-year-old man of immigrant background who had been involved with psychiatric treatment since his early teens for problems related to poor school attendance, depression, and superficial self-harming behaviors. While in individual treatment he was known to routinely miss his scheduled appointments, to show up at unscheduled times, and to seek out personal information about his therapists so as to contact them at home, particularly at late hours. When assigned to group treatment Tony was extremely reluctant to join the group, attended the initial session but immediately informed the group members that he doubted whether the group would be "enough" for him. During subsequent sessions, Tony looked tearful, and at the end of the sessions, which were held in the evenings, he would linger, expressing his fears regarding going home to an empty apartment. For the first five sessions the co-therapists responded in a neutral fashion to these behaviors, and Tony would eventually wander off on his own and return as scheduled for the next session. At the sixth session, Tony arrived early and was there to greet the therapist who was on this occasion leading the group alone as her co-therapist was ill. Tony spent the pregroup period describing how terrible his week had been and how he didn't think anything could help him. During group, he looked pained and distant, unresponsive to the contributions of the other group members, but attracting their support and interest. At the end of group he again stayed on while the therapist closed up, expressing fears regarding his ability to get home on his own. Tired after a long day, exasperated, and against her own better judgment, the therapist said, "Come on, I'll give you a ride home, I'm going that way anyway." Later that evening Tony showed up at the emergency room of the local hospital in a high state of anxiety, where he described being so sick that "his therapist had to take him home earlier in the evening." He was sent home in the early hours of the morning, and en route he attacked an elderly woman on the street, his first documented assaultive activity.

Acceptance and Tolerance

In the fourth and positive outcome of the projective identification process, the therapist absorbs, contains, and integrates the negative projections by maintaining a healthy self-interest and tolerance for her or his own retaliatory feelings and by not acting on them through withdrawal, attack, or rescue. This latter form of psychological processing by the therapist provides the essential ingredients for sustaining and advancing the therapeutic process. The IGP therapeutic strategies were designed to support the therapists' capacities for adequately processing frustrating and anxiety-provoking patient behaviors and projections. Therapeutic derailments result when therapist responses reflect their own escalating anxiety and anger. These damage the process, and the patient merely reexperiences with the therapist the negative relationships that repeatedly occur outside of the therapeutic situation.

According to IGP, therapeutic derailment occurs when the therapist fails to process adequately the patient's negative projections. Ogden's views about the effects of poorly processed projected contents are readily observable in the interactions with borderline patients; when they feel misunderstood and when they are the recipients of negative reactions, they verbally and behaviorally communicate their feelings of resentment and disappointment. The cue to the therapist that a negative therapeutic reaction has occurred is obvious.

Wachtel's (1980) formulation of how accommodation and assimilation apply to the transference paradigm extends Ogden's view of the function of projective identification. According to him, all perception is a selective construction influenced by external phenomena and internal schemas. In Piagetian (1954) terms, the processes of assimilation and accommodation shape and change the self-schemas. Schemas are derived from learning experiences in which information (cognitive and affective) is assimilated and accommodated. When the process of assimilation operates in the absence of accommodation, new information is made to fit old schemas that remain largely unaltered. When the process of accommodation can be accessed, shifts in self-schemas occur: The schema accommodates the new input and is thereby changed in the process.

Wachtel suggests that patient transference reflects a self-schema characterized by a predominance of assimilation and underutilization of accommodation: The therapist is accommodated to experiences shaped by previous relationships. In transference schemas, affective and defensive processes are played out in the context of interpersonal transactions. Defensive operations skew and distort perceptions, so that the appraisal of affect-laden interpersonal events results in confusion and ambiguity; accommodation is less efficient, and old schemas prevail. The management of confusion requires accurate judgments about the source of the stimulus. For example, is the other person clearly construed (is he as he appears?), or has the other person's response been elicited by the observer? With healthier personalities the range of elicitations from others is broader, thus the self-responses are more complex and complete. With pathological personalities the range of elicitations from others is narrower and often stereotyped, resulting in limited feedback.

Wachtel's theoretical model for explaining the mechanisms operative in transference provide a cognitive structure for understanding Ogden's views of the process of projective identification. Both models suggest that for severe personality disorders archaic, stereotyped mental representations of self in relation to others (self-schemas) are repeatedly assimilated in unaltered forms; consequently, accommodation is restricted. What is projected on to the therapist is assimilated to experiences that were shaped by earlier experiences, and current perceptions of the therapist that do not fit the old schemas fail to be accommodated. It is hypothesized that when the cognitive-emotional dissonance is managed effectively during projective identification, the new learning is accommodated and assimilated to altered schemas. This can only occur if the patient and therapist can tolerate the experience of confusion and ambiguity without disrupting the therapeutic dialogue, thereby advancing the search for new meanings. Because the patient has had a paucity of experience in tolerating and managing confusion it is the therapist who must initially accommodate this process. Subsequently, and following repeated "tests" of the therapist's sustaining capacities, the patient, through the process of identification, can accommodate new information about the therapeutic relationship and thus begin to alter self-schemas. It follows that these shifts in the patient's schemas will affect positively the negotiation of other current and future relationships.

Constructs of projective identification, assimilation, and accommodation are also important to understanding therapists' attitudes and behaviors. Searles (1986) warns that while the therapist is expected to absorb the borderline patient's projected distress, she or he must at the same time recognize that the therapist is also the cause of the distress and that there is some reality to even the most bizarre patient projections. Thus, it is equally important that the therapist be aware of her or his own contributions to the transference-countertransference matrix.

For therapists, cognitive generalizations about the self that have been derived from the past are reflected in all their role functions, including the therapeutic role, and guide the processing of self-related information contained in personal, social, and professional interpersonal encounters. In personal and social relationships, therapists have more latitude for expressing emotions associated with cognitive information processing. When information is inconsistent with self-schemas and arouses anxiety, they can call upon a wider repertoire of mental and behavioral activity to reduce anxiety and restore a secure self-schema. The activity can include avoidance mechanisms such as transforming anxiety into other emotions such as anger and withdrawal. In contrast, in their professional roles therapists are more restricted in the ways in which anxiety can be managed; not only are negative affects, which are transformations of anxiety, to be contained, but also therapists are expected to manifest empathic responses that communicate to the demanding, hostile patient that he or she is worthy of concern and care. Via clinical training in psychoanalytic psychotherapy, a personal analysis, and clinical experience in general, therapists acquire ways of thinking, and behaviors that permit productive and helpful therapeutic activity. With more stable, higher functioning patients, therapists are more capable of being empathic with the patient's subjective states because these reflect self-schemas that are more consonant with what the therapist can acknowledge in herself or himself. With severely pathological patients, therapists are more vulnerable to experiencing painful levels of anxiety because the patient's projected feelings and attitudes are frequently discrepant with the therapist's experiences and expectations. Habitual therapeutic endeavor does not elicit predictable patient responses. When therapist expectations are not confirmed, anxiety and confusion are the outcome.

As suggested, no training can adequately prepare a therapist for dealing with borderline patients' projections; sooner or later all therapists are pushed into making mistakes; that is, they inadvertently match the patient's hopes for rescue or fears of rejection. Sandler (1976) suggests that if therapists are able to tolerate this see-saw process and cope with the distortions of their conceptions of themselves induced by the patients' projections, they can then make use of this important source of information about the patients' internal representations of self in relation to other. This is the core therapeutic task to be addressed by all therapists who attempt to work with borderline patients; in other words, management of the therapist's subjective reactions are the sine qua non for effective therapeutic activity.

In the IGP model of treatment therapists are trained to monitor their subjective reactions so as to detect the experience of anxiety. Anxiety functions as a cue for deciphering the patient's expectations. In turn such a cue initiates a process for containing the anxiety before it is transformed into other emotions that lead to therapeutic error. During the course of training and consultation therapists develop considerable capacity for examining and managing effectively their subjective affective states during the interactions within the group. However, we believe that only ongoing consultation promotes a group environment that is responsive to patient expectations because the therapists are given the support they need to sustain therapeutic activity that promotes the avoidance of error and its management when it occurs.

Ogden (1979) and Wachtel's (1980) theoretical paradigms were developed for dyadic, psychoanalytic psychotherapy. In group psychotherapy the application of projective identification has not been well developed since Wilfred Bion's (1961) important observations on the mental life of groups. In addition to describing the archaic fantasies that develop in groups Bion believed that projective identification provided the vehicle for understanding group functioning and that the group therapist could facilitate the work of the group only by being aware of the process within herself or himself; these subjective affective experiences served as the major source for interpretation of group member behavior. Horwitz (1983) has shown how Bion's perspective of projective identification functions in groups within certain interpersonal transactions such as, for example, the notion of role-suction (a group member is coerced by group forces to fulfill a particular role for the group), use of a group member as spokesperson, and the occurrence of scapegoating. However, both Bion and Horwitz viewed the process of projective identification as separate from the phenomena of transference and countertransference.

Despite theoretical differences on the function of certain mental states (projective identification, transference and countertransference) in the treatment of borderlines, clinicians agree that therapists' subjective responses are useful for understanding what the patient projects on to the therapist. The management of therapist subjective experiences in psychodynamic approaches centers on the use of interpretations in response to both transference demands and projective identification (Bion, 1961; Horwitz, 1983; Kernberg et al., 1989). In contrast, IGP not only avoids interpretations but affirms the patient's views and attempts to maintain a "level playing field." However, therapist deviation from these therapeutic stances is anticipated. More important, IGP focuses on the early recognition of therapeutic errors and specifies the actions to be taken to recover from them when they occur. It is hypothesized that this activity (the commission of and recovery from thera-

peutic errors) is an important mutative agent for the positive development of the group and for the growth of its individual members.

Applications of the Theoretical Paradigm

During the training of the therapists in the IGP model of treatment,
theoretical hypotheses about the function of projective identification
and the transference-countertransference meanings of interactions
within the group are discussed and illustrated through the use of
excerpts from transcripts of treatment sessions. Moreover, the focus of
the consultation sessions while a group is in progress is to examine
therapists' subjective reactions and how these relate to the way they
behave within the group. In each instance the aim is to understand the
interpersonal issue being transacted, as illustrated by the following
excerpt.

PATIENT 1: Do you find that you can understand what we've been
    through, like . . . you haven't been through it, right?

PATIENT 2: Or have you?

PATIENT 1: Have you been through the counseling? Can you identify
    with us?

THERAPIST A: Sometimes you can understand people when you haven't
    been through exactly the same thing.

PATIENT 3: Is that a yes?

PATIENT 2: That's not an answer.

PATIENT 4: It's kind of a "no."

PATIENT 5: Yet we're supposed to be directing ourselves. . . .

In this dialogue the message to the therapists is reasonably direct: "Are
you capable of understanding us?" The response from the therapist
conveys anxiety about being competent. It constitutes a therapeutic
error, as confirmed by the patients' subsequent responses. All five
patients in the group join in the attack; they have detected accurately
the ambiguity of the therapist's response; their anxiety is heightened
and they become counterdefensive.

As the dialogue continues the therapists attempt several empathic
interventions, as for example, "So are you saying it all feels confusing,
what we are doing?" These comments do not alter the defensive, counterdefensive dialogue. The patients continue with comments such as,
"But if they haven't been through what we've been through, what do

they have to share?" and "There's a lack of communication from the leaders." As the patients continue expressing their criticisms of the leaders, they point out group issues that concern them most; members who "monopolize the meeting with their problems," patients are cut off at the end of the session without warning, and they are frustrated by having to complete research forms at the end of the sessions. The therapists' anxiety continues to be evident; in response to the anger about completing the research forms, Therapist B states, "It's hard for me to comment on that, the forms have to do with the study. I think all of you are aware of that." The patients' subsequent responses reveal once more that the therapeutic error has been reinforced; they begin to argue about the group structure, therapist leadership, and the utility of the research forms. Finally, Therapist B makes an intervention in which the patients' views are affirmed and refers to aspects of the group structure that are unalterable. "It's hard to get a happy medium between enough structure that would be helpful for the group and too much structure like the research forms that make you angry. It is hard to find the right structure. Certainly the forms are part of the structure, and the end of the session when we are out of time is part of the struc-ture." This therapist intervention is followed by between-patient, and between-therapist-and-patient dialogue on what they can negotiate about the group structure. The patients ask to be forewarned about when the session ends, and could they have the option of taking the forms home to complete and return the following week. The therapists agree to both requests. The patient dialogue then shifts to talk about disappointment with parents in the past, accepting them in the present, and continued efforts at negotiating new ways of relating to their par-ents. The parallels between this group material and what has just tran-spired with the therapists is clear; the phases of disappointment, anger, acceptance, and negotiation were played out with the therapists in the group. The experience in the here-and-now, face-to-face contacts with others has led to one level of resolution and to discussing problem solving outside of the group.

This example of therapeutic error can be addressed in two ways: (1) how could it have been avoided?, and (2) How is an error managed once it occurs? To avoid the error, the therapists would have had to acknowledge within themselves the mounting anxiety about having their competence challenged. Then they would have been in a better position to understand and process the group message—"Are you competent?"—and the meanings of this message—"Can you manage us, contain us, rescue us if we get into trouble?" The needed therapist response is an honest one: "No, we have not been through what you've been through." Later when a patient asks if the therapists have been "through the counseling," their response is honest, "Yes" if they have been in therapy, "No" if they haven't. These responses avoid therapeutic error because the therapists avoid falling prey to the patients' projections; they confirm neither competence nor incompetence but represent a forthright acknowledgment of the current transaction, that is, an anxiety-provoked patient demand is met with the truth, unencumbered by counteranxiety on the part of the therapists. The task for the group and the therapists is to address the residual anxiety and disappointment.

The selected excerpt also illustrates how a therapeutic error can be managed once it occurs. The therapists become aware of the fact that their attempts to alter the negative course of the dialogue are ineffective. Even when they switch to empathic responses the patients' demands for a show of competence continue. Despite the heightened tension in the group, the therapists demonstrate that they are able to tolerate the attacks because they do not escalate their frustration or defensiveness. Finally when the demand for more structure is acknowledged as legitimate and the nonnegotiable limits are addressed (completing the research forms and ending sessions on time), the patients shift from angry criticism to problem-solving negotiation; that is, *they* become competent and achieve their goals. As suggested, it was not surprising that the group talk then shifted immediately to a discussion about negotiating difficult relationships with parents. Although there is no way of confirming our speculation, we believe that the effective management of therapeutic error functions as a mutative agent within the group process and advances the therapeutic work. However, whether it contributes to *individual* patient change is unknown.

In another example of therapeutic error, the effects of therapists' failure to intervene is illustrated. In the 12th session of one of the groups treated in the trial one patient starts the session by announcing that she had taken two extra pills in addition to her regular dose of prescribed antidepressant medication. Neither the other group members nor the therapists respond to this information. A little later in the group the same patient states that she had in fact taken four extra pills. When this communication produced no response, the patient talks about her near-fatal overdose the previous year. Other group members ignore her and begin to report their own experiences with overdoses and other suicidal attempts. As the tension and anxiety escalates, the patients begin to show one another scars on their arms, wrists, and one neck scar resulting from previous attempts at self-harm. The atmosphere in the group turns to contagious hysteria. Two group members interject rather macabre jokes in a seeming attempt to diffuse the anxiety. The group leaders did not intervene, and eventually the members went on to discuss other current life problems. However, following the group session both therapists received phone calls from several patients who were worried about their own and other patients' suicidal impulses. The therapists acknowledged their concerns and reassured the patients about the opportunity to discuss their worries at the next group session.

It was hypothesized that the therapists' passivity and failure to intervene heightened the patients' anxiety to the point where they actually began to compete for who had engaged in the most frightening suicidal attempt. The therapists heard the first patient's call for rescue but did not intervene for fear of fulfilling the projected wish for a savior. When the same patient repeated and intensified the suicidal message and when the other patients rapidly escalated talk about their suicide attempts both therapists were overwhelmed; they dealt with their anxiety by joining in the laughter in response to the macabre jokes.

Failure to intervene when material about suicidal ideation or attempts has been introduced constitutes a major therapeutic error. Although IGP techniques are intended to avoid exaggerated responses to discussions of suicide and to avoid assuming responsibility for the patients, topics of self-harm are to be taken seriously. The therapist's attitude needs to be one of interest, care, and concern.

In all of the groups treated with IGP, there were numerous examples of therapeutic management of suicidal threats as material about self-harm was introduced by one or more patients at almost every group session. For example, during the early part of a fourth group session one of the patients states, "I'm going to end up walking out of here because I don't want to hear about any of your problems." She adds that she had never wanted to be in a group in the first place but none of the doctors at the hospital would take her on as a patient; thus, she had no choice about coming to the group. Several of the other patients try to ask questions and offer support but are immediately rebuffed by the patient:

THERAPIST: Are you worried about whether you will get what you need [from the group]?

PATIENT: I'm not going to get them in this group, I doubt it very much. I don't want to listen to anybody else's problems.

[Another patient's attempt at support is rejected:]

PATIENT: I am fed up with getting help. I put on a nice front so everyone thinks I'm all right and nothing is going to happen—yet I
keep telling them.

THERAPIST: Are you saying that you're wanting to harm yourself?

PATIENT: You've got that right.

When the therapist begins to ask who the patient has talked to about
her suicidal thoughts, she readily reveals that she has told her husband
and the welfare worker. She also reveals that the doctor who prescribes
and monitors her medication has given control over the drug to her
husband, but that she has access to other drugs that are equally lethal.
Despite a group dialogue that engages her to examine the meanings of
her suicidal wishes, the patient remains angry, rejects the group, and as
she gets up to leave the session states that the research assistant can get
in touch with her.

In this segment, the patient's message to the group and the therapists
is clear: She is not getting enough, and the suicidal talk is a form of
blackmail that is nonetheless taken seriously by both the therapists and
the other group members. One of the therapists acknowledges that the
patient's message has been heard ("Are you wanting to harm yourself?") and taken seriously ("Whom have you talked to?"), and the
group members fulfill the patient's wishes for rescue and simultaneously challenge her reasons for wanting to harm herself. However, when
the patient leaves the group asking that the research assistant call her,
neither the group members nor the therapists are concerned that the
patient will act on her threats. All have shown considerable concern,
but none have assumed responsibility for the patient's behavior.

Consultation and the Management
of Therapeutic Derailments

The training model for IGP strongly supports the use of ongoing consultation throughout the therapeutic process. As has been illustrated,
therapists who are well trained and well experienced in the treatment
of patients with BPD are nonetheless vulnerable to their own subjective
reactions to the therapeutic transactions. Thus, anxiety, anger, and frustration can be inadvertently expressed in such a way that the group
process is derailed and one or more patients suffer specific negative
consequences. It is hypothesized that the consultant can remain more

objective about the therapeutic process because her or his emotions are less apt to be aroused as she or he is not an active participant in the group. In our experience this hypothesis was not always supported. The consultant can be vulnerable to the demands of certain patients through either a process of identifying with the therapists and their mounting anxieties or the failure to monitor their own subjective reactions. For example, among all of the patient styles of behavior observed in the groups, the pseudo-competent patient was the most difficult to tolerate by both the therapists and the consultant. Although the therapeutic team understood the defensive function of the "co-therapist" behaviors of pseudo-competent patients, more therapeutic derailments and disruptions occurred with these patients. The consultant and therapists shared their frustrations and anxieties with these patients but lagged in their attempts to formulate empathic therapeutic strategies for their management. Because these patients were "very competent" at maintaining a distance from the pain and shame underlying their pseudo-competence, the competence of the therapeutic team was severely challenged. Perhaps the ultimate threat to any therapist is the admission of his or her own helplessness and hopelessness. Thus, like the patients, the therapeutic team attempted to ward off the most intolerable of affects, anxiety, and despair by counterdefensive maneuvers. Therapists and consultants can insulate themselves from their therapeutic failures by resorting to professional platitudes, such as "the patient is not ready for treatment" or "the patient has such deep-seated problems that she or he cannot benefit from this form of treatment." We learned from the experience of treating five groups of BPD patients with the IGP model of treatment that consultants, like therapists, make errors and that their responsibility for recognizing and recovering from therapeutic derailments cannot be ignored. As will be illustrated in chapter 7, a pseudo-competent patient in one of the groups was not well managed, and both consultant and therapists shared the responsibility for the failure.

Summary

The intersubjective nature of therapeutic work suggests that errors will occur because therapists are required to process both the patients' and their own anxieties. If, as has been suggested, borderline patients are more apt to project stereotyped self-schemas that reflect negative early life experiences, and if they are less able to accommodate information from new experiences, then the therapist is left with the task of absorbing the projections, reflecting on their meanings, containing her or his own anxiety, and responding to reassure the patient that the projection has not been reinforced but positively altered. In the IGP model it is hypothesized that all patient–therapist transactions revolve around a dialogue about the interactions between patient and therapist self-schemas. The risk is that the patient's projected negative and restricted self-schemas will overwhelm the therapist. The hope is that the therapist possesses more varied, flexible, benign, and positive self-schemas. It is the responsibility of the therapist to process the patient's projections regardless of their harmful contents. In a group context, one borderline patient's projections invariably reflect those of several other group members; thus, the therapist's processed response is equally available for introjection by all group members. The therapists are also better able to process the meanings of the patients' projected self-schemas in a group context. Co-therapists share the intensity of the projections with each other and with the group members, and the risk for therapeutic error is reduced.

The availability of consultation throughout the therapeutic process of an IGP group is essential to the maintenance of an appropriate therapeutic stance. However, consultants are also vulnerable to their own subjective reactions and can influence negatively the transactions within the group. Thus when considering the sources of therapeutic derailments, the behaviors, attitudes, and inputs of the consultant need to be examined as intensively as those of the therapists. Only with openness in the team consultation process is it possible to be effective in maintaining the proper therapeutic course of IGP.

By monitoring the levels of anxiety (both their own and the patients'), the therapists can anticipate the risk of therapeutic error. This means that work with borderline patients using the IGP model of therapy (and probably most other approaches with BPD) requires the therapists to tolerate the experience of large doses of anxiety due to the ambiguity and uncertainty experienced during the processing of the patient's projections because the therapists cannot know a priori the meanings of each projection. Theoretical assumptions and prior clinical experience can only instruct therapists on the probable cognitive processes, but the anticipation of an anxious state when working with borderline patients can allow therapists to retain a healthy self-interest in their work with these often difficult-to-help patients.

7

Training of Therapists

Review of Standardized Models of Psychotherapy Training

The purpose of any psychotherapy training program is to ensure competent performance of a specific treatment model. An adequate level of competence would require the trained therapist to demonstrate each of the following:

1. Theoretical framework that supports the content and context of the model of therapy
2. Capacity for integrating conceptual formulations of clinical problems with the meanings of individual patient's narratives about their current and past life experiences
3. Knowledge of the research literature and empirical evidence supporting selected therapeutic strategies
4. A skillful use of the prescribed intervention techniques
5. Ability to vary technique according to the process of the interactions both within therapeutic sessions and across the span of the entire treatment
6. Knowledge about when to apply and withhold intervention techniques
7. Capacity for accurate empathy, genuineness, and warmth (Rogers, 1957)
8. Ability to create an interpersonal context (therapeutic alliance) that supports mutual learning and growth
9. Absence of therapist characteristics and behaviors that could interfere with both the creation of a constructive therapeutic alliance and the optimal application of the prescribed interventions.

In the 1980s research on psychotherapy efficacy has developed and promoted the use of manuals to help therapists to acquire competence in a particular treatment approach (Dobson & Shaw, 1988; Rounsaville, O'Malley, Foley, & Weissman, 1988; Strupp & Binder, 1985). Manual-guided training differs from standard psychotherapy training programs by providing detailed instructions on the use of prescribed techniques. Furthermore, the manuals were developed to describe treatment approaches for specific diagnostic groups (Beck, Rush, Shaw, & Emery, 1979; Klerman, Weissman, Rounsaville, & Chevron, 1984; Kernberg et al., 1989; Luborsky, 1984; Strupp & Binder, 1985).

The aim of manual-guided training is not to teach fundamental psychotherapy principles and skills but to shape and reinforce in experienced therapists those skills that are part of the experimental treatment approach and new skills, attitudes, and behaviors unique to the new method of intervention. Thus, in most efficacy treatment trials only experienced psychotherapists have been selected for training and after relatively brief training, they achieved high levels of competence (Rounsaville et al., 1988; Shaw & Dobson, 1988). Most of the manual-guided training programs have the following format:

1. Review of the manual and relative theoretical papers
2. One or more didactic seminars to discuss and illustrate key treatment strategies
3. Supervision of one or more training cases followed by assessment of therapist competence.

Of all of the training ingredients special emphasis is placed on supervision, which most often includes observation of videotaped trainee treatment sessions.

The success of any psychotherapy training program is judged according to specific competency criteria:

1. Are therapist's attitudes, behaviors, and interventions faithful to the specified treatment?
2. Is an adequate level of skill acquisition maintained for the duration of the treatment?
3. To what extent are skill application and relationship development optimally integrated?
4. Are high levels of competency in the treatment model related to outcome?

All four questions have been addressed with positive results. Rounsaville et al. (1988), and Shaw and Dobson (1988) found that experienced therapists achieved competency readily, developed supportive relationships with their patients, and maintained a constructive working stance for the duration of the treatment. Two studies also support the correlation between adherence to manual-guided interventions and outcome. Luborsky and colleagues (Luborsky, McLellan, Woody, O'Brien, & Auerbach, 1985) found that therapists who were more faithful to the manuals achieved better results. O'Malley et al. (1988) showed that high competency ratings of Interpersonal Psychotherapy (IPT) trained therapists were predictive of greater patient improvement. Rounsaville et al. (1988) showed similar posttraining findings but caution that high adherence to a psychodynamically based therapy such as IPT may simply characterize inherently good therapists.

Although study findings demonstrate the feasibility of using manual-guided training programs for achieving competency, the relationship between specific active ingredients (techniques) of a treatment model and achieved patient outcomes is unknown. Might relationship factors such as accurate empathy, unconditional acceptance, and warmth contribute as much to positive outcomes as skillful application of technique? The manuals developed to date do not provide the opportunity for answering this question because emphasis has been placed on technique acquisition. Even though required therapist attitudes and general behaviors are described, instructions for acquiring the ideal interpersonal therapeutic stance are not well developed. Not surprisingly, in the NIMH Treatment of Depression Collaborative Research Program (Elkin, Parloff, Hadley, & Autry, 1985) experienced therapists who had demonstrated high levels of competence in their clinical work prior to training were readily trained to high levels of competency in the experimental treatments and achieved the best outcomes. Did these therapists have the "right stuff" prior to being trained? Does the "right stuff" include a healthy dose of personal qualities that contribute positively to the interpersonal dimension of any form of psychotherapy?

Interpersonal Group Psychotherapy Training Format

The training program for the IGP therapists shares the aims of other efficacy treatment programs. Effective training programs are essential for clinical research whose task is to demonstrate posttreatment outcome effectiveness. Sorting out the differences between training and treatment effects is particularly important when the patient population, BPD patients, is known to be difficult to engage in any treatment program. Might there be an interaction between level of therapist competency and early dropout from the treatment? When a group format is used, evaluation of the model must show that the interventions and their expected effects can be detected across group member–therapist

interactions. To meet these challenges it was decided that only therapists who answered the following criteria would be invited to participate in the research treatment trial:

1. Minimum of 5 years postdegree training experience in dynamic
psychotherapy
2. Some experience in individual treatment of BPD patients
3. Some experience in conducting group psychotherapy with psychiatric patients
4. Willingness to examine subjective reactions within a structure of
training seminars, observation of treatment sessions, and postsession
consultations.

The training consists of two parts; four half-day didactic seminars,
and consultation for the duration of the 30-session treatment. Each pair
of co-therapists is trained separately. The training sessions occur at
biweekly intervals and include "homework" assignments between sessions. A group is assigned for treatment after the therapists' completion of the didactic seminars.

DIDACTIC SEMINARS

Session I: Introduction to IGP

Prior to the first session, the therapists are given two papers to read:
Dawson's (1988) description of relationship management psychotherapy from which IGP was adapted, and an outline of the key assumptions of IGP:

1. Importance of the relational meanings of within-group transactions versus the content of what is transacted
2. Importance of therapists' subjective reactions for understanding
group member interactions
3. Expectation of therapeutic derailment or error and general strategies for correcting errors and for maintaining or regaining positive
therapeutic attitude (including the role of supervision)
4. Significant differences between IGP interventions and interpretive, dynamic group psychotherapy.

In the first didactic seminar the distributed materials are discussed
and the therapists are asked to raise questions about the assumptions
underlying the IGP model of treatment. The effects of the IGP
approach on the manifest behaviors of borderline patients, which most
therapists have observed in their own clinical work, is emphasized and
illustrated with transcribed segments from individual treatment ses-

sions with borderline patients. Examples of two contrasting treatment dialogues follow. In each, the patient and therapist are transacting their respective views of the merits of therapy.

Treatment Dialogue I

PATIENT: I always thought anxiety was just being a little bit shaky and having a few butterflies. To me it's like everything is falling apart, that nothing is stable around me, that there is nowhere to run for help.

THERAPIST: You know, I think part of what has happened, and it's happened today, is that if people try to help or give any ideas, even if they are not the right ones, you . . .

PATIENT: [Interrupting] It's because a lot of the ideas that people have given me [pause]. I was just so damn fed up with a lot of the things that were suggested [referring to previous treatment].

THERAPIST: I'm not saying that you weren't.

PATIENT: It's not that I don't want help, it's just that [pause] if it's too complex or too Mickey Mouse, I say "forget it" and people say "you're resisting."

THERAPIST: Is that what I'm saying?

PATIENT: I don't know.

THERAPIST: I'm not saying that you are resisting; what I'm saying is that you're getting angry at people who offer help.

Treatment Dialogue II

PATIENT: I spent another night in the hospital last night.

THERAPIST: Did you?

PATIENT: Mm hmm.

THERAPIST: Is that something you want to talk about?

PATIENT: I refused to be admitted.

THERAPIST: Oh?

PATIENT: I don't want to be in the hospital. I'm tired of being in the hospital. It never helped. Over the years I've got nothing out of therapy and kept quitting. I had a therapist before. I'll be perfectly honest with you, I don't know what the hell he did for 2 years, but it sure as hell wasn't anything that lasted.

THERAPIST: This therapy may not offer you anything more.

PATIENT: There has to be a better way of living for me. I hate myself. All I do is turn all my feelings inside. I just get too afraid to say anything. It's just easier to keep it inside. I don't know how to get angry.

THERAPIST: It's hard to know how to get angry.

PATIENT: I'm just angry that everyone is trying to control my life, angry about what my mother did to me when I was growing up. I can't tell her that. I'm just angry all the time because it's the whole world's fault that I'm fucked up, and I know it's not.

THERAPIST: That's a difficult position to be in.

From these transcribed segments of actual sessions with borderline patients the trainee therapists begin to appreciate the differences between the more confrontational, interpretive approach in Dialogue I and the more tentative, affirming, reflective approach in Dialogue II. Focus is placed on observing the patients' responses to the therapists' interventions in each segment. In Dialogue I, the patient persists in defending her position, disregarding the therapist's attempts at understanding and explaining the patient's anger about failed treatments. They remain "stuck" in the transaction. In Dialogue II, the patient's responses to the therapist's interventions reveal her fears of losing control over her anger and her despair that anything will ever change, even with therapy. The therapist does not try to convince her otherwise but affirms her perceptions of reality.

A number of contrasting segments are provided for analysis and discussion. In this manner the therapists gradually begin to grasp the overall approach of IGP and can see the aims and outcomes of the interventions. They also become aware of the fact that none of the IGP interventions are unique or unknown to them; rather, certain interventions that were included in their general repertoire of therapeutic behaviors are now extracted and identified as appropriate responses to the observed within-session meanings of the patient–therapist interactions.

Session II: IGP Technique

In the second training session, categories of therapist actions that adhere to the IGP treatment model are distinguished from actions that deviate from the model. To assist in this task, a list of interventions and their operational definitions are given to the therapists. Interventions that best represent the model are discussed and illustrated from transcripts of therapeutic dialogue. Interventions that are more likely to represent therapeutic error are also identified. The intervention list includes the following key strategies:

Note. All therapist statements are phrased in a tentative format. The option to respond is left to the patient.

Explanatory statements. An explanation about an observation, thought, or feeling is provided. That is, a new construction is offered, a new way of observing behavior, thoughts, or feelings.

Exploratory information-gaining statements. Information is asked for. Included here are empathic statements that are viewed as exploratory hypotheses about how the patient is feeling.

Questions. Statements that question the patient's observations.

One-sided commentary. Statements that reflect on one side of an issue.

Two-sided commentary. Statements that reflect on two (or more) sides of an issue.

Reiteration. Statements that paraphrase what has been said, general commentary that encourages more dialogue, or Rogerian-type (1957) repetition of the last phrase.

Confirming. Statements that agree with or confirm the patient's viewpoint.

Reflecting Doubt or Confusion. Statements that reveal the therapist's lack of knowledge or understanding.

During the second training session transcripts of a variety of therapeutic dialogues with borderline patients are used to illustrate both "on-model" and "off-model" interventions. There is considerable discussion about judging the effects of any intervention. The therapists are encouraged to observe patient responses and determine whether the process is maintained in a balanced fashion or whether polarization is the outcome. Two dialogues used in the training follow. One illustrates what we identify as a "negative down spiral," and the other illustrates a "balanced working" dialogue.

Negative Down Spiral

PATIENT: I'm a rotten mother. My husband's a single parent half the time. The rest of the time he's trying to cope with me. End up with a profession that I hate. End up stuck in it. Too afraid to do anything about it.

Therapist: Except that you're taking this part-time course at the university.

Patient: That. Nothing will ever come of that. Nothing ever comes of anything I do.

Therapist: Well, I hear you saying that's what will come of this therapy. But one of the things I'm well aware of is that despite what you're saying now, you did complete four years of university and that you have accomplished things in your life.

Patient: It just feels hopeless. I just want to crawl inside myself. I don't sleep. I feel lethargic, and I just totally withdraw—don't want to see anybody, and I don't want to talk to anybody.

Therapist: So it sounds like you need people but only if it's with the right dose. If it's too much it's overwhelming. If it's too little it's frightening.

Patient: It's just that when I'm depressed people are telling me what to do. "You shouldn't feel this, and you shouldn't feel that," and what am I supposed to say, "right, I shouldn't feel it"? What am I supposed to do—just turn it off? I shouldn't be thinking of my mother anymore. I should have put it away. My relationship with her affected every other relationship I ever had.

Therapist: I guess there are a lot of feelings about your mother that haven't been worked through. You can't let go until the feelings tied up with her are gone.

With the exception of the last intervention, all of the therapist's statements are "off-model." The therapist initially attempts to meet the patient's despairing statements with encouraging comments, but these are rebuffed by the patient. Then, the interpretation that explains to the patient her reactions to needing people leads to a response that telling her how she should or should not feel doesn't help. The last therapist response is partially on-model in that it shows empathic understanding; however, the second half of the statement tends to repeat the "instructive" quality of the earlier interpretation.

The trainee therapists are asked to consider the "message" that the patient wishes to convey to the therapist. They learn that in the IGP model of treatment the process, rather than the content, of the dialogue is emphasized. Regardless of which patient is speaking, they are to detect which wish, which demand is being expected of the therapist. In the dialogue the patient seems to be expecting the therapist to be as fed up with her as she is with herself; the therapist, like the patient, will reject her angry, depressed, incompetent self. In order to avoid confirmation of the patient's worst fears, the therapists are asked to generate "on-model" responses to the patient's dialogue. In this example, "on-model" responses would be "no response" (that is, leave the patient to develop her own theme), brief reiterations such as "You feel stuck," or brief empathic statements such as "Sounds like you are feeling pretty awful about a lot of things." These therapist statements are intended to convey two things:

1. The patient's message has been heard.
2. The therapists can tolerate the patient's frustration, anger, and disappointment with herself, with the therapists, and with others.

In the context of the group these therapist behaviors demonstrate that both the therapists and the group as a collective body can tolerate and manage interpersonal transactions that are painful, do not lead to rejection, and for which there are no immediate answers.

Balanced Working Dialogue

PATIENT 1: We don't get any feedback from you people. We discuss things and find that we have a lot in common, but you're supposed to be our main source.

PATIENT 2: Information and teaching?

PATIENT 3: That's why I'm here. I'm here to learn—none of us know what we are doing.

PATIENT 1: Could you two tell us what your roles are?

PATIENT 4: I agree with some of what you are saying—other things I'm not so sure about. I find that we are struggling with things, and the response we get is "well it's hard to know" or "maybe it will, maybe it won't." You know like it's so . . .

PATIENT 3: Patronizing?

PATIENT 4: Well, wishy-washy.

PATIENT 2: I've found with other counselors I would talk for a while, they would be thinking of things, and they would ask a question or come out with something really astounding—it gave me a different perspective. I already know the things I tell you people; I'm looking to being led into having more insight into myself.

PATIENT 4: Yeah. We are not expecting answers, the answers have to

come from us—when I went to a counselor she told me that I
talked in circles. She would stop me and ask questions.

PATIENT 2: It might'be an idea if we came up with a topic—like something that a lot of people have in common; we could talk about
how we've dealt with it in the past. Now we kind of go blindly
into things—direction would be nice.

THERAPIST A: I hear some of you saying more direction would be helpful and other saying the answers have to come from you—waiting and letting it come out of yourselves. You know there are
really no experts here.

PATIENT 5: I've been in another group [AA] with no leader—people get
help from the feedback from each other.

PATIENT 4: But we are all agreeing about needing direction.

PATIENT 2: Yeah, I agree.

THERAPIST B: It would be nice to think that somebody did have the
answers. I wish I did. And it would be kind of nice to know
which direction to take to find answers. It's hard to feel that
sometimes things are just unclear.

PATIENT 3: Well if we come up with an answer, great, that's terrific. I'm
glad that we can do that. But we miss it—obviously we've
missed a few answers in our lives or we wouldn't be here.

In this dialogue the group members' message to the therapists is
quite clear; the therapists are incompetent, provide no leadership, and
have no answers. However, despite agreement within the group that
the therapists are "wishy washy," the patients maintain in their dialogue with one another, a relatively balanced process; on the one hand
they challenge the therapists, and on the other hand they talk about
having to find answers within themselves, to choose topics, and the
benefits of gaining feedback from one another. Therapist A's response
simply reflects back the balance, that is, the wish for direction versus
the answers coming from the group members. By adding that "there
are no experts here" the therapist attempts to address more directly the
patients' wishes for rescue by competent therapists. The therapists
avoid falling prey to rescue strategies because then each patient could
confirm a sense of self as incompetent and helpless. When two patients
try to return to the wish for "direction," therapist B confirms again that
the therapists do not have the answers and adds empathically how
hard it is to be "unclear." The next patient statement states more clearly
than any other the pain and sadness of having lived a life "missing a
few answers."

Trainee therapists readily identify their own impulses to show their competence, to say "something really astounding." Initially, they have difficulty identifying with Therapist A who communicates that the therapists are no more competent than the patients ("there are no experts here") and can accept more readily the position taken by Therapist B who acknowledges the shared wish to have answers but voices empathic understanding about the discomfort experienced when things are not clear. During this part of the training, trainee therapists discover that their previous clinical knowledge and experiences are applicable to understanding the meanings of the group process. What differs are the intervention strategies. All of the therapists trained in the trial were well versed in the principles and techniques of psychoanalytic psychotherapy; thus they were accustomed to using the techniques of interpretation, confrontation, clarification, and so on. Consequently, each therapist confronted a phase of the training in which he or she felt deskilled. They began feeling comfortable and confident using IGP strategies only after they were able to witness their effects on the group.

Session III: Therapist Subjectivity and the Management of Therapeutic Error

Between the second and third training sessions the therapists are given copies of two papers (Ogden, 1979; Wachtel, 1980) to read to prepare for the discussion of therapists' subjective responses in psychotherapeutic work with borderlines. The therapists' previous clinical experiences with borderline patients are discussed, and the therapists are invited to compare their concerns about working with borderline patients in individual psychotherapy and working with a homogeneous group of these patients. The therapists consistently report their anxieties about borderline patients' high potential for engaging in impulsive, self-destructive behaviors and for dropping out of treatment. The connection between these anxieties and committing therapeutic error is introduced. The fact that in the IGP treatment model therapeutic error is expected is stated emphatically. The detection and management of therapeutic error form part of the therapeutic strategy of IGP, as do the anticipation and avoidance of error wherever possible. We point out to the therapists that appropriate behaviors and attitudes for good therapeutic work are well understood, but that the ubiquitous human tendency to intervene or behave in a nontherapeutic manner is less well understood. The Ogden (1979) and Wachtel (1980) papers are presented as an integrated framework for conceptualizing the process through which therapeutic error occurs and is managed. Also emphasized is the reciprocal nature of the constructs discussed—how projective identification, assimilation, and accommodation can be applied to understanding the therapists' participation in the commission of and recovery from therapeutic error. (Essentially, the material of chapter 6 is presented for discussion in the didactic seminars and supervision sessions.)

Session IV: Integration of Conceptual and Strategic Principles

This session is used to review and reinforce the conceptual and clinical principles covered in the first three training seminars. This is done in the context of anticipating the therapists' experiences with their first IGP group. A list of possible group events is distributed and discussed in terms of their management. Because the therapists have had previous experience as group therapists, many of their questions have to do with the task of integrating group-focused techniques into IGP strategies.

Because many borderline patients are at high risk for engaging impulsively in self-harming behaviors, trainee therapists are particularly concerned with managing these behaviors in the group. Typical "acting-out" behaviors are discussed, with suicidal acts and self-mutilation topping the list. The therapists fear within-group contamination, that the self-destructive wishes of one patient might precipitate similar behaviors in other patients. Although the potential for contamination is always present in any group, the therapists learn to focus on the nature of the dialogue among patients when suicidal wishes or threats are raised in the group. If the patients maintain a balanced discussion about the management of the potential for self-harm (e.g., "Why? You'd only lay a guilt trip on your family. Whom can you talk to?" etc.), then the therapists need not intervene. If, on the other hand, a number of patients begin to agree that the only way to stop the pain is to commit suicide, then the therapists intervene. The trainee therapists learn that in both dialogues the message is the same "rescue me/us"; however, in the first transaction, the reciprocal roles taken by the patients play out both sides of the dilemma (hopelessness versus hopefulness); in the second transaction the balance is tipped to hopelessness, and the therapists' intervention provides empathic concern but avoids rescue. The therapists learn that part of the discussion of every group session is concerned with some form of self-harm; they also learn the importance of understanding the message that accompanies each communication.

Other difficult patient behaviors, such as repeated absences, unscheduled contacts, prolonging sessions, tardiness, silences, nonverbal communications, are discussed in the context of the "messages" conveyed to the therapists by each behavior. The therapists are encouraged to express their anxieties and concerns as they anticipate managing behaviors that could result in patients leaving the group and ultimately in the disintegration of the group. In this regard they welcome the supervision phase of the training during which their first experiences with an IGP group can be observed and discussed.

CONSULTATION

Assumptions

To be practiced effectively, IGP presumes a co-therapy model and consultation as an ongoing requirement for maintaining the specified therapeutic attitudes and techniques. Because borderline patients provoke in their therapists exaggerated responses that are difficult to contain, consultation provides support and direction for making neutral observations about the interpersonal meanings of group transactions. Traditionally, clinicians have assumed that well-trained, experienced, and highly skilled therapists are able to avoid therapeutic error or recover very rapidly when it occurs. Contrary to these beliefs, psychoanalytic training, a personal analysis, and the greatest amount of experience cannot protect therapists from strong negative reactions to borderline patients (Higgitt & Fonagy, 1992; Pines, 1990; Sandler, 1976). Therapists with even less training and experience are at greater risk of provoking negative therapeutic responses in their borderline patients. Adler (1985) suggests that effective psychotherapeutic work with borderlines may be achieved only when ongoing consultation from a colleague is available.

In the IGP model of treatment, consultation advances the therapeutic work by acknowledging the fact that therapeutic errors or deviations from the recommended therapeutic attitudes are inevitable when treating borderline patients. For the IGP therapists the most important task is the recognition and management of their subjective reactions within the context of the treatment dialogue. When this is adequately managed, treatment progresses; when it is ignored or badly managed, treatment ruptures and eventual failed outcomes are the result.

Process

In IGP a collaborative model of consultation is used. The therapist trainees, like the consultant, are experienced therapists. They have much to contribute to the understanding of the group process and its management. What they most need is help in shifting from the use of techniques with which they are very familiar to the use of techniques that they initially experience as aimless and lacking in substance. Several strategies are used to support therapist learning:

1. All treatment sessions are observed by either the consultant or the research assistant behind a one-way mirror.

2. Postsession consultations are held weekly for the first half of the scheduled 30 treatment sessions, then biweekly for the second half.

3. During the treatment sessions the therapists could leave the group to consult with the observer(s). The patients had given written consent to have the sessions audiotaped and observed. The structure of the consultations during the group sessions may have illustrated the balance between therapist competence and incompetence; that is, therapist incompetence was "witnessed" every time one of the therapists left the session for a behind-the-mirror consultation, although there was no way of confirming this hypothesis.

In postsession consultations transcripts or audio tapes of the sessions were used to examine the process. The aim was to search for key "messages" communicated to the therapists and then appraise whether an intervention was required, whether interventions made responded to the "message," and whether there were possible alternate interventions. The working stance in the consultation sessions was one of shared confusion, mutual support, and considerable doses of good humor. The humor helped alleviate the anxiety about working with a group of difficult patients using a method that requires the tolerance of confusion and the acceptance of negative subjective reactions while maintaining a genuine interest in each patient's painful life experiences.

Because the therapists had treated borderline patients in individual psychotherapy, they were well aware of the subjective negative reactions typically evoked by these patients. Thus, they were well prepared to discuss similar subjective reactions as they were experienced in the group sessions. In each group there were always one or two patients with whom the therapists felt especially frustrated and angry. Often, these were the pseudo-competent patients who resisted involvement in the group and challenged the therapists' competence. The dilemma that the therapists had to confront was the containment of their negative reactions while attempting to restore an empathic stance. The management of negative subjective reactions was much assisted by the presence of co-therapists in the group. While one therapist worked on containing his or her reactions the other was usually able to attend more fully to the group process. Each therapist felt supported by the other's presence. The role of the consultant was to acknowledge the therapists' feelings and then attempt an analysis of patient "messages" to be understood from the nature and intensity of the therapists' subjective reactions. Therapists were also able to observe that their negative reactions toward a particular patient were similar to group member reactions to the same patient. These observations served to support hypotheses about the "message" intended in the patient's provocative behavior.

Because the IGP model emphasizes the commission of therapeutic error as an inevitable occurrence throughout the duration of the treatment, trainee therapists were less likely to be anxious or defensive about looking at what went wrong during a group session. They learned to observe patients' responses to their interventions. If an intervention was followed by patient dialogue that was balanced rather than polarized, then that intervention was judged to have facilitated the process. When, in contrast, a therapist intervention failed to help the patients to recover a balance or even reinforced polarization, the effects were readily observable in subsequent group member interactions. The role of the consultant was to support the therapists in their development of strategies for judging the efficacy of their work within and across the treatment sessions.

The general importance of consultation was also emphasized. Problems evoked by the patients (threats of self-harm, threats to terminate therapy, threats of losing control, etc.) and those evoked by the clinical institution (patients hospitalized or offered alternate treatments without consultation with the group therapists, etc.) are common occurrences, and consultation can be an effective tool for dealing with these. The ultimate aim of consultation is to avoid therapeutic error and thus maintain each patient in a constructive therapeutic environment.

Although the consultant's task is well understood by the treatment team, it is important to maintain an atmosphere of openness that allows the therapists also to examine the consultant's reactions to the group process and to individual patient responses. As discussed in chapter 6, the consultant is also vulnerable to subjective reactions to patient input in the group. Thus, when a consultant fails to process her or his own exaggerated subjective responses, the supervision of the cotherapists can be skewed so that the potential for therapeutic derailments within the group are reinforced.

Evaluation of Training Reliability and Validity

A study was conducted to assess the effectiveness of the training program. The purpose of the study was to answer two questions:

1. Did the trained IGP therapists use more "on-model" than "off-model" interventions?
2. Did the IGP treatment model differ technically from the comparison treatment model (individual psychoanalytic psychotherapy)?

The data for the reliability study consisted of transcripts of two early and two mid-therapy sessions for the first and fifth groups treated with IGP during the trial. In order to demonstrate that the therapist interventions in the two treatments did in fact differ, the co-therapist interventions in the fifth IGP group were compared with interventions used by therapists with two patients treated with individual psychotherapy.

Three judges (social work graduate students) were trained to use a coding system reliably. The coding system consisted of 14 categories of therapist interventions (see appendix, part I). It was expected that the IGP treatment would have fewer occurrences of interpretive statements delivered in a "certain" format than the individual treatment and that, overall, the IGP treatment interventions would be more frequently framed in a "tentative" format. These expectations were supported. In addition, the IGP therapists used "two-sided commentary" more frequently than the comparison treatment therapists.

The results of the study showed that the IGP therapists were able to alter their previous therapeutic stance and carry out the IGP model of treatment consistently. The IGP treatment model could also be distinguished on essential treatment interventions from individual psychoanalytic psychotherapy.

Summary

A unique factor in the training was the special emphasis placed on detecting and managing therapeutic derailments. Most other forms of psychotherapy presume that with sufficient training and clinical experience therapeutic error can be avoided and, if it occurs, that counterproductive aspects of countertransference are at work. The IGP treatment model was developed from the conviction that therapeutic errors are inevitable when working with borderline patients and that the use of co-therapists and consultation provide the structure for recognizing errors more immediately when they occur and for developing strategies to mend disruptions to the therapeutic process.

The format used to train each pair of co-therapists was successful in ensuring consistent adherence to the prescribed treatment model. Over the course of training the therapists acquired expertise and became comfortable with the IGP strategies. They understood the rationale for selecting certain modes of intervention and rejecting others. During the treatment comparison trial, five pairs of co-therapists were trained successfully to use IGP. All independently reported that they much preferred being in a room with a co-therapist and a group of these patients than being alone with one borderline patient. They felt that when they used the IGP model of treatment their capacities for being empathically therapeutic were much more available to them; thus, there was more focus on liking their work with the patients, rather than dreading their contacts with them.

8

Interpersonal Group Psychotherapy: An Illustration

Introduction

An analysis of an entire group process is presented to illustrate the major group themes, their contextual meanings, and the therapists' responses. In addition, the responses of several patients selected from three diagnostic subgroups of the borderline disorder are used to illustrate differences in their respective contributions to the process. The diagnostic groups resulted from a qualitative analysis of several assessment measures used in the random control trials (RCT) and yielded three BPD subgroups: a Dependent group, a Substance Abuse group, and an Impulsive Angry group (see chapter 2). A brief description of each subgroup illustrates the primary criterion differences among the patients.

DEPENDENT SUBGROUP

Three female patients met the dimensional criteria for the Dependent (D) subgroup. All were in their late twenties. One was employed. Although the other two were unemployed, both had held jobs in the past. All three lived on their own. Their symptoms included overdrinking, depression, suicidal ideation, and one of the three had been hospitalized frequently following suicidal attempts. The main concern for each of them was their inability to maintain intimate relationships. None of the patients in the D subgroup had engaged in abusive relationships; however, their expectations of others were constantly frustrated. One had been married for 5 years and had been devastated when her husband left. The other two had lived in common-law relationships for various periods; all intimate relationships had ended badly. Generally, symptoms were exacerbated following these losses. The patient with the frequent hospitalizations masked her severe bouts of depression that preceded the suicide attempts by being frenetically busy; there were no quiet spaces in her life. Her greatest frustration and embarrassment were that she could not initiate or maintain gratifying relationships with men.

In terms of past history, one of the three D subgroup patients had been sexually abused in early childhood by a family friend, but the other two had not experienced either sexual or physical abuse. All reported that they had been harshly disciplined and emotionally neglected. Their parents tended to be unpredictable; they were either overly critical or overly indulgent. Despite these childhood experiences, the patients in the D subgroup took some pride in the fact that they had left home in late adolescence, had been self-supporting, and had managed the practical aspects of everyday living rather well. All had been in psychotherapy for various periods and the experience had been a positive one.

SUBSTANCE ABUSE SUBGROUP

Two patients met criteria for the Substance Abuse (SA) subgroup. One was a male in his early forties and the other, a female in her early thirties. The male patient had had a series of disappointing relationships with women; two marriages that had ended in divorce and several common-law relationships that had also ended unhappily. The patient felt exploited by women, and it seemed that no matter how hard he tried to please them, the relationships inevitably failed. He had a 20-year-old son who lived in another city with whom he had little contact. The patient was unemployed but in the past had held responsible management jobs. Severe states of depression and lengthy bouts of drinking had precipitated job losses. During the 2 years prior to joining the group the patient had attended Alcoholics Anonymous (AA) and had remained alcohol free. However, he continued to worry about whether he would be able to work again. He was responding well to a maintenance dose of an antidepressant. This patient described early childhood experiences of neglect; his parents were both alcoholics, and their marriage, which was in constant turmoil, ended in divorce when the patient was in mid-adolescence. He left home shortly thereafter, worked initially in unskilled jobs but later attended night school, obtained various office jobs, and eventually was promoted to middle management positions.

The second SA patient was a female in her early thirties. She reported a history of mutually violent relationships with men and problems with alcohol and drug abuse (mainly marijuana and cocaine). She drank heavily on a daily basis and used marijuana several times a day. She seemed to manage adequately other aspects of her life, was self-supporting, and had some rewarding social contacts with women friends. The patient did not view herself as having problems with substance abuse because her drinking and drug taking had been a daily occurrence for many years and did not interfere with her work. She was also convinced that she did not drink or smoke marijuana in response to stress or depression. The patient's entire focus was on how to deal with the men in her life. She would become quickly and intensely involved with each new man she met and would hold high expectations that the relationship would fulfill her ideal of a nurturing, caring, intimate bond. In fact, she seemed to choose men who were very dependent and/or demanding of her attention and care. The relationships resulted initially in repeated episodes of angry and often physically violent exchanges followed by painful separations. The patient described her early life experiences with her family as cold and indifferent. Her mother died when she was 6 years old, and her father made adequate housekeeping arrangements for the family, but the patient felt permanently bereft of a mother to whom she could turn for affection and care. She and her siblings took responsibility for their own emotional needs and ceased to rely on their father. The patient did well in school and was successfully employed as an office supervisor.

Impulsive Angry Subgroup

Two female patients met criteria for the Impulsive Angry (IA) subgroup. Both were in their late thirties, had been in a series of common-law relationships, and had children. Both were unemployed but had worked intermittently in the past. One of the IA patients had been repeatedly hospitalized over a period of many years for severe bouts of depression and suicidal attempts. Her relationships with men had been fraught with conflict and abuse. She had been raped several times. Her three adolescent children were largely managed and cared for by their father as the patient was frequently depressed and would isolate herself from the family. She felt that her angry reactions were out of her control; as a result, there were frequent, impulsive manifestations of her rage reactions within and outside the family. The patient's mother had died 10 years previously, and the patient had not been able to mourn the loss. At age 5 when her father abandoned the family, she had managed that loss by clinging to her mother. She would fabricate illnesses in order to avoid school. The patient resented her morbid attachment to her mother and continued to feel that she had never satisfied her mother; nothing she had done had been good enough. She viewed previous therapeutic experiences negatively. Apart from protecting her from risk of suicide, her stays in hospital had not helped, and she had pursued outpatient psychotherapy intermittently. Invariably, the therapists disappointed her.

The second IA patient had also been hospitalized following suicidal attempts, but less frequently. She had daily rage reactions directed at her common-law partner and her 8-year-old daughter. Her relationships with men, including her current mate, were fraught with conflict. This relationship seemed to have survived because of his passivity and tolerance of her angry outbursts. She felt that the only control she had over these intense aggressive reactions was to avoid contact with others. She had given up seeing friends because they invariably let her down. In early childhood the patient had sustained repeated separations from her parents due to their severe marital difficulties; she and her siblings were left with relatives or in foster care for varying periods. During latency and adolescence she had been sexually abused by a relative. She persisted in resenting her mother's denial of this event. The patient left home early and had worked consistently for 10 years. She worked intermittently after having her daughter. As her depressive symptoms and impulsive self-destructive behaviors escalated, she was less able to work outside the home, manage household tasks, or discipline her daughter. This IA patient had highly negative experiences with the psychiatric health care system. She felt that she had been manipulated, ignored, and ultimately rejected by all therapists with whom she had had contact.

These brief vignettes of the three diagnostic subgroups of BPD who participated in one of the IGP groups tested in the trial provide background for understanding their participation in the group. In chapter 9, a discussion of the 12-month follow-up interviews with patients in each subgroup is also provided to demonstrate the continuity across three domains of the psychotherapeutic process: differentiating diagnostic features, unique styles of participation in the group, and independent perceptions of change posttreatment.

Description of the IGP Process

In chapter 7 four phases of the IGP process were identified: search for boundaries, attack and despair, mourning and repair, and integration of self-control. Although these four phases of group process have been identified to describe the aims, focus, and actual experience with IGP, they have parallels in group process phases typical of other models of group psychotherapy, such as the phases of preaffiliation, power and control, cohesion, differentiation, and ending (Budman, 1989; Yalom, 1975). The notion of "phase" captures the cluster of interactions that portray the core group themes. The themes were introduced early in the group process but were continually addressed with varying levels of intensity across the 30 sessions of the treatment. Fragments of three themes were introduced within the first three group sessions. The remaining theme (integration of self-control) was more evident during the latter half of the therapy, particularly during the last 10 sessions.

The discussion of the group process demonstrates how rapidly each theme was introduced and how the themes provide the ongoing focus of the work. The management of the contextual meanings of the themes as portrayed in group member interactions and in member–therapist interactions illustrates the therapeutic work and its effects. The processes of the three patient subgroups is highlighted.

Sample Segments from Beginning Group Sessions

At the beginning of the first session one of the therapists reviews the structure of the group (time, place of meetings, and duration of sessions). After a brief silence the following exchange takes place.

THERAPIST: I don't know how we want to get rolling today.

[One of the IA patients responds by suggesting that the members introduce themselves, which they proceed to do.]

OTHER PATIENT: I don't know exactly how you want us to start.

THERAPIST: There are no set rules; you may find it helpful to say a bit about yourselves; you may have other things you want to say. [Short silence]

MALE SA PATIENT: Well I know why I'm here. I've been depressed a lot because things don't work out for me. I've had to get counseling for that and also for different types of problems in my life. I'm an alcoholic but don't drink now. I've had marriage breakdowns, relationship problems. I'm the type of person who worries about things and am very insecure and very distrusting. I feel that way toward everybody.

[Following this patient's disclosure of his problematic life experiences, three other patients tell equally painful stories in rapid succession.]

IA PATIENT 1: I'm like you; we have some things in common. I've had a couple of rapes, a lot of hurt, some relationship breakdowns, and I've been distrusting of the whole universe. I'm trying to trust, it's not easy.

D PATIENT 1: I've never been in a group, but I'm, in a way, looking forward to this. Already listening to you there are some similarities—depression, suicide attempts. I want my life to change. I've gone forward and then slid back. I turned to suicide when I couldn't fight anymore. I want to be around people, to get acceptance. I'm afraid of being depressed; I want to learn how to deal with it.

D PATIENT 2: I've had a lot of your experiences. No matter how good life would be in the past, horrible things would happen, and like you're back where you started; you feel just as awful as you did before. Most of my life I've been more depressed than happy. I used suicide attempts and alcohol to get away from the pain.

[While these four patients corroborate each other's experiences, the other IA patient is able to identify with their maladaptive ways of coping but does not tell a story about her problems.]

IA PATIENT 2: When you're angry you go into hiding; you struggle and get nowhere. I go forward and then hit a brick wall. I've tried to climb it, go through it, go around it; sometimes it works, sometimes it doesn't.

The third patient from the D subgroup is silent and does not tell her story until the midpoint of this first group session. The second SA subgroup patient did not come to the first session.

As is obvious from this material, four of the patients readily reveal painful life experiences without knowing whether the group members or the therapists warrant their trust. Their stories might be understood as containing wishes for immediate acceptance and relief; however, these expectations of others are not grounded in observations or judgments about whether the others can or are willing to meet their needs. The risk for disappointment is high. Despite this risk, by telling their stories unguardedly, the patients are able to quickly identify with each other's pain and experience some relief because of it. One patient says, "It's nice to know I'm not the only screwed up person in the world. It's nice to have company."

The messages to the therapists are clear: Can the therapists be trusted? Will the therapists be able to contain the chaos? Will they have answers? Or will they, like the patients, give up in despair? Through the use of a relatively neutral statement, one of the therapists reiterates the patients' overall concern and reinforces their control over the process: "There seem to be some similarities and differences in the group; are you wondering how much you will be able to learn from one another?" The repeatedly suicidal patient agrees, and goes on to compare her ways of harming herself with those of other group members. Whereas they use drugs and alcohol, she thinks of suicide a lot. She had been in psychotherapy, but it hadn't always helped. She suspects that the wish to harm herself is connected to her anger and frustration when she is disappointed by lovers and friends. This patient then launches into a long monologue in which she moralizes about the behavior of "dys-functional families" who abuse their kids. She wants to gain control over her anger before she has kids. She refers to her own childhood; it was like a "roller coaster." Her parents would give her everything one moment and then the next moment, "nothing; you'd be told you were stupid, spoiled, and bad." She ended her story with an extended "speech" about change and making life better because she deserved it. She used jargon such as "you need to be good to your inner child" and "developing self-awareness is basic to therapy."

In this long, rambling monologue this patient revealed her style of interpersonal communication. Regardless of the words used, her mes-sage is the same, "things may be bad but you can change if you want to." This patient came to be referred to as "pseudo-competent" because her behavior appeared to reflect a level of competence that, within the framework of IGP, would require reinforcement by the therapists. But as the dialogue in the first session progressed the patient became more frantic about maintaining a competent role; references to problem states were followed by numerous self-injunctions such as "I have to learn to love myself," "I can't depend on other people to affirm me and tell me I'm good," "I have to make time for myself, I have to be good to me." To reinforce her competent role the patient refers to a counselor she has had. "She always asked, 'What are you going to work on this week?'" Her counselor explained things; told her how to take small steps to change specific behaviors. The message to the therapists is twofold: (1) I need to appear competent because it is my best survival mechanism; and (2) will you (therapists) be as competent as my coun-selor?

The therapists respond to the dual messages throughout the session with statements to the group such as "sounds like people are talking about the struggle between being able to accept the good parts of yourselves and still being able to handle the side that doesn't work so well." Later, in response to a patient's hopelessness about changing, one of the therapists makes an empathic statement; "that's a real worry about what to do; will anything be helpful, will you be able to make any changes?"

With only a half hour left in the session the therapists are aware that one of the IA patients has not spoken except for a brief statement at the beginning of the session about hiding when she is angry. The therapists now bring her into the discussion.

THERAPIST 1: There has been a lot going on here, and [patient's name], I notice that you seem to have a lot going on inside; I don't know, do you?

SILENT PATIENT: Just listening.

THERAPIST 2: [Trying to deal with her silence less directly] People seem to be saying that mostly they find that talking helps—but sometimes it may be hard to talk.

[This empathic statement is responded to by other patients.]

SA MALE PATIENT: [To the silent IA patient] Are you not used to being in a group?

SILENT IA PATIENT: I've never been in a group before.

SA MALE PATIENT: In the AA group at first I couldn't talk at all. It helped to listen too, because sometimes I was the one that talked all the time and I never got anything out of it; so I learned to listen.

[One of the D patients adds more supportive comments.]

SILENT IA PATIENT: By the sounds of it you've all had counseling, I haven't.

OTHER PATIENT: [Quickly] I haven't either.

Finally the silent IA patient tells her story in the form of a long, disjointed monologue; over a period of 2 years she had spent a lot of time in a psychiatric hospital. She has had many angry altercations with a neighbor; her partner is not helpful; she almost killed her daughter when in a fit of rage; has been on all sorts of medication; was abused as a child; was in a foster home; left home at 16; doesn't want to do to her daughter what was done to her; has attempted suicide and thinks about it all the time. In this monologue the patient showed that, when anxious, her thinking becomes disorganized; she perseverates and has difficulty finding closure for her story. Like the other patients, she reveals many painful current and past life experiences. However, in contrast to the other patients, the affective components of this IA patient's story show the intensity of her anger and disappointment with people in her life. Although she is aware that she frequently loses control, she feels helpless about being able to harness abusive behaviors. The patient's message to the therapists is direct: Will she overwhelm them with her uncontainable rage? Will they be able to rescue her from her self-destructive impulses?

As the session draws to a close, one of the therapists refers to the "difficult experiences everyone has been talking about; feelings are tense, and it is hard to draw the session to a close." Following this statement, the male SA patient says that he wants to say one thing to the IA patient: "I was told by a counselor once that if we've been abused, we abuse; it's like a vicious cycle. I was relieved to hear this; I don't know if that helps you?" This supportive intervention from the only male patient in the group characterized, in part, his style of communicating in the group. He was often thoughtful, direct, and sometimes blunt. He frequently provided a balanced view of his life experiences; he had survived many crises but felt more in control since attending the AA meetings and being on medication. He said that he did not know why he didn't feel as sorry for himself as he used to; maybe he had "hit bottom" for the last time during his last hospitalization. He had done a lot of thinking, and the hospital staff had been there for him when he needed them. He came to realize how he used to let other people rule him. He also learned to "let go of the past." He was aware that disasters in his life were related to the past but that "to dwell on it is not going to help today." From the onset of the group it appeared that the adjunct treatments (AA and medication) were essential ingredients of his progress and contributed favorably to his participation in the group and eventual outcome.

Each patient's "search for boundaries" is expressed in this first session. The self-harming patient from the D subgroup communicates that by appearing competent she will master the anxieties associated with being in a group of patients who are feeling as vulnerable as she is. By giving advice to herself and others, she tests whether there exists in the group a secure place for her. The angry patient from the IA subgroup attempts to maintain a semblance of boundary between herself and the others by initially remaining silent. When she finally does engage with the group, her self-boundaries are at risk; her story is disjointed, confusing, and infused with strong emotions (anxiety and anger). In contrast, the male patient from the SA subgroup appears more self-contained. His boundary maintenance is assisted by the concurrent treatments (AA and medication); he also seems to have benefited from his most recent hospitalization during which he modified some expectations of self and others.

The "attack and despair" theme is introduced in the first session in the discussion of disappointments with important people in the patients' lives. Parents, spouses, and lovers have not met their expectations; many of the patients expressed hopelessness about ever being able to have their expectations met because all previous efforts to achieve this outcome had failed. A fragment of the "mourning and repair" theme appears in the male SA patient's dialogue in which he says that he does not want to dwell on the past any longer, even though he knows that many of his problems are linked to the past. Possibly he had already engaged in a mourning process and now was more invested in repairing or altering images of himself in relation to significant others.

Observations of the first group session interactions show that the patients took major responsibility for the work of the group. The therapists were technically accurate in representing the IGP intervention strategies. Patient dilemmas were reiterated, polarized positions were avoided, and the notion of "not knowing" or "not having the answers" was communicated empathically. The patients' views of their life circumstances were respected and affirmed.

In the second session two competing issues are central to the discussion; feeling rageful and losing control versus "quick-fix" solutions. Both issues seem to encapsulate the wish for more effective self-boundaries and the accompanying hope for rescue. The male SA patient is absent, but the other SA patient attends for the first time. Following introductions one of the D subgroup patients refers to the fact that the angry IA patient had ended the previous sessions discussing her problems. In response, the patient immediately responds with a long story about getting angry with her daughter, involvement with the school principal, and her partner's failures as a father. She ends by asking the group, "Have any of you experienced a rage?" The D patient responds that everyone has experienced rage. The IA patient continues in a rambling, befuddled dialogue about medications, competing advice from various doctors, the role of the school counselor, and not having anyone to talk to. Several patients question her about her situation. Then the pseudo-competent patient proposes a number of quick-fix solutions. She provides a list of ways to be good to one's self; how you have to keep trying; how you have to balance what you have to do with planning special treats for yourself, and so on. Several patients challenge her but she persists in providing "answers." Other patients ignore her. The angry IA patient talks about how her anger toward family members has resulted in a loss of control and violent behavior toward her daughter and partner. She states, "I'm doing exactly the same thing to them as my mother did to me." Other patients make similar connections for themselves, but all despair that anything will change. For example, in discussing a recent breakdown of a relationship with a man she had been living with, one of the patients from the D subgroup talks about her options for coping with her rage, "I had four choices; I could have stayed, I could have killed him, or killed myself, or I could leave." She left him but continues to have some contact with the hope that she won't need to for much longer.

The therapists' interventions reiterate the dilemma portrayed in the competing themes with statements such as, "It sounds like people are really hoping that things are going to be different but don't really know if they can be." In response to this therapist, a patient from the D subgroup says, "That's something you said last week." This marks the beginning of a more open manifestation of the "attack and despair" theme, which becomes more strongly evident in subsequent sessions. Later in the session the same patient asks, "I wonder if stabler people than ourselves get just as angry as we do?" and a few minutes later talks about a male friend who "mentally" abused her and whom she no longer trusts. The therapists missed the message intended in these statements: Do the therapists "mentally abuse" (they just repeat what they said the previous week)? Are the therapists "stabler"? Can they be trusted? The therapists fail to intervene, and the outcome is a polarized, defensive exchange between this D patient and the pseudo-competent patient:

Pseudo-Competent Patient: Why are you letting him [referring to patient's male friend] have control over you?

[The patient denies.]

Pseudo-Competent Patient: You're still attached emotionally, therefore he dictates how you relate to yourself. Does he deserve to have that much control over you? What are you going to do about it?

D Patient: [angrily] I don't know; if I knew I wouldn't be here.

[At this point one of the therapists intervenes empathically.]

THERAPIST: It's a struggle to know what to do.

Other patients join in and empathize with the D patient. One patient talks about a recent rejection by a man and how she would like a second chance to do it right. In this context, one of the therapists takes the opportunity to include the new SA patient who has been silent throughout the session, and asks, "Is there something you connect to? You've been kind of quiet." This patient readily responds with her story of recently leaving a man who was verbally abusive to her; it took strength because she loved him. The pseudo-competent patient persists with injunctions about the "need to love yourself before loving others." Again, she is challenged by other patients, and the dialogue shifts to talk about how hate for others can be turned on the self. During this exchange the effects of a patient's interpretation of the angry IA patient's refusal to eat are seen.

PATIENT: When you hit your daughter it's really your rage at yourself
          for not nurturing yourself with food, I think. You want your
          daughter to be responsible; but you won't do it for yourself.

ANGRY IA PATIENT: [Perceiving the interpretation as an attack] I know
          that my daughter did not deserve to be hit; but I am strict with
          her; she [the daughter] is good when I'm around and terrible
          when I'm not.

The therapists have difficulty closing the session. The patients' wishes for secure connections have not been met. Attack and despair has been repeated among patient pairs. The pseudo-competent patient "attacks" through her admonishing directives to several patients, one of the D patients despairs, and the angry IA patient becomes more angry. Another patient "attacks" with an interpretation of the IA patient's behavior and is responded to defensively. The messages to the therapists convey several expectations: Will the therapists secure the boundaries within and among the group members? Can they tolerate the attacks without retaliation? Will they come to their rescue when self-harm seems to be the only option? On several occasions the therapists failed to intervene when an intervention was needed; however, when they did intervene, their responses were empathically communicated and resulted in important shifts in the patients' polarized dialogue.

During the latter half of the third session the focus shifts to a discussion of negative early life experiences with parents and how several of the patients continue to struggle with the effects of having been abused, neglected, and unloved. The angry IA patient states that she abuses her daughter because she only learned "bad parenting" from her mother; but more recently her mother has acknowledged the mistakes she made with her children and is remorseful. One of the therapists reflects on this patient's wish to come to terms with the disappointment and anger at her parents and adds, "I see a lot of heads nodding, as if you know what that is like." Several patients talk about "understanding," "forgiving," "confusion between anger and the wish to forgive," and "is it necessary to forgive." Others want to know how to deal with parents currently because their parents haven't changed. One of the therapists reiterates the dilemma, "How to forgive when you still have a whole lot of hurt, anger, and disappointment?" All of the patients become intensely involved in this dialogue, which introduces the next and most protracted phase of the group, that of mourning ungratified expectations and repairing negative images of the self in relation to other. In approaching this theme the patients address the central focus of IGP, which is to understand and facilitate attempts to modify patient expectations of significant others and manage the task of mourning lost hopes and wishes. In this process the aim is to shift self-schemas that reinforce a negative, depleted self-image to other ones that reflect an empowered, hopeful perception of the self in relation to significant others.

From the third through to the seventh session the group repeatedly attacks the therapists for their inadequacies in directing the group. They challenge the therapists:

PATIENTS: What are your roles in the group? What methods do you use for helping us?

THERAPIST: You know this is really your group and the way that this group is organized is that it's a psychotherapy group . . . [hesitation] . . . uhm, what that means is that it's the group's opportunity to make their own goals.

PSEUDO-COMPETENT PATIENT: So actually when it comes down to it, you can leave, and we can do our own problem solving?

[Subsequent attempts by the therapists to recover balance in the dialogue are not effective.]

THERAPISTS: It sounds like you want something different from us; maybe we could try to talk about that.

Both in the tone of voice and the content of their interventions the therapists reveal their anxieties about being attacked and about the failure of their efforts to appease the patients' demands. It is in this type of situation that a therapeutic derailment is likely to occur; that is, when therapist anxiety mounts in direct proportion to the patients' escalating anxieties and frustrations. Thus deviation from the prescribed therapeutic stance is understandable.

As the patients persist in attacking the therapists for not providing what is needed the meanings of their anxieties are revealed. One patient reports that she loses her "security" when she comes to the group:

PATIENT: I lose it because you are not participating. You're up here, you're our authority figures, but big deal; you're just sitting here. . . . I feel like—it sounds paranoid—but I feel like I'm being watched over; just don't make a wrong move. I'm not sure I can be real in here. I'm very good at jumping on everybody else when they have a problem, but I won't say anything about my problems because I'm afraid; I don't feel secure enough to do it.

The therapists ignore this plea for an empathic affirmation of the members' perceptions of the group; that is, that the task (talking about personal problems) and the structure (group) are not only incompatible but frightening. Following this patient's disclosure of the reasons for her anxieties other group members begin to tell the therapists how they should behave.

PATIENT 1: You have to throw in more objective comments, not just 10-second reiterations of 15 minutes of conversation.

PATIENT 2: If the conversation is going around in circles, I see it is your role to intervene to give us some guidance.

[Again the therapists miss the message]

THERAPIST: It raises the question of how leaders know when to be involved, when it's more helpful not to be involved.

PATIENTS: Take a chance. That's what life's all about. I mean we're taking chances here, and it requires you to take a risk.

THERAPIST: I guess we aren't always helpful, and not in the way that you need.

Eventually the therapists recover their empathic stance and let the group know that they understand the group members' disappointments in the therapists. Later the other therapist acknowledges that the patients' concerns about being themselves in the group reflect accurately the situation they are in, that is, not knowing whom you can trust.

In the fourth group session the attack and despair theme is followed by a beginning recognition of the need to mourn what has been lost. At the beginning of the session several members start to talk about setting group goals and again attack the therapist for failing to provide leadership: "What's the point of having them [the therapists] here; they just say 'it could be this, or it could be that.' We could play a tape recorder and have that comment played every time." The therapists agree with the patients' assessment of their involvement; it is true that they do not offer what the patients want; what would the patients like to see happen? A discussion around goals follows, and individual patients identify specific relationship problems they want to deal with. A repeated theme of how to cope with parents who are not going to meet their needs becomes the focus of the discussion. Referring to his father, the male SA patient states that he has to accept the fact that his father is not going to be what he wants.

SA Patient: It's like mourning; you have in your mind this mental
image of the father that you want.

[Other patients join in to identify their own goals. As the session progresses some begin to wonder about attitudes to life events.]

Patient 1: Life is a struggle and you just have to make an effort to be
comfortable with yourself and other people all the time; you
always have to work hard at it.

[One of the therapists agrees.]

IA Patient: It can't be easy walking in here and dealing with us every
week; they [the therapists] have to work at it some days.

Patient 2: In the real world it's hard, in here it's safe.

In this session the therapists are tested for their capacity to tolerate the group members' attacks and feelings of hopelessness; when they sustain the attacks with equanimity, empathic understanding, and continuity of care they earn the patients' trust. Then, shifts in the patient's perceptions of the therapists and the therapeutic task occur. For the patients, accepting what is is the prelude to giving up what cannot be.

Sample Segments from Middle Group Sessions

A persistent concern in the group was the fear that intense anger could not be expressed, would not be tolerated, and, if expressed, might lead to rejection and expulsion from the group. The pseudo-competent patient talks about her anger toward a male friend who is not as available to her now as he used to be; he is always making excuses to avoid meeting. She says that she shouldn't be angry:

PATIENT: I'd like to be able to release that anger and to get it outside of me without being told, "you shouldn't feel that way." It's not his fault; I don't think it's a matter of right or wrong. I'm angry, and that's okay, and I should allow myself to feel that way.

THERAPIST: Do you feel like it's okay to express the anger here? Can we handle it?

Neither the patient nor other group members respond to the question; rather, they focus on how the pseudo-competent patient might manage her anger in relation to her friend and help her reflect on the meaning of the friendship and how much support she had derived from it. Others join in with the wish to have someone they can count on and the disappointment when that person lets you down. One of the therapists makes the following interpretation:

THERAPIST A: Is it the same way here? I wonder if there is a parallel between here and what you are all talking about, that is, wanting support and feeling disappointed and angry when you don't get it. I guess, I'm wondering if there is a parallel between wanting more support from B [other therapist] and me and feeling some disappointment and anger at us. Is it okay to express that, to just talk about feelings as they come up. Can we handle that here?

PATIENT 1: It's hard. It's really scary.

[The patients spend some time talking about how to express their anger toward one another.]

PATIENT 2: It would be nice if I could feel free and be able to say, "You're an asshole," that is, without you being offended.

PATIENT 3: I would be offended

MALE PATIENT: We could develop proper methods of communication.

PSEUDO-COMPETENT PATIENT: You could express anger provided you explained why, such as "Your actions are making me feel angry; I didn't mean to hurt you.

MALE PATIENT: Is this a safe enough group for us to release emotions
     including anger?

Although there is some agreement about what emotions the group can
tolerate, one patient says that the group will "need objectivity from
you two [the therapists]. If our emotions aren't going to be quite so
controlled, like we need someone to have a look and to give it some
direction because emotions don't have a lot of direction." A therapist
responds, "Is it that you're wondering if you can depend on A [co-
therapist] and me to step in when it's necessary to be helpful to the
group so that things don't get too escalated?" Several patients voice a
need for the therapists' involvement "even before it escalates." The
members begin to talk about situations that make them angry and how
they have attempted to control the anger. One of the IA patients says,
"I think that's where abuse comes from; like a person will feel a lot of
anger inside, and they suppress it, and they don't know how to get rid
of it, so they take it out on something that's very safe, someone that
trusts them." Although some patients agree, they back away from the
anxiety provoked by this patient's insight and talk about getting rid of
anger by taking it out on inanimate objects such as pillows, or going
for a fast walk, or being direct and telling someone that they're acting
like a jerk. One of the therapists acknowledges the different ways to
cope with anger and then refocuses on the angry IA patient's earlier
anxiety about going to see her GP later that day but feeling enormously angry with him.

THERAPIST: Does any of this connect with you, any of these ideas for
     how to handle anger?

IA PATIENT: I end up turning it inside like other people. I give off the
     wrong impression, and then I push people away. People seem to
     be pushing away from me, and it ends up that I have nobody.

[Several other group members identify with her and tell stories about how
the expression of anger has resulted in rejection.]

As members tested the group's and the leaders' tolerance for the open
expression of anger there was increasing comfort with the processing
of all painful emotions, including rage. In the management of group
member interactions around the expression of anger, the angry IA
patient made some obvious shifts in the ways she viewed herself and
others. Her stories became more coherent and focused; she began to

make connections between her way of communicating and the subsequent responses from others. However, not until the final three sessions was she able to see how she used isolation and withholding as a way of manipulating others' responses to her. She also began to talk about taking some responsibility to control how she "come[s] across" and that she has "got to see that they behave that way because I'm so negative." The pseudo-competent patient made few shifts and persisted in searching for safe outlets for the expression of anger such as scrubbing the floors of her apartment. She also became more frustrated as her advice to the group members ceased to be considered. The male SA patient was an involved participant in the group and was open about his failed attempts to cope with anger in the past. Now he was angry less often because he asserted himself more effectively and made sure that he separated out what was important for him from what others expected of him.

Many versions of the intertwining of the three IGP group themes were played out through the duration of the treatment. The attack and despair theme was often expressed through polarized dialogue in which two or more patients took opposite positions. In one session, an argument erupts between the pseudo-competent patient and another patient who had asked the group how she can control her anger toward her mother whom she finds is intrusive and who "digs deliberately" to make her angry. The pseudo-competent patient insists that the patient's anger is her problem; therefore she is responsible for knowing the meanings of her anger; she can't change others' attitudes, but she can change her own, and so on. In response, and with the support of several other group members, the patient wonders why it is that only her mother is able to make her feel so rotten; she has come to realize that her mother's love is conditional. The pseudo-competent patient continues to challenge the whole group with injunctions about knowing the source of angry feelings before you can control them. The therapists' efforts to address the polarized dialogue and gain feedback from other group members ("What are other people in the group thinking about this?") do not shift the dialogue.

This exchange shows how polarized dialogue is a failed dialogue. It illustrates how the group members enact competent-incompetent roles in a defensive, circular fashion. Polarized dialogue is a signal to the therapists that an intervention is needed. The aim is to shift from positions of wrong or right to a position of uncertainty and confusion that allows for the possibility of new perceptions, feelings, and thoughts to be processed. In the session a shift takes place when the therapists acknowledge the difficulty of expressing anger.

THERAPIST A: Is it that there are a lot of different ways of keeping anger from escalating that work differently for different people?

THERAPIST B: Is the struggle here that either someone has to be right or someone has to be wrong?

PATIENT: I feel insulted when the other person always thinks they are right [probably this message is intended for the pseudo-competent patient] . . . [in a sad tone of voice] it would be nice if sometimes someone could admit that you are right.

The between-member talk returns to a discussion of anger and how to recognize "the breaking point." Despite the pseudo-competent patient's attempts to tell the group what to think and how to behave when feeling angry, the members individually and collectively are able to maintain a balanced discussion about hurt feelings, angry responses, and the management of the accompanying disappointment.

By the 17th session the group theme of mourning and repair is central to the dialogue. The patients talk about the people in their lives who have disappointed them most, in particular their parents.

THERAPIST: Is there some sadness about feeling that you were not taken care of?

PATIENT 1: What she's saying is our parents didn't take care of us emotionally so we're not taking care of us emotionally.

PATIENT 2: [Later in the session] I think we feel unworthy, and that's why it's hard for us to take care of ourselves. It's like why should we bother, we're not worth it? But I think we are trying to learn that we are worthy.

[The patients' sadnesses about earlier losses escalate and there is a discussion about crying and its containment.]

PATIENT 3: I'm having crying fits. They come out of the blue. One minute I'm fine, then the next I'm dissolved in tears in the corner somewhere. Can someone tell me what's happening, can someone give me an idea, an insight somewhere?

MALE PATIENT: I can only share that it happens to me on occasion when I'm actually feeling great. I think it's great actually because at one time I could never cry at all.

These two patients identify with each other as they piece together their respective stories about what might be associated with crying. The patient who initiated the dialogue says that sometimes she just wants to be left to cry and doesn't want to be asked "what's wrong?" Talk about sad feelings and feeling sorry for oneself engages most of the members. Although the male SA patient had participated initially in this dialogue, his anxiety begins to escalate, and he tries to convince himself that he is in better control. "I can't let myself get like that (sad and hopeless) because I'm in trouble if I do. Like, I may not come out of it. I have to keep busy, I have to keep on top. I have to push myself." He goes on to talk about how he has reduced self-expectations. "I think I have more balance than I used to." He then gives several examples about not feeling guilty when he doesn't accomplish what he had set out to do; not feeling guilty when he doesn't live up to others' expectations. "I used to let others push me, and I used to get angry at someone pushing me; now I don't have to get angry, it's just that if I can't do it, I can't do it, I'm sorry. I think I look after my own welfare now, whereas before I was always trying to please everybody else." And later in a discussion about the management of depression the same patient connects suicidal thoughts to feeling guilty and being hard on himself. He says that he knows that a lot of it was tied up with his past. He had to let that go; "I had to let go of a lot of shit from before and forget; and I had to find things that would make me happy, and no one was going to do it for me." Although this patient still felt concerned about returning to drinking for solace and being depressed and suicidal, he also was able to mourn what could not change. He, more than any of the other patients, seemed determined to consolidate the gains he had made.

In the 20th session an important exchange between the pseudo-competent patient and the angry IA patient illustrates how open criticism in the group was handled. The group is again dealing with being direct with one another without being "hurtful or damaging." The angry IA patient says that each week she feels that she can't talk about herself because all of the attention goes to one person. With support from the therapists and from the group, she reveals her fears about being directly critical of a group member. She can't bring it up because "it's offending someone else by being angry about it." She refers to the current session and how she wanted to talk about what had happened to her on a recent evening, but she rarely gets five minutes to say something; the attention always goes to the same group member. She then extends her concern to the other IA patient whom she feels has not been able to tell her story because of one group member monopolizing the time. The group "talks around" the issues for some time, but eventually the pseudo-competent says that she knows that she is the person who is being singled out as monopolizing the group:

Pseudo-Competent Patient: Why it's so painful is that I know she's right. It makes me angry with myself. It makes me want to hurt myself, it makes me want to leave. By saying that I know that I'm not giving you [the IA patient] the freedom to be able to say that to me directly because you'll feel that you will hurt or offend me.

Angry IA Patient: Well we are going to get somewhere because you are right. Just like you said, how do you go about not offending someone? Because that's not what I'm trying to do. I know when C (one of the D subgroup) said that she didn't want to hear about suicide that she didn't want to offend me; it was just her personal feelings, but it still hurt. Then after you leave you begin to build up a wall.

Pseudo-Competent Patient: It hurt because I know that it's true. People have told me that before. People used to get angry with me because I was always the center of attention; it's hard for me to say that.

These two patients have an exchange in which they reassure each other that it was okay to be open, and they tell each other that they will feel comfortable bringing things up in the future. The IA patient says, "I don't want you to hide, but it's going to be hard," and later adds, "now the group can get on with it, I've been carrying this around with me for a while." The remainder of the session focuses on this issue, and the angry IA patient later suggests that "maybe it's the group's fault as well? That everybody kind of encouraged that to happen?" One of the therapists pursues this point and asks, "It seems you're raising the issue that this is a shared problem?" The group takes up this possibility, and several members acknowledge how they use different strategies to gain attention. However, the pseudo-competent patient's hurt at being singled out as monopolizing the group is not adequately managed by either the therapists or the other group members. A distinction is not made between her contributions to the group and what she needed from the group. In effect, the pseudo-competent patient was silenced by the angry IA patient and no one came to her rescue. As the IA patient suggested, "it's the group's fault"; all (therapists included) inadvertently colluded to achieve this unspoken aim. Although group members were able to reflect on how they are perceived in the group and how to exchange feedback about intensely experienced emotions when they feel ignored or left out, this learning took place partially at the expense of one of their members. This vignette shows how a patient's apparent competence is in fact a plea for understanding and help with underlying feelings of vulnerability and helplessness. As will become evident in the subsequent discussion of the group process, the failure to identify empathically the pseudo-competent patient's despair contributed to the return of suicidal behaviors.

During the mourning and repair phase of group dialogue the accompanying theme was to understand suicidal ideation and attempts. Discussion of suicidal ideation, gestures, and attempts occurred at every group session. The group members discussed in some detail the events in their lives that triggered thoughts of suicide and how to manage the impulse to harm themselves. The tone of the discussion frequently communicated the sadness and emptiness that they shared, but the content of the dialogue was usually balanced as the members drew on each other's support as they processed their separate versions of suicidal risk. When the risk of suicide with any one group member was apparent but not discussed, the therapists addressed the risk directly by asking, for example, "Are you thinking of harming yourself?" However, neither the therapists nor the group members recognized the intensification of the pseudo-competent patient's depression and risk of self-harm.

At the 21st session the pseudo-competent patient monopolizes the session by expounding on "theories" about the causes of suicidal behavior. Although she acknowledges that controlling her suicidal impulses is difficult for her, she persists in invoking possible solutions. She feels that she should be able to control the impulse to hurt herself. In her perception, the self-harm is directly related to feeling depressed and helpless. Group members offer support and suggestions as to how the patient might control her impulse to harm herself. The therapists miss the "message" in the pseudo-competent patient's despair about not being able to control the wish to commit suicide. Moreover, the therapists and group members failed to empathize with the patient's anxiety at having had her role in the group challenged by the IA patient the preceding week. The resurgence of the attention-seeking behavior is an appropriate response for this patient because it represents her most successful strategy for warding off intolerable levels of anxiety. However, because this pseudo-competent patient has previously appeared to have the "answers" to both her own and other patient's dilemmas, the therapists and the group members failed to see that her focus on theories and solutions to suicidal behavior indicated that she was now at risk of attempting suicide. The group members responded to her in the same style as she had communicated to them; "There has to be a solution; when faced with suicidal thoughts you just have to try harder." One of the therapists challenged the group by stating that "theories" about suicide were not of much help unless you tried to apply them to yourself. This injunction silenced the pseudo-competent patient.

At the following session the therapists report to the group that the pseudo-competent patient has been hospitalized because of fears that she might harm herself and would not be returning to the group. Several of the patients are puzzled about the pseudo-competent patient ending up in hospital. Her problems had not appeared to be as severe as their own; she seemed to have the answers to most things. The patients do not engage in discussing their concerns about losing a group member, even when given the opportunity to do so. The angry IA patient seems to be relieved; she thinks that the group should get on with talking about their problems. Perhaps her relief was shared by the other group members and the therapists. The therapists acknowledge in the consultation meeting between sessions that they had missed the contextual meanings of the pseudo-competent patient's renewal of efforts to be the center of attention in the group. Clearly, the intervention that challenged the patient to apply theory about suicidal wishes to themselves has been perceived accurately by the pseudo-competent patient as rejection. Her response in the form of taking herself to a psychiatric emergency service is a healthy one and through hospitalization she is receiving the protection she needs. However, the hospital staff failed to consult with the group therapists and recommended that the patient leave the group and attend a day treatment program instead. This response from the hospital staff further compromised the clinical management of this patient.

For the remainder of the group session, the patients discussed issues to do with their lack of control over certain life situations. Whereas they cannot change others' behaviors they have control over changing their expectations of others. Two of the patients talk about having recently confronted their mothers with some old hurts and how, much to their surprise, their mothers have responded well. Both felt that it was now possible to build different relationships with their mothers. They also altered their expectations of their mothers. One patient said, "Maybe our blowup was healing. My mom and I get on better now. She can still get to me, but I don't have to freak on it anymore."

Another patient adds, "Until we [referring to herself and her mother] had the explosion we couldn't even be friends; now we are." She went on to talk about having a better understanding of her mother's life experiences and how her mother's hardships got in the way of good mothering.

The mismanagement of the pseudo-competent patient within the group illustrates the problems in managing a style of behavior that is aggravating to both the therapists and the other group members. The therapists may have felt that their therapeutic roles were usurped by this patient, and possibly their frustrations and anxiety about containing the patient's effect on other group members led them to inadvertently collude with them in ejecting her from the group. The patient needed to continue to express her frustration and disappointment about not being able to occupy the central role in the group. When challenged in the 20th session by the angry IA patient, she had struggled to find an alternate niche in the group but found that she was more comfortable with giving advice to herself and to the group, even though her advice was increasingly ignored. With the negative therapist intervention she realized that the therapists had missed her plea for help; thus, going to the emergency service had been the healthy way to deal with escalating feelings of despair. The therapists realized that when their repeated attempts to engage the patient in more self-reflection during the earlier phase of the group had failed, they had felt anxious about finding a way of coping with the patient's protective, pseudo-competent behavior. They became increasingly inactive in responding empathically to the patient. The consultant also missed the fact that the therapists' inactivity in relation to this patient was a clue to their increasing helplessness at changing her involvement in the group.

Sample Segments from Later Group Sessions

The integration of self-control is evident during the latter 10 sessions of the group. Group members begin to anticipate the ending of the sessions and know that the last five sessions will be spaced at 2-week intervals. The discussion focuses on what has been learned and the frustration and disappointment about what has not changed. The content of the dialogue identifies differences between members, whereas in the first half of the therapy the emphasis was on sameness. Although talk about difference is helpful as each patient begins to value his or her own uniqueness, the responsibility for one's actions is also acknowledged. In this process, some of the patients had difficulty processing the feedback they received from the group. The interaction between the pseudo-competent patient and the angry IA patient illustrates this process and also its mismanagement. A similar transaction occurred between the same IA patient and a patient from the D subgroup who was the only patient who had no history of suicidal attempts. The challenge was initiated by the latter patient. Frequently, in previous sessions the angry IA patient would say that something was bothering her but then would refuse to discuss it. In various ways each of the patients let her know how frustrated they were with her. Eventually, some group members stated that they would not make great efforts to involve the IA patient in the group; they would leave it up to her to decide her own level of involvement. In the 27th session several patients are talking about how they have taken control over some aspects of their lives.

PATIENT 1: You helped me see other directions for my anger. I'm not as
    angry as I used to be. I can still get that angry, but I don't direct it
    like I used to. My anger was totally out of control at one time. It
    doesn't take me over like it used to. I don't know what specifi-
    cally helped it, but something in here helped me find direction
    for it.

[A little later in the session the D patient says that she learned a lot about herself and others in the group but had to continue the "healing" on her own. She compared the group to one-to-one therapy.]

D PATIENT: There's not much feedback in the sharing of emotions. But
    in here there's lots of it and I relate to a lot of it. . . . Just to know
    that I'm not alone where before I thought I was the only one that
    went through this garbage.

[The IA patient "dampens" the enthusiasm in the group by saying that the group members are not friends but acquaintances. She never felt that she was the only one with problems.]

IA PATIENT: I'm looking at everyone else and feeling so bad for them
    thinking what the hell am I doing. I don't feel sorry for myself at all.

Later she adds that she has given up trusting friends because when she got "sick mentally" a neighbor she thought had been her friend rejected her, and "that was a blow." Both the therapists and the D patient reiterate that by expecting nothing you protect yourself from being hurt. Then the D patient says: "I want to understand what's going on between you [IA patient] and me. We've had lots of disagree-ments in previous sessions; even when we go for coffee after the sessions there is a lot of tension between us." A lengthy argument follows. Through attacks and counterattacks the D patient communicates how she has felt continually rejected by the other patient. She says: "No matter how hard I tried to get to know you, you gave me the silent treatment." In response the IA patient says: "I felt mad at you and upset because you wouldn't let me talk about suicide." The D patient replies: "Talk about suicide makes me angry because I can't accept that you would want to take your life." Another patient interjects that talk about suicide frightened her as well. The therapists speculate that maybe the anger was substituted for the anxiety associated with the feelings that precipitate the suicidal wishes. "Maybe it's easier to be angry rather than think about what led up to feeling suicidal." Both the D patient and another patient reinforce this connection and add that the IA patient has a right to talk about suicidal thoughts even if these feelings get stirred up in others. The D patient says that she no longer wants to be blamed for why the IA patient refused to talk in the group. As this dialogue progresses the sadness about unfulfilled expectations comes to the foreground of the discussion.

THERAPIST: It's scary to feel you need people.

IA PATIENT: You hit the nail on the head. You guys are all I got.

D PATIENT [empathically] Then don't push us away.

[The IA patient starts to sob.]

In the following session, mourning the loss of the group continues. The two patients described in the dialogue refer to the preceding session and reveal what they learned from each other and from the group.

IA PATIENT: You know how you said to me that I, . . . no, I'll put it dif-
        ferently—like how I set you off—but I find that it's not just you. I
        do it to other people too. . . . Maybe I put everybody else off, too,
        but I don't realize that I'm doing it. So that is one thing that
        maybe I've got out of this. Maybe I needed the explosion that you
        and I had between us. . . . It makes me more aware that I'm doing
        it, and it makes me aware that I've got to control it.

D PATIENT: [Affirming these observations and identifying with the IA
        patient] It's a good reflection. . . . I realize that I operate that same
        way. I can bring out the beast in people and not even think that
        I'm doing it; it's my tone, my facial expression, and my actions
        . . . it's a real good reflection.

IA PATIENT: That's exactly right.

OTHER PATIENTS: It's not what you say but how you say it. And it's my
   actions that always speak louder than words.

[The IA patient then goes on to talk about how angry she had been after the
previous session, but how beneficial it had been.]

IA PATIENT: I needed it, and I realize it now. I found that all along I had
   trouble getting along with people. I always blamed myself, but
   now I know where to start; I know what to watch for.

Both patients had wished that the other had called during the interven-
ing week but neither had. Both affirmed the wish to mend the breach
and learn from it. Both refer to feedback in the past from doctors,
nurses, and friends; they had been told how their behaviors had
"turned off" others. The IA patient talks about insights gained.

IA PATIENT: I didn't realize that I was that bad until I thought about
   how I must have upset the nurses when I was in hospital; I then
   automatically thought about how I seem to trigger something off
   in you [the D patient] to make you react the way you did, and I
   felt like—I'm doing that; it's not other people's fault.

THERAPIST: It sounds like you're saying that although there have been
   some disappointments from this group, some painful issues,
   there's some other things that have been gained.

IA PATIENT: You know, you're right; I never really looked at it that
   way, because one of my biggest problems is getting along with
   other people.

D PATIENT: I think we all have that problem because we have a hard
   time relating to ourselves so we put it on other people.

This latter exchange between group members demonstrates the
patients' beginning capacities to control behaviors and emotions that
are perceived to cause painful interpersonal experiences and frequent
disruptions. The angry IA patient's insights are particularly important
for her because she had repeatedly expressed her anxiety about
becoming involved in the group; yet, she had attended more regularly
than any of the other patients (29 of 30 sessions). It is also clear that
gaining control over emotional reactions is most meaningful for the
patients; and of all of the painful emotions that they must process, the
experiencing of anger is the most problematic. If anger can be controlled, then other emotions and associated problems become more
manageable.

The last five sessions of the 30-week therapy are held every second week. The purpose is to have the patients experience some separation from the group while still retaining the opportunity to discuss their respective reactions to ending the group. In the 28th session the patients mentioned their attachment to one another and how important the group has been. They talked about maintaining contact but also acknowledged that it may not be possible; members need to get on with their own lives. The main shift that was obvious in the group dialogue was a growing sense of control over their independent destinies. It was manifest in the way in which they talked about life after the group ends. All of the patients had relinquished versions of the self as victim; they discussed being in control of themselves in relationships. The angry IA patient said that she has a better idea of how she used isolation to avoid being hurt in relationships. However, it did not appear that she had achieved much understanding about how she used suicidal threats as a way of reassuring herself that others cared about her. The male SA patient felt that he had made gains from the therapy but had wanted the group to continue. The group meetings defined his week, and he would miss them. However, he also felt confident that he would be in control of his life situation without further therapeutic contacts. Another patient focused on changes she had made in managing conflicts in important relationships. She reported a hurtful event that had occurred between her and her best friend. Subsequently, they talked about it, "I made it through whatever it was that she let me down; she made it through it too, and we're stronger for it."

Three of the original seven patients who started in the group went on to other treatment programs. As reported, the pseudo-competent patient was involved in a group program for patients who self-harm. The angry IA patient attended a 3-month day treatment program during which she had her medication reassessed and altered. The other IA patient wanted to do some more work on the insights gained while in the group and was referred for individual psychotherapy. At 24-month follow-up six of the seven patients were not in therapy and were maintaining the gains made. The angry IA patient met with a psychiatrist biweekly to have her medication monitored and to have a "chat."

This overview of the process of one of the groups treated in the comparison trial illustrates the therapeutic management of the contextual meanings of the patients' expectations of the therapists and the therapy. As was demonstrated, the patients, when given the opportunity, took major responsibility for the work of the group. They were articulate, insightful, and highly motivated to change. They were also well aware of the impact of their emotions; apart from their association with self-harming behaviors, emotions were experienced as debilitating. Most were managed adequately in the group. The experience in this group illustrates the difficulties in managing patients who appear to be competent and whose style of communication is primarily one of advice giving. Although these patterns of defensive maneuvers are well-known, their clinical management is challenging. The risk of therapeutic failure may be higher with these pseudo-competent patients than with the IA patients whose attacks of the therapists' inadequacies are usually more direct.

The major therapeutic task in each group treated in the trial involved the recognition, differentiation, tolerance, and containment of powerful emotions, in particular, rage and despair. The group structure offered a safe environment for testing intense feelings with which all of the group members could identify. They could express potentially violent forms of anger that in other contexts would lead to disruption and loss. The expression and management of anger within the group may have provided the most valued learning experience for all of the patients. When the anger was managed more effectively, the mourning and repair process progressed and led to integration of self-control in many sectors of the lives of these troubled patients.

9

Conclusion

Treatment Outcome

The merits of any newly developed treatment program must be determined through the careful appraisal of treatment results. The essential question to be answered is, What form of treatment, for what duration, produces the greatest benefits for which diagnostic group of patients? Although borderline patients comprise between 13% and 15% of psychiatric outpatients, only two treatment comparison trials have been conducted: Marsha Linehan and her colleagues' (1991) cognitive-behavioral treatment of chronically parasuicidal borderline patients, and the treatment comparison trial in which IGP was tested. Both trials used group models of intervention for the experimental treatments but differed in terms of the comparison treatment; Linehan used "treatment as usual in the community," which included any number of models of treatment (individual psychotherapy, day treatment, pharmacotherapy, etc.). In contrast, IGP was compared with psychodynamic individual psychotherapy; the intent was to choose a comparison treatment that best represented the typical form of psychotherapy offered borderline patients in psychiatric outpatient clinics. It was also thought that a psychodynamic approach to individual psychotherapy with borderlines would best emulate the form of treatment prescribed for borderlines in the literature (Kernberg, 1975; Waldinger & Gunderson, 1987). Both treatment comparison trials showed positive results. Linehan et al. (1991) showed that at 12 months following assessment the patients treated with the experimental treatment (Dialectical Behavioral Therapy, DBT) had fewer parasuicidal (any intentional self-harming action) behaviors and fewer days in hospital than the control group, but the two groups did not differ on self-report measures of depression, hopelessness, reasons for living, and suicide ideation. That is, both groups improved equally on these dimensions. Of note is the fact that the groups did not differ on the proportion of parasuicides that were actual suicide attempts.

The treatment trial in which IGP was compared with individual psychodynamic psychotherapy showed that borderline patients benefit from both forms of treatment. Outcome was measured through patient self-reports of depression, general symptoms, social behavior, and specific behavioral problems such as the management of angry and violent behavior. When interviewed at follow-up therapists who had engaged in the IGP model of treatment reported more satisfaction with their therapeutic experiences than those in individual psychotherapy. The IGP therapists valued both the co-therapy and group structure of the treatment. They reported that previous anxieties that were typical when initiating a course of individual psychotherapy with a borderline patient were much diminished as they engaged in the IGP process. The fact that a shared state of confusion was an expected dimension of the treatment allayed many of their fears about being in a room with a group of impulsive, demanding patients. Each IGP therapist reported that it was possible to develop empathic connections with each of the patients, even though the continuity of their empathic responses varied both within and across the therapeutic sessions. The time-limited boundary of IGP also provided both therapists and patients with a predictable, safe time frame in which to carry out their work. In contrast, the therapists who conducted the individual comparison treatment were often unaware as to why their patients terminated treatment; in their view the treatments had not been completed.

Follow-up interviews conducted 12 months posttreatment are reported for the three clusters of patients discussed in chapter 8. The two patients in the Impulsive Angry (IA) subgroup continued to make progress. Both felt that the most important change was that their expectations of others had been lowered; therefore they had moderated their demands. For example, one IA patient realized that she was not very tactful and was working hard to change that. Both felt that their ability to communicate more openly and clearly had improved; they were in better control of their interactions with their children and their mates. One of the patients talked about her drive to change; she felt 85% of the change that was needed was in herself. The other had joined a group in a community mental health program and talked about liking the leader and how sad she felt when the group ended. She felt that she managed her temper more effectively. Both of the IA patients knew that some things were not going to change, and when they worried about this, thoughts of self-harm reoccurred; but neither had made any suicidal attempts. When asked about her thoughts about the IGP experience, one IA patient said that "it was a farce; everyone kept talking, but nothing was accomplished." She added that the therapists never said a word, "so what was their purpose?" She hadn't liked the group the whole time she attended. Despite this patient's negative recollections of her experiences in group, she clearly had benefited from it. Her own strong motivation to change had sustained her in the group, and despite her reluctance she had become intensely involved with the other members, and she did make some important gains. During the last few sessions of the group she had actually acknowledged that it was her participation in IGP that had helped her most despite her comments about the futility of the group at follow-up. The other patient was more ambivalent about her experience with IGP. She had liked the other group members, had felt that she could be forthright with her opinions, and had learned some things about herself; however, the group had not gone on for as long as she would have liked. She had also hoped to make enduring friendships within the group, but this had not happened.

The three patients in the Dependent subgroup varied in their responses to IGP. One patient was enormously positive about her experience with the other group members and the therapists. She had never previously been in group psychotherapy and at the onset of IGP had been skeptical about what could be accomplished. However, she felt that she had gained considerable control over her anger toward family members who had disappointed her so much in the past. She now expected less and felt that as a result she was often surprised when unexpected support and affection was forthcoming from them. She had still not found the ideal mate but was hopeful that she would. Although she was working, she was not satisfied with her job, but she was looking to find something more suitable.

A second patient in the D subgroup felt that the group had been helpful because she now felt good about herself. However, she was still unemployed and worried that living on welfare might become a permanent way of existing. She met with friends regularly and managed her daily responsibilities well. She did tend to go to bars too much but did not feel that she resorted to drinking to alleviate anxiety and depression as she had in the past.

The pseudo-competent patient from the Dependent subgroup who had dropped out of IGP had participated in a day treatment program

for about 3 months but had not found it helpful; she felt especially negative toward the psychiatrist who had initially recommended the referral to the program and had refused his recommendation for intensive
individual psychotherapy. Following the experience with the day treatment program the patient learned about a special program for suicidal
patients at a hospital in another city. She applied and was admitted for
an intensive 2-week program. She felt she had benefited; she learned
that her emotional reactions and depressions were connected to her
patterns of intense involvement with men who always disappointed
her. Although the patient reported that she was not depressed, her
affect during the follow-up interview was flat. She talked about trying
to control her emotions by taking "one thing at a time." She was
involved in various exercise classes, went swimming, and walked a lot.
She was also taking better care of her appearance and was getting positive feedback from her employer and co-workers. However, when
asked about friends and family, it appeared that the patient did not
have many close relationships and had not found the ideal mate. When
asked about the IGP group she felt that "it had been good in a sense"
but did not know if it had helped much because she never felt accepted
by either the therapists or the other group members. Her admission to
hospital when she left the group had been a repetition of what had
been happening to her in the 3 years prior to attending the group;
when she became depressed and suicidal, hospitalization seemed to be
the only answer. She felt that the group she had attended during the
intensive 2-week treatment program had been more useful because the
leaders focused on suicidal behaviors. She felt that she needed to deal
with "concrete issues" and that the IGP experience had not helped her
with that. The patient's leaving the group was understandable. Her
need for attention and her need to control the group had not been well
managed. Although the patient had made some gains from the IGP
experience and from subsequent treatments, at follow-up she appeared
fragile and in need of more therapy. She was "hanging on" and managing but still longing to develop an intimate relationship with a man.

The male patient in the Substance Abuse (SA) subgroup reported
that he was doing well and had never been as happy. He said, "I'm a
different person; people used to have power over me, especially
women. Now they don't. I just do what I want." He was dating a
woman whom he felt was different from the women who had disappointed him in the past and was hopeful that things would work out
for them. He didn't need to be taken care of so much as before and as a
result had lowered his expectations of others. He had not attended AA

meetings since beginning IGP. He did not miss the meetings and had not resumed drinking. However, it appeared that he had become "addicted" to bingo, which he played most nights of the week. He did not feel that he was a chronic gambler; he controlled how much he spent on the bingo and often won enough money to pay for the games. He liked the socializing at the bingo games and had come to know some of the regulars. He had found a part-time job as a clerk in the office of a friend's business. He earned enough to maintain himself in a small apartment, although he lived a frugal existence. The patient continued to take antidepressant medication. Sometimes he thought about "going off of it" but was afraid of "sliding back." The only therapeutic contacts he had were regular appointments with a psychiatrist to monitor his medication. In response to questions about his experience in the IGP group, the patient said that he had found it very helpful. Although he had been in AA groups for many years, he had not learned things about himself until he attended the IGP group. He was comfortable with the other patients and had learned a lot from them; he also valued being able to help them. He talked about the therapists; he felt secure with them, and because of them "the group was done really well." His only regret was that the group had not lasted long enough; more sessions would have helped and "maybe the others wouldn't have had to go for more treatment." He viewed his experience in the group as advancing a positive therapeutic continuum that had been initiated during his hospitalization just prior to joining the group. He was motivated to continue the work of therapy and thus from the onset of the group was positively disposed to change despite the other patients' reluctance to join in the work of the group.

The other SA patient had gained more control over her angry reactions when men in her life disappointed her. Although she continued to search for the ideal mate, she was more cautious about engaging in new relationships with men. She was still successful at her job but had not altered her drinking and drug-taking habits. The patient felt that the group had been helpful but that she possibly had not given it a chance because she had found it difficult to involve herself in the group. She had learned a lot by listening to the other group members.

These brief vignettes of the follow-up contacts with three patient subgroups describe the quality and quantity of change in important domains of the patients' lives. For example, for the male SA patient, the group experience extended the therapeutic work initiated previously. In contrast, the pseudo-competent patient from the Dependent subgroup continued to need attention, and her flat affect at follow-up was symptomatic of how hard she was trying to maintain control in the face of unmet needs. She had made some gains, and possibly her experience in the IGP group helped her better manage the intensive 2-week experience in the group that focused on the management of suicidal behavior. The other two patients from the Dependent subgroup had made significant changes in their lives. The patients from the IA subgroup had made important gains, as for example achieving increased control over angry reactions. However, one of the patients denied that the group contributed to her increased self-control, despite evidence to the contrary.

For borderline patients, IGP is more cost-effective than open-ended individual psychodynamic psychotherapy. Even with a co-therapy group model of treatment, patient–therapist contact time is considerably reduced. Typically, seven patients were treated in each group, for 30 sessions by two therapists—an equivalent of 90 hours (1 and ½ hours per session × 30 sessions × 2 therapists), which compares favorably with 210 contact hours if the same 7 patients were treated by individual therapists for 30 sessions. In addition to the cost benefits, general outpatient psychiatric services that develop group models of intervention such as IGP could help allay therapists' frequent "allergic" reactions when confronted with the prospects of treating borderline patients. In tandem, the "bad press" that accompanies BPD patients might be tempered. This viewpoint is stressed by Vaillant (1992) in the title of a recent article "The beginning of wisdom is never calling a patient a borderline." Vaillant argues that the borderline label often reflects the clinician's subjective response rather than diagnostic accuracy; thus, in any encounter with borderline patients, therapists' attitudes influence both their perceptions and management of this group of patients. The IGP model of treatment pays special attention to therapists' subjective reactions and endorses the view that patients with BPD share a universal need for care, respect, and empathic response. When these elements are provided in a therapeutic context, the patients' abilities to make choices and to control their destinies are enhanced.

Integration of Etiologic, Diagnostic, and Intervention Hypotheses

All approaches to the treatment of BPD patients assume links between specific etiologic hypotheses, unique diagnostic dimensions, and well-defined therapeutic principles and strategies. In designing and testing IGP, each of these domains of the disorder and its treatment focused on understanding the complex phenomena that define the nature and function of interpersonal relationships. Thus, developmental antecedents that contribute to information processing about self–other relationship schemas in an interpersonal space influenced by strong emotions (either positively or negatively valenced) were linked to salient diagnostic dimensions. These included the borderline patients' chronic problems in establishing and maintaining caring relationships, their confusion about their own and others' motivations and emotions, and the use of impulsive, self-destructive behaviors in response to repeated disappointments and frustrations with important people in their lives. The IGP model of treatment directly addresses the etiologic and diagnostic hypotheses about the meanings of borderline patients' views of themselves and others, including therapists. The therapists are trained to monitor the meanings of group member interactions within the context of the patients' expectations of the therapists. Their therapeutic responses are focused on avoiding the replication of negative interpersonal transactions so typical of the histories of borderline patients. The ultimate goal of IGP is to help the patients to achieve altered and more benign representations of themselves in relation to others.

The IGP model of treatment replicates many of the strategies advocated by other clinicians who in their work with borderline patients have modified traditional psychoanalytic techniques. In the IGP approach the patients' perceptions of their life circumstances, past and current, are affirmed by the therapists. Initially in therapy there is no other reality but that represented by each patient in the group; that is, whatever the confusions and distortions present in the group, the task for the therapists is not aimed at providing reality-orienting interpretations or clarifications but, rather, at attempting to understand the message being conveyed to them. How are the therapists being perceived? What is being expected of them? Will they be vulnerable to the expression of strong emotions? Can they tolerate the confusion and ambiguity? When the patients' motivations are well understood, the therapists avoid the pitfall of reinforcing for the patients their worst fears about rejection and abandonment. When the patients' expectations are not understood, then the risk of therapeutic derailment is heightened. Because IGP describes "markers" for recognizing when the patient–therapist process is in trouble, the therapists detect when a derailment has occurred, and they take steps to shift the process back on course. The strong emphasis on understanding the types and functions of therapeutic derailments is a unique feature of IGP. The time-limited, group format, and co-therapist model also provide a parsimonious approach to the treatment of borderline personality when typically long-term, intensive individual psychoanalytic psychotherapy has been considered the optimal treatment of choice. Finally, therapist satisfaction in treating borderlines using IGP is an important feature of the potential utility of this model of treatment in general outpatient psychotherapy clinics.

The Management of Therapeutic Derailment

An important feature of IGP is the management of therapeutic derailment. Experienced clinicians can distinguish when a therapy is proceeding well from when it is faltering; however clinicians are less likely to identify the point in the interaction that signaled the risk of derailment. Through close observation of the group processes during each IGP group conducted in the comparison trial it was possible to identify "markers" that alerted the therapists that the interaction was either "stuck" or progressing rapidly toward a derailment. That is, when the therapists were unable to decipher the meanings of the patients' expectations of them, their interventions and the patients' subsequent responses demonstrated that the patients were at risk of having their most negative expectations confirmed. In descriptive terms, individual patient "stories" ceased to be expanded by the input of other group members. The stories became circular or "died," and the atmosphere in the group became infused with large doses of anxiety, hopelessness, and/or rage. The duration of any derailment depended on the progression from a "stuck" discourse to the expression of despair or rage by most of the group members. Another important feature of the derailment process was the effect of its adequate management on the progress of the treatment. When the therapists acknowledged that they did not have the answers and demonstrated that they could not fulfill the patients' expectations of rescue, the patients shifted to problem-solving talk and to the task of relinquishing expectations that could not be fulfilled. This process of letting go of unrealistic hopes was especially evident during the terminating phase of each group; the patients contrasted gains that had been made with a discussion of problems that persisted. This "summing-up" process illustrated the degree to which individual self-control had been achieved; each patient reflected on his or her independent capacities for managing future interpersonal crises.

We learned from our experiences with implementing IGP within the context of a large clinical trial that the whole treatment team is vulnerable to inappropriate subjective reactions to individual patient behaviors or to group interactions in the course of carrying out the treatment. As indicated, the pseudo-competent patient presented special challenges to the therapeutic team. We learned that because these patients are in fact competent in controlling the group process, the therapists are at risk of engaging in a therapeutic-skills competition. The therapists' accompanying anxiety and anger are understandable. We observed that under these conditions it was especially important for the consultant to acknowledge her or his own subjective reactions to the process. Linehan has also identified a similar borderline patient type which she describes as "the apparently competent woman" (Linehan, 1993). It may be that in any treatment program for patients with borderline personality disorder, therapists need to be alerted to the potential effect on the process of those patients who defend against their own vulnerabilities by functioning in a controlling and competent manner. If this behavior is responded to in a counter defensive manner as was the case in one of the IGP groups discussed in chapter 8, these so called pseudo competent patients will experience failed outcomes.

The Importance of Training

The IGP model of treatment was designed and tested in a treatment comparison trial with stringent criteria to ensure that therapists were adequately trained to apply the study treatments reliably. The same rigorous training criteria should be used for initiating the IGP model of treatment in any clinical setting. As stated, only therapists who have experience in treating borderline patients individually and who also have experience with group psychotherapy should be trained to use IGP. Because IGP specifically addresses a group of severe personality disorders patients who are at high risk of harming themselves, it is not a treatment that can be practiced by inexperienced therapists. Because much emphasis is placed on understanding the therapists' subjective reactions to patients in the context of the inordinate amount of confusion generated in group sessions, therapists who are trained in IGP must be prepared to examine openly their individual subjective reactions. Only through this careful self-monitoring is it possible for the therapists to understand their own contributions to the interaction. During the training, the aim is to establish a collegial environment in which the risk of criticism is low and the opportunity for learning is high.

Application of IGP in Clinical Settings

Although IGP was tested on patients with a BPD diagnosis, it is expected that the treatment model might be equally suitable and effective with groups of patients who do not share the same personality disorder but share similar levels of severity. For example, a mixed-diagnosis group could include patients with borderline, narcissistic, dependent, and obsessive personality disorders. The aim would be to choose patients with similar interpersonal problems, but who might present differently. However, the same inclusion-exclusion criteria discussed in chapter 2 should apply. It is also important to use a standardized screening device such as the SCID (Spitzer, Williams, & Gibbon, 1987) to check the reliability of the Axis II diagnoses. The actual effectiveness of IGP with a mixed group of personality disorders would need to be tested.

For the treatment comparison trial, the IGP model of treatment consisted of 30 sessions; however, each patient was in contact with the project 3 to 4 months prior to beginning treatment. Because randomization to treatments was used, a pool of 16 to 20 qualifying patients was accumulated prior to each wave of assignment to treatment; that is, each patient had equal chance of being assigned to either treatment. During the waiting pretreatment period, each patient was in continual contact with the research assistant who scheduled a number of appointments for the completion of the study measures and maintained regular telephone contact with each patient to keep them informed about when treatment might begin. These research contacts no doubt functioned as supplementary treatment sessions, especially as the research assistant was trained to use strategies that paralleled those used in the IGP model of treatment. Thus, to assess the effects of IGP it is important to factor into the treatment time the additional 3 to 4 months of pretreatment research contacts. In a clinical setting a pretreatment time interval will be necessary in order to screen a sufficient number of patients for assignment to an IGP group, depending on the rate of referral of suitable patients. To replicate the duration of patient contact used in the treatment comparison trial it is recommended that the number of group sessions be extended from 30 to 45. Alternately, patients could be offered 1 year of treatment but would receive approximately 45 sessions because of holiday and vacation breaks. An extended time frame for the treatment might also be more beneficial for those patients who had greater difficulty engaging in the group process. Even when the group treatment is extended, it would still be more cost effective as compared to the same number of individual psychotherapy sessions for each patient.

Between 30% and 40% of patients dropped out of treatment within the first five group sessions. Reduction of this high dropout rate might be controlled through brief weekly individual contacts with each patient during the initial phase of treatment. Budman (1989) instituted this practice during a study of patients with personality disorders treated with group psychotherapy. The individual sessions were especially useful for the borderline patients and markedly reduced the dropout rate (personal communication). Within the IGP context it would be important to establish a priori a specific structure and duration for the individual sessions. Both therapists would meet with each patient, and the technical strategies used in IGP could be replicated in the individual sessions. This would include communicating to each patient at the time of referral to IGP that, in addition to the pregroup session, a specific number of individual sessions are available to each patient if she or he wishes to use them.

The limitations of the IGP model of treatment include the following:

1. It is not any more effective for substance abusing borderline patients than any other form of treatment. Until these patients are able to exercise some control over their addictions, such as attending AA meetings, they are less likely to benefit from any form of psychotherapy.

2. Patients who protect themselves from acknowledging their own scarred images of self by adopting pseudo-competent roles in any therapeutic situation may benefit less from a model of treatment such as IGP that is based on the premise that patients are competent and that their view of the world is to be affirmed. Pseudo-competent patients have all of the "right" answers and provide them in liberal doses for the other group members but in so doing avoid acknowledging their own vulnerabilities. These patients may need longer therapies to repeatedly test expectations of others and to be reassured that they will not be punished or abandoned when they forgo the competent stance and reveal their painful life experiences. If the IGP time boundaries were extended to 1 year, the pseudo-competent patient might have a better opportunity to relinquish this interpersonal pattern of behavior in favor of alternate strategies for engaging with significant others.

3. Even though all patients made moderate to notable gains, a small number chose to continue therapeutic work in individual psychotherapy. By their own reports the patients felt that their experiences in the group had helped them to make better use of the subsequent individual therapy sessions. In these instances IGP functioned

both as a vehicle for change and as a support for continuing in individual psychotherapy. In this regard the group was especially effective for those patients who had previously had repeated failures in individual treatment.

4. The IGP model does not include other family members in the treatment paradigm. Some borderline patients could benefit from both marital and family forms of treatment (Shapiro, Shapiro, Zinner, and Berkowitz, 1977). Some might need support in accessing services from community social welfare agencies. Others could benefit from a trial of psychotropic drugs, especially when they meet criteria for Axis I affective disorders. Thus, for some borderline patients a multimodel approach to treatment (Waldinger, 1992) may be the most beneficial, and IGP would be but one factor contributing to change.

Summary

In many respects the IGP treatment model is not dissimilar from other forms of dynamic group psychotherapy. The unique difference is that much of the work of the group is focused on recognizing and mourning the loss of the wished-for fantasies imbedded in interpersonal relations. Historically, when these fantasized wishes were frustrated and the borderline patient responded with impulsive, self-destructive behaviors, the mourning process and the accompanying pain was circumvented. In IGP, the fantasized wishes are expressed and measured against the reality of each patient's personal life situation. Each patient has the opportunity to give and receive empathic understanding for the shared losses of the hopes and expectations that cannot be realized. It is the successful management of this process within the context of IGP that advances the therapeutic work. The therapists are inevitably the targets for much of the anxiety and frustration that accompany the relinquishing of unattainable wishes. However, when mourning has been accomplished, reduction in the quantity and intensity of debilitating behaviors is the outcome. Thus, the progress made by patients in their capacities to mourn the past within the process of IGP is measured in terms of changes in the concrete behaviors of everyday living, such as improved and more stable living arrangements, stable employment, and a more predictable and satisfying social life, including improved relations with intimate others.

In summary there is no evidence as yet to suggest that any one approach to the treatment of BPD is more effective than any other. As reported, both the Linehan, Armstrong, Suarez, Allmon, & Heard

(1991) study and the treatment comparison trial that tested IGP showed that BPD patients improve in all forms of treatment. Linehan's model of treatment targets parasuicidal behavior and patients treated with DBT show fewer parasuicidal behaviors than the comparison group. The results of both comparison trials showed that there were lower dropout rates when compared with rates of dropout for BPD patients treated in general psychiatric services.

It may be that ultimately the most effective and parsimonious model is a staged approach that combines different models of treatment. Borderline personality disorder patients with extensive histories of impulsive and self-destructive behaviors coupled with no fruitful work experience may need either the structure, support, and direction of an educational behavioral approach such as Linehan's (1993) or the neutrality and affirmation of the IGP approach in order to achieve control over these behaviors. Once this is accomplished, individual dynamic psychotherapy may add depth and stability to individual patient changes in behavior and understanding of self. Future research could add useful information about the optimal match of patient profile and treatment strategy. As illustrated, subgroups of the borderline disorder exist. It may be that any matching program will need to take into account the differences across subgroups to formulate treatment plans that respond best to the needs of patients in each subgroup. The uniqueness of each patient's contribution to the treatment encounter will show us the way.

Appendix

IGP Training Materials

Part I

Therapist Interventions

Below are listed categories of therapist statements/interventions. After each statement indicate whether you think it is on-model, off-model or could be both.

EXPLORATORY—INTERPRETIVE—CERTAIN

The therapist provides an explanation about the patient's thoughts, behaviors, or feelings in a definitive manner.

On-model_____   Off-model_____   Could be both_____

EXPLORATORY—INTERPRETIVE—TENTATIVE

The therapist provides an explanation about the patient's thoughts, behaviors, or feelings in a neutral, tentative manner.

On-model_____   Off-model_____   Could be both_____

EXPLORATORY—INFORMATION GAINING—DIRECT FORMAT

The therapist asks for information—for example, "How do you feel when your boyfriend walks out in a huff?"

On-model_____   Off-model_____   Could be both_____

EXPLORATORY—INFORMATION GAINING—INDIRECT FORMAT

The therapist asks for information—"Is that something you would like to talk about?"

On-model_____   Off-model_____   Could be both_____

GENERAL COMMENTARY

The therapist provides a neutral or reflective comment in response to something the patient has just said.

On-model_____ Off-model_____ Could be both_____

ONE-SIDED COMMENTARY
The therapist reflects on one side of an issue in a tentative format.

On-model_____ Off-model_____ Could be both_____

TWO-SIDED COMMENTARY
The therapist reflects on both sides of an issue in a tentative format.

On-model_____ Off-model_____ Could be both_____

REITERATION
The therapist repeats or briefly paraphrases what the patient has just said.

On-model_____ Off-model_____ Could be both_____

INTEREST IN PATIENT'S NARRATIVE
The therapist shows interest in the patient's narrative (e.g., patient's interests, hobbies, type of employment, etc.).

On-model_____ Off-model_____ Could be both_____

ADVICE GIVING
The therapist gives advice.

On-model_____ Off-model_____ Could be both_____

SUPPORTIVE STATEMENTS
The therapist makes a supportive statement that characterizes the patient's behavior.

On-model_____ Off-model_____ Could be both_____

ANSWERING QUESTIONS
The therapist answers patient's enquiries (including enquiries about the therapist).

On-model_____ Off-model_____ Could be both_____

THERAPIST CONFIRMING
The therapist agrees with or confirms patient's viewpoint.

On-model_____ Off-model_____ Could be both_____

REFLECTING DOUBT OR CONFUSION
The therapist makes statements that reveal a genuine lack of knowledge or understanding.

On-model_____ Off-model_____ Could be both_____

Part II

Tentative Words

The IGP model of treatment recommends the use of tentative phrasing in interventive strategies. The use of tentative language can help therapists to learn to express uncertainty about the issues patients bring to therapy. Some examples follow:

Could, Could be, Could it
Do I understand
Do you think
Don't know if
I seem to have the feeling
Gather
Guess
How about
I imagine
I seem to have the impression
Kind of
Is it a little like
Looks to me
May have
Maybe
Might, might be
One approach may be
One way of looking at it
One way of seeing things
Partly
Perhaps
Probably
Puzzled, puzzling
Same time (at the same time)
Could you be saying
Does it seem like
Somehow
Sometimes
Sort of
Sounds like, sounds to me like
Not sure
In a way
What if
Wonder, wondering
Wouldn't it be nice if
You think maybe

Part III

Treatment Dialogue I

P: I always thought anxiety was just being a little bit shaky and having a few butterflies. To me, it's like feeling like everything is falling apart, that nothing is stable around me, that there is nowhere to run for help.

T: You know, I think part of what has happened, and it's happened today, is that if people do try to help or give any ideas, even if they are not the right ones, you reject them.

On-model_____   Off-model_____   Could be both_____

If off-model, what would you have said?

P: [Interrupting] It's because a lot of the ideas that people have given me . . . . I was just so damn fed up with a lot of the things that were suggested.

T: And I'm not saying that you weren't . . .

On-model_____   Off-model_____   Could be both_____

If off-model, what would you have said?

P: It's not that I don't want help, it's just that . . . if it's too complex or too Mickey Mouse, I say "forget it" and people say "you're resisting."

T: Is that what I am saying?

On-model_____   Off-model_____   Could be both_____

If off-model, what would you have said?

P: I don't know.

T: I'm not saying that you are resisting; what I'm saying is that you're getting angry at people who offer help.

On-model_____   Off-model_____   Could be both_____

If off-model, what would you have said?

P: The only help they offer is to string nuts or bolts or something like that, that makes me feel worse. It makes me feel like a nut case.

T: Well, what makes you feel good? What could they offer that would make you feel good?

On-model_____   Off-model_____   Could be both_____

If off-model, what would you have said?

P: Oh God, who knows?

T: So there is no answer. Whomever offers help is . . .

On-model_____   Off-model_____   Could be both_____

If off-model, what would you have said?

Treatment Dialogue II

P: I know what it's like. I mean before I used to be in a group, and I just sat there and said nothing. I was too scared because I didn't have anything to say.

T: To be honest this could be the same. The group might not have anything to offer you. It might not have anything to offer you at this point.

On-model_____   Off-model_____   Could be both_____

If off-model, what would you have said?

P: I know. I've talked to a lot of people about being nuts. I mean you wonder who is going to help. I don't get anywhere and I'm sort of stuck now. I'm having a hard time making a decision whether I should leave this guy I'm living with. He has beat me up a lot. I don't know whether I should leave him and nobody has helped me. Everybody just says do what you want. I know that if I throw him out, I'll probably end up letting him come back. . . . I don't know, I'm pulled every which way.

T: The advice you get from a group like this might be wrong. It might be the wrong advice.

On-model_____   Off-model_____   Could be both_____

If off-model, what would you have said?

P: My friends don't say what to do; they are afraid to say. They say, "Well, you'll have to decide." See, I'm not worried about being hurt; we've been through a lot together. I don't care what other people think or anything like that. I'm more worried about me and him.

T: Sounds like a difficult position you're in.

On-model_____   Off-model_____   Could be both_____

If off-model, what would you have said?

Treatment Dialogue III

P: Do you want to hear about my experiences as an adolescent? What somebody did to me?

T: Well, I'm not. . . does it feel like that would interfere with telling us why you are here?

On-model_____   Off-model_____   Could be both_____

If off-model, what would you have said?

P: Well this, this . . . . She was a woman. She used to yell at me. I was pretty nervous, fragile then, I felt anyway. She was too tough [chuckles].

T: So if you think about therapy, you need therapists who don't yell at you.

On-model_____   Off-model_____   Could be both_____

If off-model, what would you have said?

P: Right. I mean I just thought she was a horrible person, I really do think she's horrible. I think she's very moody, more than me even. And, and. . . I think she probably yelled at everybody. . . and I was impatient with most people. I mean, I was very young then. I was 15.

T: Do you have a sense that you do things that contribute to it?

On-model_____   Off-model_____   Could be both_____

If off-model, what would you have said?

P: Well, I guess she didn't think that I took the counseling seriously.

T: I see.

On-model_____   Off-model_____   Could be both_____

If off-model, what would you have said?

P: Yeah.

T: Were you moving or making any progress or interested in making progress?

On-model_____   Off-model_____   Could be both_____

If off-model, what would you have said?

P: Yeah, I was. I think she . . . I really think she thought I was a spoiled kid.

T: What gets people feeling that about you?

On-model_____   Off-model_____   Could be both_____

If off-model, what would you have said?

[Later in the same session]

P: But as far as keeping people away, you know, I'm not very good in social situations. I just can't handle them. I would be ignored and, you know, I just couldn't take it.

T: Do you have a sense of what you would like to happen at a party if you went to a party?

On-model_____   Off-model_____   Could be both_____

If off-model, what would you have said?

Treatment Dialogue IV

P: I spent another night in the hospital last night.

T: Did you?

On-model_____   Off-model_____   Could be both_____

If off-model, what would you have said?

P: Mm hmm.

T: Are you still an inpatient there, or did they just rehydrate you and send you out?

On-model_____   Off-model_____   Could be both_____

If off-model, what would you have said?

P: No, I refused to be admitted.

T: Uh huh. What hospital was that?

On-model_____   Off-model_____   Could be both_____

If off-model, what would you have said?

P: The one nearest my home.

T: And how come you refused to be admitted?

On-model_____   Off-model_____   Could be both_____

If off-model, what would you have said?

P: Because I don't want to be in the hospital. I'm tired of being in the hospital.

T: Who took you there?

On-model_____   Off-model_____   Could be both_____

If off-model, what would you have said?

[Later in same session]

P: I just don't believe that 30 weeks of therapy are gonna lead to anything except creating more problems for me. It's just another on-again, off-again bullshit.

T: I think one way to avoid it becoming, you know, the on-again, off-again bullshit you've gone through before is to try and figure out what's happened that you got caught up in the on-again, off-again bullshit.

On-model_____   Off-model_____   Could be both_____

If off-model, what would you have said?

P: Over the years I've got nothing out of therapy and kept quitting. I had a therapist for 2 years. I'll be perfectly honest with you, I don't know what the hell he did, but it sure as hell wasn't anything that lasted.

T: Mm hmm. What is it that you're looking for out of therapy?

On-model_____   Off-model_____   Could be both_____

If off-model, what would you have said?

P: There's just gotta be a better way of living for me. I hate myself. All I do is turn all my feelings inside.

T: What feelings?

On-model_____   Off-model_____   Could be both_____

If off-model, what would you have said?

P: Anything that's negative, that I think somebody might reject me for.

T: You do it for them first?

On-model_____   Off-model_____   Could be both_____

If off-model, what would you have said?

P: I just get too afraid to say anything. It's just easier just to keep it inside. I don't know how to get angry.

T: Do you get angry perhaps in other ways? Rather than getting angry and saying, you know, "I'm really angry with you, I'm pissed off, and this is what I'm pissed off about." Do you get angry in sort of different ways?

On-model_____   Off-model_____   Could be both_____

If off-model, what would you have said?

P: I'm just angry that everybody's always trying to control my life, angry about what my mother did to me when I was growing up. I can't tell her that. I'm just angry all the time because it's the whole world's fault that I'm fucked up, and I know it's not.

T: But it's hard for you to let go of that anger.

On-model_____   Off-model_____   Could be both_____

If off-model, what would you have said?

P: I don't know what to do with it. [short pause] I just turned out to be a big failure.

T: How's that?

On-model_____   Off-model_____   Could be both_____

If off-model, what would you have said?

P: I'm not good at anything that I do. I hate everyone and everything. I try new things, but they just don't work out.

T: What about that night course you're taking at college?

On-model_____   Off-model_____   Could be both_____

If off-model, what would you have said?

P: Nothing'll ever come of that. Nothing ever comes of anything I do.

T: Well, I hear what you are saying, but you know you have accomplished things in your life.

On-model_____   Off-model_____   Could be both_____

If off-model, what would you have said?

[Later in the same session]

P: It just feels hopeless. Makes me feel uncomfortable. I just want to crawl inside of myself. I don't sleep. I feel lethargic, and I just totally withdraw— don't want to see anybody and I don't want to talk to anybody. I just want to be left alone. Then I feel worse.

T: Cause you. . . . So it's almost like you need people but only if it's with the right dose. If it's too much, it's overwhelming. If it's too little, it's frightening.

On-model_____   Off-model_____   Could be both_____

If off-model, what would you have said?

P: It's just that when I'm depressed—at the best of times, people are telling me what to do. When I'm depressed, it's even worse. You shouldn't feel this, and you shouldn't feel that, and what am I supposed to say—right, I shouldn't feel it? What am I supposed to do—just turn it off?

T: Mm hmm. I guess there's a lot of feelings that haven't been worked through. You can't let go till the feelings that are tied up are gone.

On-model_____   Off-model_____   Could be both_____

If off-model, what would you have said?

Treatment Dialogue V

P: I didn't want to hear bad things in the group; like everyone is gonna talk and I won't wanna talk, you know.

T: What makes you nervous about that?

On-model_____   Off-model_____   Could be both_____

If off-model, what would you have said?

P: Cause I'm afraid I won't talk, and if I don't talk . . .

T: Some people are quieter than others sometimes . . . especially if they feel uncomfortable. Are you worried about that happening?

On-model_____   Off-model_____   Could be both_____

If off-model, what would you have said?

P: Yeah.

T: Is there something we could do to make you feel more comfortable? Help you be more at ease?

On-model_____   Off-model_____   Could be both_____

If off-model, what would you have said?

P: Not really, it's just like . . . say somebody has a problem and somebody says, well I think you should do this about it or that. Is that sort of what . . . we're gonna be getting at?

T: Sometimes. Sometimes you might get more than one suggestion, and some of them might be helpful and some of them might not be.

On-model_____   Off-model_____   Could be both_____

If off-model, what would you have said?

P: Like you mean giving suggestions?

T: . . . is that good or is that bad?

On-model_____   Off-model_____   Could be both_____

If off-model, what would you have said?

P: That's good. That's good. Somebody would say, 'What do you think?' and maybe . . .

T: So, that would help bring you out, would it, if they called on you like that?

On-model_____   Off-model_____   Could be both_____

If off-model, what would you have said?

P: Yeah . . . something like that would help.

T: Fair enough, so when you are silent for a long time, do you want us to ask you?

On-model_____   Off-model_____   Could be both_____

If off-model, what would you have said?

P: Yeah, that would help because I have a feeling I would never talk. . . at least if I feel like saying something at the time I have something to say about it.

T: Okay.

On-model_____   Off-model_____   Could be both_____

If off-model, what would you have said?

P: Somebody asks me, I might say it, but if no one asks me, I won't say it.

T: Do we ask twice? Like if we ask twice and there's still silence. . . ?

On-model_____   Off-model_____   Could be both_____

If off-model, what would you have said?

P: Are you making fun of me or what?

T: No, no, it's a serious question. If we ask once and you still don't feel like talking, can we ask again or would that make you more uncomfortable?

On-model_____   Off-model_____   Could be both_____

If off-model, what would you have said?

P: I think I need to be pushed.

T: So ask again?

    On-model_____   Off-model_____   Could be both_____

    If off-model, what would you have said?

P: Like, yeah, but you don't have to jump on my case or anything.

T: I could ask you, all right?

    On-model_____   Off-model_____   Could be both_____

    If off-model, what would you have said?

P: Just wait a little while and ask another time . . . easy.

References

ADLER, G. (1985). *Borderline psychopathology and its treatment.* New York: Jason Aronson.

AINSWORTH, M. D. S. (1985). Patterns of infant-mother attachments: Antecedents and effects on development. *Bulletin of the New York Academy of Medicine, 61,* 771–791.

AINSWORTH, M. D. S. (1989). Attachments beyond infancy. *American Psychologist, 44,* 709–716.

AINSWORTH, M. D. S., BLEHAR, M. E., WATERS, E., & WALL, S. (1978). *Patterns of attachment.* Hillsdale, NJ: Erlbaum.

AKISKAL, H. S. (1981). Subaffective disorders: Dysthymic, cyclothymic and bipolar II disorders in the borderline realm. *Psychiatric Clinics of North America, 4,* 25–46.

AKISKAL, H. S. (1992). Borderline: An adjective still in search of a noun. In D. Silver & M. Rosenbluth (Eds.), *Handbook of borderline disorders.* Madison, CT: International Universities Press.

AKISKAL, H. S., CHEN, S. E., DAVIS, G. C., PUZANTIAN, V. R., KASHGARIAN, M., & BOLINGER, J. M. (1985). Borderline: An adjective in search of a noun. *Journal of Clinical Psychiatry, 46,* 41–48.

ALEXANDER, F. (1957). *Psychoanalysis and psychotherapy: Developments in theory, technique and training.* New York: Norton.

AMERICAN PSYCHIATRIC ASSOCIATION (1980). *The diagnostic and statistical manual of mental disorders* (DSM III) (3rd ed.). Washington, DC: Author.

AMERICAN PSYCHIATRIC ASSOCIATION (1987). *The diagnostic and statistical manual of mental disorders* (DSM-III-R) (3rd ed., rev.). Washington, DC: Author.

ANDRULONIS, P. A., & VOGEL, N. G. (1984). Comparison of borderline personality subcategories to schizophrenic and affective disorders. *British Journal of Psychiatry, 144,* 358–363.

ANDRULONIS, P. A., GLUEK, B. C., STOEBEL, C. F., VOGEL, N. G., SHAPIRO,

A. L., & ALDRIGE, D. (1981). Organic brain dysfunction and the borderline syndrome. *Psychiatric Clinics of North America, 4*, 47–66.

BARASCH, A., FRANCES, A., HURT, S., CLARKIN, J., & COHEN, S. (1985). Stability and distinctiveness of borderline personality disorder. *American Journal of Psychiatry, 142*, 1484–1486.

BATTEGAY, R., & KLAUI, C. (1986). Analytically oriented group psychotherapy with borderline patients as long term crisis management. *Crisis, 7*, 94–110.

BATTLE, C., IMBER, S., HOEHN-SARIC, R., STONE, A., NASH, E., & FRANK, J. (1966). Target complaints as criteria of improvement. *American Journal of Psychotherapy, 20*, 184–192.

BECK, A. T., RUSH, A. J., SHAW, B. F., & EMERY, G. (1979). *Cognitive therapy of depression.* New York: Guilford Press.

BECK, A. T., WARD, C. H., MENDELSOHN, M., MOCK, J., & ERBAUGH, J. (1961). An inventory for measuring depression. *Archives of General Psychiatry, 4*, 561–571.

BELL, M., BILLINGTON, R., & BECKER, B. (1986). A scale for the assessment of object relations: Reliability, validity and factorial invariance. *Journal of Clinical Psychology, 42*, 733–741.

BELL, M., BILLINGTON, R., CICHETTI, S., & GIBBONS, J. (1988). Do object relation deficits distinguish BPD from other psychiatric groups? *Journal of Clinical Psychology, 44*, 511–516.

BELLAK, L. (1980). On some limitations of dyadic psychotherapy and the role of group modalities. *International Journal of Group Psychotherapy, 30*, 7–21.

BELLAK, J., & SMALL, L. (1978). *Emergency psychotherapy and brief psychotherapy* (2nd ed.). New York: Grune & Stratton.

BION, W. (1961). *Experiences in groups.* New York: Basic Books.

BLATT, S., & LERNER, H. (1983). The psychological assessment of object representations. *Journal of Personality Assessment, 47*, 7–28.

BOWLBY, J. (1973). *Attachment and loss* (Vol. 2). New York: Basic Books.

BOWLBY, J. (1979). *The making and breaking of affectional bonds.* London: Tavistock.

BOWLBY, J. (1980). *Attachment and loss. Vol. 3. Loss, sadness and depression.* New York: Basic Books.

BOWLBY, J. (1982). *Attachment and loss* (Vol. 1, 2d. ed.). New York: Basic Books.

BOWLBY, J. (1988). Developmental psychiatry comes of age. *American Journal of Psychiatry, 145*, 1–10.

BRADLEY, S. J. (1979). The relationship of early maternal separation to borderline personality in children and adolescents: A pilot study. *American Journal of Psychiatry, 136*, 424–426.

BRANDCHAFT, B., & STOLOROW, R. D. (1987). The borderline concept: An intersubjective view. In J. S. Grotstein, M. F. Solomon, & J. A. Lang (Eds.), *The borderline patient: Emerging concepts in diagnosis, psychodynamics, and treatment.* Hillsdale, NJ: Analytic Press.

BRETHERTON, I., & WATERS, E. (Eds.). (1985). *Growing points of attachment theory and research.* Monographs of the Society for Research in Child Development, 50 (1–2, Serial No. 209).

BRETHERTON, I., RIDGEWAY, D., & CASSIDY, J. (1990). The role of internal working models in attachment relations: Can it be assessed in 3-year-olds? In M. Greenberg, M. Cummings, & D. Cichetti (Eds.), *Attachment beyond the preschool years.* Chicago: University of Chicago Press.

BRETHERTON, I., BIRINGEN, Z., RIDGEWAY, D., MASLIN, C., & SHERMAN, M. (1989). Attachment: The parental perspective. *Infant Mental Health Journal, 10,* 203–221.

BRIERE, J., & ZAIDI, L. Y. (1989). Sexual abuse histories and sequelae in female psychiatric emergency room patients. *American Journal of Psychiatry, 146,* 1602–1606.

BRYER, J. B., NELSON, B. A., MILLER, J. B., & KROL, P. K. (1987). Childhood physical and sexual abuse as factors in adult psychiatric illness. *American Journal of Psychiatry, 144,* 1426–1430.

BUDMAN, S. H. (1989). *Personality disorders, group therapy and change.* Washington, DC: U.S. Department of Health and Human Services.

BUIE, D., & ADLER, G. (1982). The definitive treatment of the borderline personality. *International Journal of Psychoanalytic Psychotherapy, 33,* 531–546.

BURKE, W. F., SUMMERS, F., SELINGER, D., & POLONUS, T. W. (1986). The comprehensive object relations profile: A preliminary report. *Psychoanalytic Psychology, 3,* 173–185.

BUSS, D. M., & PLOMIN, R. (1986). The EAS approach to temperament. In R. Plomin & J. Dunn (Eds.), *The study of temperment: Changes, continuities and challenges.* Hillsdale, NJ: Erlbaum.

CAMPOS, R. (1988). Comfort measures for infant pain. *Zero to Three, 9,* 6–13.

CAMPOS, J. J., CAMPOS, R. G., & BARRETT, K. C. (1989). Emergent themes in the study of emotional development and emotion regulation. *Developmental Psychology, 25,* 394–402.

CAMPOS, J. J., BARRETT, K. C., LAMB, M. E., GOLDSMITH, H. H., & STEINBERG, C. (1983). Socioemotional development. In P. Mussen (Series Ed.) & J. J. Campos & M. H. Haith (Vol. Eds.), *Handbook of Child Psychology. Vol. 2: Infancy and developmental psychobiology.* New York: Wiley.

CAMRAS, L., GROW, J., & RIBORDY, S. (1983). Recognition of emotion expression by abused children. *Journal of Clinical Child Psychology, 12,* 325–328.

CAREY, W. B. (1986). Interactions of temperament and clinical conditions. In M. Wolriach & D. Routh (Eds.), *Advances in developmental and behavioral pediatrics* (Vol. 6). Greenwich, CT: JAI Press.

CHATHAM, P. (1985). *Treatment of the borderline psersonality.* New York: Jason Aronson.

CHESS, S., & THOMAS, A. (1984). *Origins and evolution of behavior disorders.* New York: Brunner/Mazel.

CLARKIN, J. F., HURT, S. W., & HULL, J. W. (1991). *Subclassification of border-line personality disorder: A cluster solution.* Unpublished manuscript. New York Hospital-Cornell Medical Center, Westchester Division, White Plains, NY.

CLARKIN, J. F., KOENIGSBERG, H., YEOMANS, F., SELZER, M., KERNBERG, P., & KERNBERG, O. (1992). Psychodynamic psychotherapy of the borderline patient. In J. F. Clarkin, E. Marziali, & H. Munroe-Blum (Eds.), *Borderline personality disorder.* New York: Guilford.

COHN, D. (1990). Child-mother attachment of six-year-olds and social competence at school. *Child Development, 61,* 152–162.

CRITTENDEN, P. M. (1990). Internal representational models of attachment relationships. *Infant Mental Health, 11,* 259–277.

CRITTENDEN, P. M., PARTRIDGE, M. F., & CLAUSSEN, A. H. (1992). Family patterns of relationship in normative and dysfunctional families. *Development and Psychopathology, 3,* 491–512.

DAWSON, D. (1988). Treatment of the borderline patient, relationship management. *Canadian Journal of Psychiatry, 33,* 370–374.

DAWSON, D. L. & MACMILLAN, H. L. (1993). *Relationship management of the borderline patient: From understanding to treatment.* New York: Brunner/Mazel.

DEMOS, E. V., & KAPLAN, S. (1986). Motivation and affect reconsidered: Affect biographies of two infants. *Psychoanalysis and Contemporary Thought, 9,* 147–221.

DEROGATIS, L. R., LIPMAN, R. S., & COVI, L. (1973). SCL-90: An outpatient psychiatric rating scale—preliminary report. *Psychopharmacological Bulletin, 9,* 13–28.

DOBSON, K. S., & SHAW, B. F. (1988). The use of treatment manuals in cognitive therapy: Experiences and issues. *Journal of Consulting and Clinical Psychology, 56,* 673–680.

ELKIN, I., PARLOFF, M. B., HADLEY, S. W., & AUTRY, J. H. (1985). NIMH Treatment of depression collaborative research program. *Archives of General Psychiatry, 42,* 305–316.

EMDE, R. N. (1981). Changing models of infancy and the nature of early development: Remodeling the foundation. *Journal of the American Psychoanalytic Association, 29,* 179–219.

EMDE, R. (1983). The pre-representational self and its affective core. *Psychoanalytic Study of the Child, 38,* 165–192.

ENDICOTT, J., & SPITZER, R. L. (1978). A diagnostic interview: The schedule for affective disorders and schizophrenia. *Archives of General Psychiatry, 35,* 837–844.

FELDBERG, T. M. (1958). Treatment of "borderline" psychotics in groups of neurotic patients. *International Journal of Group Psychotherapy, 8,* 76–84.

FITZPATRICK, C. J. (1985). Children's development out of event-bound conception of their emotions. In I. Fast (Ed.), *Event theory: A Piaget-Freud integration.* Hillsdale, NJ: Erlbaum.

FONAGY, P. (1991). Thinking about thinking: Some clinical and theoretical considerations concerning the treatment of a borderline patient. *International Journal of Psychoanalysis, 72,* 639–656.

FONAGY, P., & HIGGITT, A. (1990). A developmental perspective on borderline personality disorder. *Revue Internationale de Psychopathologie, 1,* 125–159.

FOX, N. A. (1989). Psychobiological correlates of emotional reactivity during the first year of life. *Developmental Psychology, 25,* 364–372.

FRANCES, A. (1982). Categorical and dimensional systems for personality diagnosis: A comparison. *Comprehensive Psychiatry, 23,* 516–527.

FRANCES, A., & CLARKIN, J. F. (1981). No treatment as the treatment of choice. *Archives of General Psychiatry, 38,* 542–545.

FRANCES, A., CLARKIN, J. F., & PERRY, S. (1984). *Differential therapeutics in psychiatry: The art and science of treatment selection.* New York: Brunner/Mazel.

FRANCES, A., CLARKIN, J. F., GILMORE, M., HURT, S. W., & BROWN, R. (1984). Reliability of criteria for borderline personality disorder: A comparison of DSM-III and DIB. *American Journal of Psychiatry, 141,* 1080–1084.

FRANK, H., & PARIS, J. (1981). Recollections of family experience in borderline patients. *Archives of General Psychiatry, 38,* 1031–1034.

FRANK, N., & HOFFMAN, N. (1986). Borderline empathy: An empirical investigation. *Comprehensive Psychiatry, 27,* 387–395.

FRIEDMAN, H. J. (1975). Psychotherapy of borderline patients: The influence of theory on technique. *American Journal of Psychiatry, 132,* 1048–1052.

FRYER, M. R., FRANCES, A. J., SULLIVAN, T., HURT, S. W., & CLARKIN, J. F. (1988). Comorbidity of borderline personality disorder. *Archives of General Psychiatry, 45,* 348–352.

GELINAS, D. J. (1983). The persisting negative effects of incest. *Psychiatry, 46,* 312–332.

GEORGE, C., & SOLOMON, J. (1989). Internal working models of caregiving and security of attachment at age six. *Infant Mental Health Journal, 10,* 222–237.

GIOVACCHINI, P. L. (1987). The "unreasonable" patient and the psychotic transference. In J. S. Grotstein, M. F. Solomon, & J. A. Lang (Eds.), *The borderline patient: Emerging concepts in diagnosis, psychodynamics and treatment* (Vol. 1). Hillsdale, NJ: The Analytic Press.

GNEPP, J., MCKEE, E., & DOMANIC, J. (1987). Children's use of situational information to infer emotion: Understanding emotionally equivocal situations. *Developmental Psychology, 23,* 114–123.

GOLDBERG, R. L., MANN, L. S., WISE, T. N., & SEGALL, E. A. (1985). Parental qualities as perceived by borderline personality disorders. *Hillside Journal of Clinical Psychiatry, 7,* 134–140.

GRINKER, R., WERBLE, B., & DRYE, R. (1968). *The borderline syndrome: A behavioral study of ego functions.* New York: Basic Books.

GUNDERSON, J. G. (1977). Characteristics of borderlines. In P. Hartocollis

(Ed.). *Borderline personality disorders.* New York: International Universities Press.

GUNDERSON, J. G. (1984). *Borderline personality disorder.* Washington, DC: American Psychiatric Press.

GUNDERSON, J. G., & ELLIOTT, G. R. (1985). The interface between borderline personality disorder and affective disorder. *American Journal of Psychiatry, 142,* 277–288.

GUNDERSON, J. G., & SABO, A. N. (1993). The phenomenological and conceptual interface between borderline personality disorder and PTSD. *American Journal of Psychiatry, 150,* 19–27.

GUNDERSON, J. G., KERR, J., & ENGLUND, D. W. (1980). The families of borderlines. *Archives of General Psychiatry, 135,* 792–796.

GUNDERSON, J. G., KOLB, J., & AUSTIN, V. (1981). The diagnostic interview for borderline patients. *American Journal of Psychiatry, 138,* 896–903.

GUNNAR, M. R., MANGELSDORF, S., LARSON, M., & HERTSGAARD, L. (1989). Attachment, temperament and adrenocortical activity in infancy: A study of psychoendrocrine regulation. *Developmental Psychology, 25,* 355–363.

HARRIS, P. L. (1989). *Children and emotion: The development of psychological understanding.* Oxford: Basil Blackwell.

HARTER, S., & BUDDIN, B. (1987). Children's understanding of simultaneity of two emotions: A five-stage developmental acquisition sequence. *Developmental Psychology, 23,* 391–399.

HARTOCOLLIS, P. (1968). The syndrome of minimal brain dysfunction in young adult patients. *Bulletin of the Menninger Clinic, 32,* 102–114.

HERMAN, J. L., PERRY, J. C., & VAN DER KOLK, B. A. (1989). Childhood trauma in borderline personality disorder. *American Journal of Psychiatry, 146,* 490–495.

HIGGITT, A., & FONAGY, P. (1992). Psychotherapy in borderline and narcissistic personality disorder. *British Journal of Psychiatry, 161,* 23–43.

HORNER, H. (1975). A characterological contraindication for group psychotherapy. *Journal of the American Academy of Psychoanalysis, 3,* 301–305.

HOROWITZ, L., ROSENBERG, S., BAER, B. A., URENO, G., & VILLASENOR, V. S. (1988). Inventory of Interpersonal Problems: Psychometric properties and clinical applications. *Journal of Clinical and Consulting Psychology, 56,* 885–892.

HOROWITZ, M. J. (1991). States, schemas and control: General theories for psychotherapy integration. *Journal of Psychotherapy Integration, 1,* 85–101.

HORWITZ, L. (1977). Group psychotherapy of the borderline patient. In P. Hartocollis (Ed.), *Borderline personality disorders.* New York: International Universities Press.

HORWITZ, L. (1980). Group psychotherapy for borderline and narcissistic patients. *Bulletin Menninger Clinic, 4,* 181–200.

HORWITZ, L. (1983). Projective identification in dyads and groups.

International Journal of Group Psychotherapy, 33, 259–279.

HORWITZ, L. (1987). Indication for group psychotherapy with borderline and narcissistic patients. *Bulletin Menninger Clinic, 51,* 248–260.

HULSE, W. C. (1958). Psychotherapy with ambulatory schizophrenic patients in mixed analytic groups. *Archives of Neurological Psychiatry, 79,* 681–687.

HURT, W. S., CLARKIN, J. F., MARZIALI, E., & MUNROE-BLUM, H. (1992). Borderline behavioral clusters and different treatment approaches. In J. F. Clarkin, E. Marziali, & H. Munroe-Blum (Eds.), *Borderline personality disorder.* New York: Guilford.

HUTTENDEN, M. O., & NYMAN, G. (1982). On the continuity, change and clinical value of infant temperament in a prospective epidemiological study. In R. Porter & G. M. Collins (Eds.), *Temperamental differences in infants and young children.* London: Pitman.

HYLER, S. E., RIEDER, M. D., WILLIAMS, J. B., SPITZER, R. L., HENDER, J., & LYONS, M. (1989). The Personality Diagnostic Questionnaire: Development and preliminary results. *Journal of Personality Disorders, 2,* 229–237.

IZARD, C. E., & MALATESTA, C. W. (1987). Perspectives on emotional development. I: Differential emotions theory of early emotional development. In J. Osofsky (Ed.), *Handbook of infant development* (2nd ed.). New York: Wiley.

JONAS, J. M., & POPE, H. G. (1992). Axis I comorbidity of borderline personality disorder: Clinical implications. In J. F. Clarkin, E. Marziali, & H. Munroe-Blum (Eds.), *Borderline personality disorder.* New York: Guilford.

KAGAN, J., REZNICK, J. S., & SNIDMAN, N. (1986). Temperamental inhibition in early childhood. In R. Plomin & J. Dunn (Eds.). *The study of temperament: Changes, continuities and challenges.* Hillsdale, NJ: Erlbaum.

KAGAN, J., REZNICK, J. S., & SNIDMAN, N. (1988). Biological bases of childhood shyness. *Science, 240,* 167–171.

KASS, F., SKODOL, A., CHARLES, E., SPITZER, R. L. & WILLIAMS, J. B. W. (1985). Scaled ratings of DSM-III personality disorders. *American Journal of Psychiatry, 142,* 627–630.

KERNBERG, O. F. (1975). *Borderline conditions and pathological narcissism.* New York: Jason Aronson.

KERNBERG, O. F., BURSTEIN, E., & COYNE, L. (1972). Final report of the Menninger Foundation psychotherapy project: Psychotherapy and psychoanalysis. *Bulletin of the Menninger Clinic, 34,* whole issue.

KERNBERG, O. F., SELZER, M. A., KOENIGSBERG, H. W., CARR, A. C., & APPELBAUM, A. M. (1989). *Psychodynamic psychotherapy of borderline patients.* New York: Basic Books.

KIBEL, H. (1980). The importance of a comprehensive clinical diagnosis for group psychotherapy of borderline and narcissistic patients. *International Journal of Group Psychotherapy, 30,* 427–440.

KLEIN, D. F. (1975). Psychopharmacology and the borderline patient. In

J. E. Mack (Ed.), *Borderline states in psychiatry*. New York: Grune & Stratton.

KLEIN, D. F. (1977). Psychopharmacological treatment and delineation of borderline disorders. In P. Hartocollis (Ed.), *Borderline personality disorder: The concept, the syndrome, and the patient*. New York: International Universities Press.

KLERMAN, G. L., WEISSMAN, M. M., ROUNSAVILLE, B. J., & CHEVRON, S. E. (1984). *Interpersonal psychotherapy and depression*. New York: Basic Books.

KNIGHT, R. P. (1953). Borderline states. *Bulletin Menninger Clinic, 17,* 1–12.

KOBAK, R. R., & SCEERY, A. (1988). Attachment in late adolescence: Working models, affect regulation, and representations of self and others. *Child Development, 59,* 135–146.

KOHUT, H. (1977). *The restoration of the self*. New York: International Universities Press.

KOPP, C. B. (1989). Regulation of distress and negative emotions: A developmental view. *Developmental Psychology, 25,* 343–354.

KORNER, A. F., HUTCHINSON, C. A., KOPERSKI, J. A., KRAEMER, H. C., & SCHNEIDER, P. A. (1981). Stability of individual differences of neonatal motor and crying pattern. *Child Development, 52,* 83–90.

LEE, C. L., & BATES, J. E. (1985). Mother-child interaction at age two years and perceived difficult temperament. *Child Development, 56,* 1314–1325.

LEIBOVITCH, M. A. (1983). Why short-term psychotherapy for borderlines? *Psychotherapy and Psychosomatic Medicine, 39,* 1–9.

LESZCZ, M. (1992). Group psychotherapy of the borderline patient. In D. Silver & M. Rosenbluth (Eds.), *Handbook of borderline disorders*. Madison, CT: International University Press.

LEVINE, D. (1992). *The measurement of emotions in borderline personality disorder*. Unpublished doctoral thesis, University of Toronto.

LEWIS, M., & MICHALSON, L. (1988). *Children's emotions and moods*. New York: Plenum.

LINEHAN, M. M. (1993). *Cognitive behavioral treatment of borderline patients*. New York: Guilford Press.

LINEHAN, M. M., ARMSTRONG, H. E., SUAREZ, A., ALLMON, D., & HEARD, H. L. (1991). Cognitive-behavioral treatment of chronically parasuicidal borderline patients. *Archives of General Psychiatry, 48,* 1060–1065.

LINKS, P. (1982). The existence of the borderline diagnosis: Studies on diagnostic validity. *Canadian Journal of Psychiatry, 27,* 585–592.

LINKS, P., STEINER, M., OFFORD, D., & EPPEL, A. (1988). Characteristics of borderline personality disorder: A Canadian study. *Canadian Journal of Psychiatry, 33,* 336–340.

LIVESLEY, W. J., & JACKSON, D. N. (1992). Guidelines for developing, evaluating, and revising the classification of personality disorders. *Journal of Nervous and Mental Disease, 180,* 609–618.

LIVESLEY, W. J., & SCHROEDER, M. L. (1991). Dimensions of personality disorder, the DSM-III-R cluster B diagnoses. *Journal of Nervous and Mental Disease, 179,* 320–328.

LORANGER, A. W., SUSMAN, V. L., OLDHAM, J. M., & RUSSAKOFF, M. (1985). *Personality Disorder Examination (PDE): A structured interview for DSM-III-R personality disorders.* White Plains, NY: New York Hospital-Cornell Medical Center, Westchester Division.

LUBORSKY, L. (1984). *Principles of psychoanalytic psychotherapy—A manual for supportive expressive treatment (SE).* New York: Basic Books.

LUBORSKY, L., & CRITS-CHRISTOPH, P. (1990). *Understanding transference: The Core Conflictual Relationship Theme method.* New York: Basic Books.

LUBORSKY, L., MCLELLAN, A. T., WOODY, G. E., O'BRIEN, C. P., & AUERBACH, A. (1985). Therapist success and its determinants. *Archives of General Psychiatry, 42,* 602–611.

MACASKILL, D. (1982). Therapeutic factors in group psychotherapy with borderline patients. *International Journal of Group Psychotherapy, 32,* 61–73.

MAHLER, M. S. (1971). A study of the separation-individuation process and its possible application to borderline phenomena in the psychoanalytic situation. *Psychoanalytic Study of the Child, 26,* 403–424.

MAHLER, M., PINE, F., & BERGMAN, A. (1975). *The psychological birth of the human infant.* New York: Basic Books.

MAIN, M., & CASSIDY, J. (1988). Categories of response to reunion with the parent at age six: Predictable from infant attachment classifications and stable over a one month period. *Developmental Psychology, 24,* 415–426.

MAIN, M., & GOLDWYN, R. (1990). *Adult attachment classification system.* Unpublished coding manual, University of California, Berkeley.

MAIN, M., KAPLAN, N., & CASSIDY, J. (1985). Security in infancy, childhood, and adulthood: A move to the level of representation. In I. Bretherton & E. Waters (Eds.), *Growing points of attachment theory and research.* Monographs for the Society of Research in Child Development, 50 (1–2, Serial No. 209), 66–104.

MARZIALI, E. (1987). People in your life. *Journal of Nervous and Mental Disease, 175,* 327–338.

MARZIALI, E., & MUNROE-BLUM, H. (1987). The management of projective identification in group treatment of self-destructive borderline patients. *Journal of Personality Disorders, 1,* 340–343.

MARZIALI, E., & OLENIUK, J. (1990). Object representations in descriptions of significant others: A methodological study. *Journal of Personality Assessment, 54,* 105–115.

MARZIALI, E., & PILKONIS, P. (1986). The measurement of subjective response to stressful life events. *Journal of Human Stress, 12,* 5–12.

MASTERSON, J. F. (1981). *Narcissistic and borderline disorders.* New York: Brunner/Mazel.

MASTERSON, J. F., & RINSLEY, D. B. (1975). The borderline syndrome: The role of the mother in the genesis and psychiatric structure of the borderline personality. *International Journal of Psychoanalysis, 56,* 163–177.

MATHENY, A. P., RIESE, M. L. & WILSON, R. S. (1985). Rudiments of infant temperament: Newborn to 9 months. *Developmental Psychology, 21,* 486–494.

McGLASHAN, T. H. (1986). The Chestnut Lodge follow-up study, III: Long-term outcome of borderline personalities. *Archives of General Psychiatry, 43,* 30–40.

MILLON, T. (1987). *Manual for the Millon Clinical Multiaxial Inventory II (MCMI-II).* Minneapolis: National Computer Systems.

MILMAN, D. H. (1979). Minimal brain dysfunction in childhood: Outcome in late adolescence and early adult years. *Journal of Clinical Psychiatry, 40,* 371–380.

MUNROE-BLUM, H., & MARZIALI, E. (1986). *Objective Behaviors Index: Scoring manual.* McMaster University, Hamilton, Ontario.

MUNROE-BLUM, H., & MARZIALI, E. (1988). Time-limited, group psychotherapy for borderline patients. *Canadian Journal of Psychiatry, 33,* 364–369.

MUNROE-BLUM, H., & MARZIALI, E. (1986–1992). *Randomized Clinical Trial of Relationship Management Time-Limited Group Treatment of Borderline Patients.* Funded by Ontario Mental Health Foundation and the National Health and Research Development Program, McMaster University, Hamilton, Ontario, Canada.

MURRAY, M. E. (1979). Minimal brain dysfunction and borderline personality adjustment. *American Journal of Psychotherapy, 33,* 391–403.

NURNBERG, H. G., RASKIN, M., LEVINE, P. E., POLLACK, S., SIEGEL, O., & PRINCE, R. (1991). The comorbidity of borderline personality disorder and other DSM-III-R axis II personality disorders. *American Journal of Psychiatry, 148,* 1371–1377.

OGDEN, T. H. (1979). On projective identification. *International Journal of Psychoanalysis, 60,* 357–373.

OLDHAM, M. J., SKODOL, A. E., KELLMAN, H. D., HYLER, S. E., ROSNICK, L., & DAVIE, M. (1992). Diagnosis of DSM-III-R personality disorders by two structured interviews: Patterns of comorbidity. *American Journal of Psychiatry, 149,* 213–220.

OLENIUK, J. (1992). *Descriptions of significant others: A comparison of schizophrenic patients and borderline personality disorder.* Unpublished doctoral dissertation, York University, Toronto.

O'MALLEY, S. S., FOLEY, S. H., ROUNSAVILLE, B. J., WATKINS, J. T., STOTSKY, S. M., IMBER, S. D., & ELKIN, I. (1988). Therapist competence and patient outcome in interpersonal psychotherapy of depression. *Journal of Consulting and Clinical Psychology, 56,* 496–501.

PALOMBO, J. (1987). Self-object transference in the treatment of borderline neurocognitively impaired children. In J. S. Grotstein, M. F. Solomon, & J. A. Lang (Eds.), *The borderline patient: Emerging concepts in diagnosis, psychodynamics and treatment* (Vol. 1, pp. 317–346). Hillsdale, NJ: The Analytic Press.

PARIS, J., & FRANK, H. (1989). Perceptions of parental bonding in border-line patients. *American Journal of Psychiatry, 146,* 1498–1499.

PARIS, J., BROWN, R., & NOLIS, D. (1987). Long-term follow-up of border-line patients in a general hospital. *Comprehensive Psychiatry, 28,* 530–535.

PARKER, G. B., BARRETT, E. A. & HICKIE, I. B. (1992). From nurture to net-work: Examining the link between perceptions of parenting received in childhood and social bonds in adulthood. *American Journal of Psychiatry, 149,* 877–885.

PARKER, G. B., TUPLING, H., & BROWN, L. B. (1979). A parental bonding instrument. *British Journal of Medical Psychology, 52,* 1–10.

PERRY, J. C. (1985). Depression in borderline personality disorder: life-time prevalence at interview and longitudinal course of symptoms. *American Journal of Psychiatry, 142,* 15–21.

PERRY, J. C. (1990). Challenges in validating personality disorders: Beyond description. *Journal of Personality Disorders, 4,* 273–289.

PERRY, J. C., & KLERMAN, J. L. (1978). The borderline patient: A compara-tive analysis of four sets of diagnostic criteria. *Archives of General Psychiatry, 35,* 141–150.

PERRY, J. C., HERMAN, J. L., VAN DER KOLK, B. A., & HOKE, L. A. (1990). Psychotherapy and psychosocial trauma in borderline personality dis-order. *Psychiatric Annals, 20,* 33–43.

PERRY, S. (1989). Treatment time and the borderline patient: An underap-preciated strategy. *Journal of Personality Disorders, 3,* 230–239.

PIAGET, J. (1952). *The origins of intelligence in children.* New York: International Universities Press.

PIAGET, J. (1954). *The construction of reality in the child.* Translated by M. Cook. New York: Basic Books.

PIERSMA, H. L. (1987). The MCMI as a measure of DSM-III Axis II diag-noses: An empirical comparison. *Journal of Clinical Psychology, 43,* 478–483.

PINE, F. (1985). *Developmental theory and clinical process.* New Haven, CT: Yale University Press.

PINE, F. (1992). From technique to a theory of psychic change. *International Journal of Psychoanalysis, 73,* 251–254.

PINES, M. (1990). Group analytic psychotherapy and the borderline patient. In B. E. Roth, W. N. Stone, & H. D. Kibel (Eds.), *The difficult patient in group: Group psychotherapy with borderline and narcissistic dis-orders* (pp. 31–44). Madison, CT: International University Press.

PLAKUN, E. M., BURKHARDT, P. E., & MULLER, J. P. (1986). Fourteen-year follow-up of borderline and schizotypal personality disorders. *Comprehensive Psychiatry, 40,* 23–30.

POPE, H. G., JONAS, A. M., HUDSON, J. I., COHEN, B. M., & GUNDERSON, J. G. (1983). The validity of DSM-III borderline personality disorder. *Archives of General Psychiatry, 137,* 23–30.

QUITKIN, F., RIFKIN, A., & KLEIN, D. F. (1976). Neurological soft signs in schizophrenia and character disorders. *Archives of General Psychiatry, 33,* 845–853.

REICH, J. (1992). Measurement of DSM-II and DSM-III-R borderline personality disorder. In J. F. Clarkin, E. Marziali, & H. Munroe-Blum (Eds.)., *Borderline personality disorder.* New York: Guilford.

REICHENBACH, L., & MASTER, J. (1983). Children's use of expressive and contextual cues in judgments of emotion. *Child Development, 54,* 993–1004.

REZNICK, J. S., KAGAN, J., SNIDMAN, N., GERSTEN, M., BAAK, K., & ROSENBERG, A. (1986). Inhibited and uninhibited children: A followup study. *Child Development, 57,* 660–680.

RIESE, M. L. (1987). Temperament stability between the neonatal period and 24 months. *Developmental Psychology, 23,* 216–222.

ROGERS, C. R. (1957). *Client centered therapy.* Boston: Houghton Mifflin.

ROSENFELD, H. (1978). Notes on the psychopathology and psychoanalytic treatment of some borderline patients. *International Journal of Psychoanalysis, 59,* 215–222.

ROSENFELD, H. (1987). Impasse and interpretation. London: Tavistock.

ROTH, B. E. (1980). Understanding the development of a homogeneous identity-impaired group through countertransference phenomena. *International Journal of Group Psychotherapy, 30,* 405–426.

ROUNSAVILLE, B. J., O'MALLEY, S., FOLEY, S., & WEISSMAN, M. M. (1988). Role of manual-guided training in the conduct and efficacy of interpersonal psychotherapy for depression. *Journal of Consulting and Clinical Psychology, 56,* 681–688.

RUSHTON, J. P., FULKER, D. W., NEALE, M. C., NIAS, D. K. B., & EYSENCK, H. J. (1986). Altruism and aggression: The heritability of individual differences. *Journal of Personality and Social Psychology, 50,* 1192–1198.

RUTTER, M. (1978). Family area and school influences on the genesis of conduct disorders. In L. A. Hersov & M. Berger with D. Schaffer (Eds.), *Aggression and antisocial behavior in childhood and adolescence,* Journal of Child Psychology and Psychiatry Book Supplement No 1. Oxford: Pergamon Press.

RUTTER, M. (1980). *Scientific foundations of developmental psychiatry.* London: Heinemann.

RUTTER, M., & QUINTON, D. (1984a). Long-term follow-up of women institutionalized in childhood: Factors promoting good functioning in adult life. *British Journal of Developmental Psychology, 2,* 191–204.

RUTTER, M., & QUINTON, D. (1984b). Parental psychiatric disorder: Effects on children. *Psychological Medicine, 14,* 853–880.

SANDLER, J. (1976). Countertransference and role-responsiveness. *International Review of Psychoanalysis. 3,* 43–47.

SCHLEFFER, E., SELZER, M., CLARKIN, J. F., YOEMANS, F., & LUBORSKY, L. (1989). *Rating CCRTs with borderline patients.* Paper presented at the annual meeting of the American Psychiatric Association, San Francisco.

SEARLES, H. (1986). *My work with borderline patients.* New York: Jason Aronson.

SELMAN, R. L. (1980). *The growth of interpersonal understanding: Developmental and clinical analyses.* San Diego, CA: Academic Press.

SHAPIRO, E. R., SHAPIRO, R. L., ZINNER, J., & BERKOWITZ, D. A. (1977). The borderline ego and the working alliance: Indications for individual and family treatment in adolescence. *International Journal of Psychoanalysis, 58,* 77–87.

SHAW, B. F., & DOBSON, K. S. (1988). Competency judgments in the training and evaluation of psychotherapists. *Journal of Consulting and Clinical Psychology, 56,* 666–672.

SHEARER, S. L., PETERS, C. P., QUAYTMAN, M. S., & OGDEN, R. L. (1990). Frequency and correlates of childhood sexual and physical abuse histories in adult female borderline patients. *American Journal of Psychiatry, 147,* 214–216.

SIEVER L. J., DAVIS K. L. (1991). A psychobiological perspective on the personality disorders. *American Journal of Psychiatry, 148,* 1647–1658

SILK, K. R., LOHR, N. E., OGATA, S., & WESTEN, D. (1990). Borderline inpatients with affective disorder: Preliminary follow-up data. *Journal of Personality Disorders, 4,* 213–224.

SILVER, D. (1985). Psychodynamics and psychotherapeutic management of the self destructive character-disordered patient. *Psychiatric Clinics of North America, 8,* 357–377.

SILVER, D., & ROSENBLUTH, M. (1992). The assessment process. In D. Silver & M. Rosenbluth (Eds.), *Handbook of borderline disorders.* Madison, CT: International Universities Press.

SLAVINSKA-HOLY, N. M. (1983). Combining individual and homogeneous psychotherapies for borderline conditions. *International Journal of Group Psychotherapy, 33,* 297–312.

SMITH-BENJAMIN, L. (1992). An interpersonal approach to the diagnosis of borderline personality disorder. In J. F. Clarkin, E. Marziali, & H. Munroe-Blum (Eds.), *Borderline personality disorder.* New York: Guilford.

SOLOFF, P. H., & MILLWARD, J. W. (1983). Developmental histories of borderline patients. *Comprehensive Psychiatry, 24,* 574–588.

SOLOFF, P. H., GEORGE, A., NATHAN, R., & SCHULTZ, P. M. (1987). Characterizing depression in borderline patients. *Journal of Clinical Psychiatry, 48,* 155–157.

SPITZER, R. L., & WILLIAMS, J. B. W. (1980). Classification of mental disorders and DSM-III. In H. Kaplan, A. Freedman, & B. Sadock (Eds.), *Comprehensive textbook of psychiatry III* (3d ed., vol. 1). Baltimore: Williams & Wilkins.

SPITZER R. L., ENDICOTT, J., & GIBBON, M. (1979). Crossing the border into borderline personality and borderline schizophrenia: The development of criteria. *Archives of General Psychiatry, 36,* 17–24.

SPITZER, R. L., WILLIAMS, J. B. W., & GIBBON, M. (1987). *Structured Clinical*

Interview for DSM-III-R (SCID-II). New York: New York State Psychiatric Institute, Biometrics Research.

STALKER, C. (1993). *Quality of object relations in women victims of childhood sexual abuse.* Unpublished doctoral dissertation, Smith College, Northampton, MA.

STERN, A. (1938). Psychoanalytic investigation of and therapy in the borderline group of neuroses. *Psychoanalytic Quarterly, 7,* 467–489.

STERN, D. N. (1985). *The Interpersonal World of the Infant: A View from Psychoanalysis and Developmental Psychology.* New York: Basic Books.

STEVENSON-HINDE, J., & HINDE, R. (1986). Changes in associations between characteristics. In R. Plomin & J. Dunn (Eds.), *The study of temperament: Changes, continuities and challenges.* Hillsdale, NJ: Erlbaum.

STONE, W. N., & GUSTAFSON, J. P. (1982). Technique in group psychotherapy of narcissistic and borderline patients. *International Journal of Group Psychotherapy, 32,* 29–47.

STONE, M. H. (1993). Long-term outcome in personality disorders. *British Journal of Psychiatry, 162,* 299–313.

STROUFE, L. A., & FLEESON, J. (1986). Attachment and the construction of relationships. In W. W. Hartup & Z. Rubin (Eds.), *Relationships and development.* Hillsdale, NJ: Erlbaum.

STRUPP, H. H., & BINDER, J. L. (1985). *Psychotherapy in a new key.* New York: Basic Books.

TABACHNICK, N. (1965). Isolation, transference-splitting, and combined therapy. *Comprehensive Psychiatry, 6,* 336–346.

THOMAS, A., & CHESS, S. (1977). *Temperament and development.* New York: Brunner/Mazel.

TOPLIN, M., & KOHUT, H. (1980). The psychopathology of the first years of life: Disorders in the self. In S. Greenspan & G. Pollock (Eds.), *The course of life.* Washington, DC: U.S. Government Printing Office.

TULVING, E. (1983). Elements of Episodic Memory. Oxford: Oxford University Press.

TULVING, E. (1985). How many memory systems are there? *American Psychologist, 40,* 395–398.

TULVING, E. (1989). Remembering and knowing the past. *American Scientist, 77,* 361–367.

VAILLANT, G. E. (1977). *Adaptation to life.* Boston: Little, Brown.

VAILLANT, G. E. (1992). The beginning of wisdom is never calling a patient borderline. *Journal of Psychotherapy Practice and Research, 1,* 117–134.

WACHTEL, P. L. (1980). Transference, schema, and assimilation: The relevance of Piaget to the psychoanalytic theory of transference. *The Annual of Psychoanalysis, V (8),* 59–76.

WALDINGER, R. (1992). Multimodal treatment of borderline personality disorder. In J. F. Clarkin, E. Marziali, & H. Munroe-Blum (Eds.), *Borderline personality disorder.* New York: The Guilford Press.

WALDINGER, R., & GUNDERSON, J. G. (1987). *Effective psychotherapy with borderline patients.* Toronto: MacMillan Press.

WEISS, G., HECHTMAN, L., PERLMAN, T., HOPKINS, J., & WENER, A. (1979). Hyperactives as young adults. *Archives of General Psychiatry, 36,* 675–681.

WEISSMAN, M. M., & BOTHWELL, S. (1976). Assessment of social adjustment by patient self-report. *Archives of General Psychiatry, 33,* 1111–1115.

WELLS, M., & GLICKAUF-HUGHES, C. (1986). Techniques to develop object constancy with borderline clients. *Psychotherapy, 23,* 460–468.

WENDER, P. H., REIMHER, F. W., & WOOD, D. R. (1981). Attention deficit disorder ("minimal brain dysfunction") in adults. *Archives of General Psychiatry, 38,* 449–456.

WERNER, E. E., & SMITH, R. S. (1982). *Vulnerable but invincible.* New York: McGraw-Hill.

WEST, M., SHELDON, A., & REIFFER, L. (1987). An approach to the delineation of adult attachment: Scale development and reliability. *Journal of Nervous and Mental Disease, 176,* 738–741.

WEST, M., KELLER, A., LINKS, P., & PATRICK, J. (1993). Borderline personality disorder and attachment pathology. *Canadian Journal of Psychiatry, 38,* (Supplement I), S16–S22.

WESTEN, D. (1990). Towards a revised theory of borderline object relations: Contributions of empirical research. *International Journal of Psychoanalysis, 71,* 661–693.

WESTEN, D. (1991). Cognitive-behavioral interventions in the psychoanalytic psychotherapy of borderline personality disorders. *Clinical Psychology Review, 11,* 211–230.

WESTEN, D., LOHR, N., SILK, K., GOLD, L., & KERBER, K. (1990). Object relations and social cognition in borderlines, major depressives, and normals: A TAT analysis. *Psychological Assessment: A Journal of Consulting and Clinical Psychology, 2,* 355–364.

WIDIGER, T. A., & FRANCES, A. (1985). The DSM-III personality disorders. *Archives of General Psychiatry, 42,* 615–623.

WIDIGER, T. A., MIELE, G. M., & TILLY, S. M. (1992). Alternative perspectives on the diagnosis of borderline personality disorder. In J. F. Clarkin, E. Marziali, & H. Munroe-Blum (Eds.), *Borderline personality disorder.* New York: Guilford.

WIXOM, J. M. (1988). *The depressive experiences of adolescents with borderline personality disorder.* Unpublished doctoral dissertation, University of Michigan, Ann Arbor.

WONG, N. (1980a). Combined group and individual treatment of borderline and narcissistic patients: Heterogeneous versus homogeneous groups. *International Journal of Group Psychotherapy, 30,* 389–404.

WONG, N. (1980b). Focal issues in group psychotherapy of borderline and narcissistic patients. In L. R. Wolberg & M. L. Arons (Eds.), *Group and family therapy.* New York: Brunner/Mazel.

YALOM, I. D. (1975). *The theory and practice of group psychotherapy* (2d. ed.). New York: Basic Books.

ZANARINI, M. C., GUNDERSON, J. G., & FRANKENBURG, F. R. (1989). Axis I phenomenology of borderline personality disorder. *Comprehensive Psychiatry, 30,* 149–156.

ZANARINI, M. C., GUNDERSON, J. G., & FRANKENBURG, F. R. (1990). Cognitive features of borderline personality disorder. *American Journal of Psychiatry, 147,* 57–63.

ZANARINI, M. C., GUNDERSON, J. G., FRANKENBURG, F. R., & CHAUNCEY, A. B. (1989). The Revised Diagnostic Interview for Borderlines: Discriminating BPD from other axis II disorders. *Journal of Personality Disorders, 3,* 10–18.

ZANARINI, M. C., GUNDERSON, J. G., FRANKENBURG, F. R., & CHAUNCEY, A. B. (1990). Discriminating borderline personality disorder from other axis II disorders. *American Journal of Psychiatry, 147,* 161–167.

ZANARINI, M. C., GUNDERSON, J. G., FRANKENBURG, F. R. et al. (1991). The face validity of the DSM-III and the DSM-III-R criteria sets for borderline personality disorder. *American Journal of Psychiatry, 148,* 870–874.

ZANARINI, M. C., GUNDERSON, J. G., MARINO, M. F., SCHWARTZ, E. O., & FRANKENBURG, F. R. (1989). Childhood experiences of borderline patients. *Comprehensive Psychiatry, 30,* 18–25.

ZETZEL, E. R. (1971). A developmental approach to the borderline patient. *American Journal of Psychiatry, 127,* 867–871.

ZIMMERMAN, M., PFOHL, B., CORYELL, W., STANGL, D., & CORENTHAL, C. (1988). Diagnosing personality disorders in depressed patients. *Archives of General Psychiatry, 45,* 733–737.

Index